The issue of small islands hosting big money has been much in the media and on the policy agenda of late, and nowhere more so than the UK Overseas Territories of the Caribbean. Yet for all the attention, perhaps even notoriety, these islands remain strangely unknown, often being lumped together as inter-changeable exotic tax havens. Eschewing lazy prejudice and stereotypes of tropical bolt-holes, Thomas-James's book does what should have been done a long time ago but has not: it provides a thoroughly researched and nuanced picture of these islands' presence and participation in the global financial industry, as well as their reactions to international regulatory campaigns to counter dirty money. Focusing on Bermuda, Anguilla and the Turks and Caicos Islands, *Offshore Financial Centres and the Law* provides an invaluable resource for those interested in the real story of offshore finance.

Professor Jason Sharman FBA, *Sir Patrick Sheehy Professor of International Relations, and Head of the Department of Politics and International Studies, University of Cambridge; Fellow, King's College, Cambridge; and Fellow, British Academy*

Dr. Dominic Thomas-James' treatise takes a most interesting approach to the growing literature on anti-money laundering and anti-corruption. The text, which developed from an excellent doctoral dissertation at the University of Cambridge, tells the story from the perspective of the small jurisdiction attempting to meet the ever-increasing regulatory requirements of international conventions, and of dominant nations. By example, the FATF money laundering and terrorism financing Recommendations have acquired the status of global norms but are based on a one-size-fits-all approach. This simply does not work for all nations, particularly those who have, oftentimes through necessity, developed legitimate offshore financial sectors which now must be re-tooled to fit global norms. As the saying goes, failure is not an option, forcing small jurisdictions to either 'toe the line' or suffer the ignominy of being branded rogue nations. So, it is with the British Overseas Territories and this story that Dr. Thomas-James skillfully weaves in his timely and important work. I commend it to all who practice in this area.

Dr Peter German QC, *President, International Centre for Criminal Law Reform and Criminal Justice Policy, Canada; and former Deputy Commissioner and Director of the Financial Crime Division, Royal Canadian Mounted Police*

With Covid-19 throwing the world's economies into turmoil and with Britain, having Brexited the European Union, needing to strengthen its financial and economic ties with Commonwealth countries despite its reputation for being "the dirty money capital of Europe", this book could scarcely be more useful and timely. Dr Thomas-James throws new light on the working of British Overseas Territories as tax havens. This scholarly work examines how far international legal and regulatory standards are being achieved, where and to what extent there may be room for improvement, and what can be done to advance the reputations of the several countries concerned.

Sir Ivan Lawrence QC, *Visiting Professor of Law, University of Buckingham and BPP University; Co-Chair, Cambridge International Symposium on Economic Crime; Barrister, and Master of the Bench, Inner Temple; former Member of Parliament and Chairman, Home Affairs Committee, House of Commons*

Dr Thomas-James presents an insightful and nuanced review of the complexities of anti-money laundering compliance in offshore jurisdictions. By focusing on three British Overseas Territories – Bermuda, Turks and Caicos, and Anguilla – he is able to demonstrate both the common issues facing many offshore financial centers as well as the particularized difficulties faced by discrete jurisdictions based on their economies, the specific financial activities they foster, and international expectations. The conclusion, that there is no "one-size-fits-all" solution, should be obvious, but unfortunately is not widely recognized. Calls for strict adherence to an American or British AML structure are doomed to failure as many offshore jurisdictions lack the capital and infrastructure to implement all of the changes mandated by such an approach. Instead, Dr Thomas-James recognizes the need for bespoke solutions to particular problems. Eschewing generalities and popularized myths about offshore jurisdictions, Dr Thomas-James focuses instead on facts and detailed analyses to offer real world solutions.

Mr Adam Kaufmann, *Partner, Lewis, Baach, Kaufmann & Middlemiss PLLC, and former Executive Assistant District Attorney and Chief of the Investigations Division, New York District Attorney's Office*

The relationship between offshore financial centres and economic crime has always been controversial and particularly so in the context of the British Overseas Territories. Dr Thomas-James's book provides a welcome, indispensable and balanced guide to understanding this complex relationship and the issues that surround it.

Mr Peter Lowe, *Executive Secretary, International Chamber of Commerce FraudNet*

Offshore Financial Centres and the Law

This book considers the ability of island jurisdictions with financial centres to meet the expectations of the international community in addressing the threats posed to themselves and others by their innocent (or otherwise) facilitation of the receipt of suspect wealth.

In the global financial architecture, British Overseas Territories are of material significance. Through their inalienable right to self-determination, many developed offshore financial centres to achieve sustainable economic development. Focusing on Bermuda, Turks and Caicos, and Anguilla, the book concerns suspect wealth emanating from financial crimes including corruption, money laundering and tax evasion, as well as controversial conduct like tax avoidance. This work considers the viability of international standards on suspect wealth in the context of the territories, how willing or able they are to comply with them, and how their financial centres can better prevent receipt of suspect wealth. While universalism is desirable in the modern approach to tackling suspect wealth, a one-size-fits-all approach is inappropriate for these jurisdictions. On critically evaluating their legislative and regulatory regimes, the book advances that they demonstrate willingness to comply with international standards. However, their abilities and levels of compliance vary. In acknowledging the facilitatively harmful role the territories can play, this work draws upon evidence of implication in transnational financial crime cases. Notwithstanding this, the book questions whether the degree of criticism that these offshore jurisdictions have encountered is warranted in light of apparent willingness to engage in the enactment and administration of internationally accepted laws and cooperate with international institutions.

Dominic Thomas-James is a Postdoctoral Research Associate at Fitzwilliam College, University of Cambridge and is a Global Justice Fellow at Yale University. He is a Course Director and Tutor in International Development and International Relations at the University of Cambridge Institute of Continuing Education, and is a Member of the Cambridge Centre for Criminal Justice. He earned his Ph.D. and M.Phil. from Queens' College, University of Cambridge, and read law at King's College London. He is a Secretariat Member of the Annual Cambridge International Symposium on Economic Crime at Jesus College, Cambridge. He regularly speaks at international conferences and forums and has served as a consultant to various inter-governmental and international organisations. He is a practising barrister, called to the Bar of England and Wales by the Inner Temple, and is a Door Tenant at Goldsmith Chambers, London.

The Law of Financial Crime
Series Editor: Nicholas Ryder

Available titles in this series include:

Financial Crime and Corporate Misconduct
A Critical Evaluation of Fraud Legislation
Edited by Chris Monaghan and Nicola Monaghan

Corporate Liability for Insider Trading
Juliette Overland

Corruption in the Global Era
Causes, Sources and Forms of Manifestation
Lorenzo Pasculli and Nicholas Ryder

Counter-Terrorist Financing Law and Policy
An Analysis of Turkey
Burke Uğur Başaranel and Umut Turksen

Integrity and Corruption and the Law
Global Regulatory Challenges
Edited by Nicholas Ryder and Lorenzo Pasculli

Regulating and Combating Money Laundering and Terrorist Financing
The Law in Emerging Economies
Nkechikwu Valerie Azinge-Egbiri

Combating Corruption in the Middle East
A Socio-legal Study of Kuwait
Khaled S. Al-Rashidi

For more information about this series, please visit: www.routledge.com/The-Law-of-Financial-Crime/book-series/FINCRIME

Offshore Financial Centres and the Law

Suspect Wealth in British Overseas Territories

Dominic Thomas-James

Routledge
Taylor & Francis Group
LONDON AND NEW YORK

First published 2021
by Routledge
2 Park Square, Milton Park, Abingdon, Oxon OX14 4RN

and by Routledge
605 Third Avenue, New York, NY 10158

Routledge is an imprint of the Taylor & Francis Group, an informa business

British Library Cataloguing-in-Publication Data
A catalogue record for this book is available from the British Library

Library of Congress Cataloging-in-Publication Data
Names: Thomas-James, Dominic, author.
Title: Offshore financial centres and the law : suspect wealth in British overseas territories / Dominic Thomas-James.
Description: Abingdon, Oxon ; New York, NY : Routledge, 2021. | Series: The law of financial crime | Based on author's thesis (doctoral - University of Cambridge, 2019) issued under title: Suspect Wealth-a risk to stability, development and sustainability : the case of Bermuda, the Turks and Caicos Islands, and Anguilla. | Includes bibliographical references and index.
Identifiers: LCCN 2021002953 (print) | LCCN 2021002954 (ebook) | ISBN 9780367651091 (hardback) | ISBN 9781003127864 (paperback) | ISBN 9780367651107 (ebook)
Subjects: LCSH: Banks and banking, International—Law and legislation—Great Britain—Territories and possessions. | Banks and banking, International—Law and legislation—Bermuda Islands. | Banks and banking, International—Law and legislation—Anguilla. | Banks and banking, International—Law and legislation—Turks and Caicos Islands.
Classification: LCC KD1737.F67 T46 2021 (print) | LCC KD1737.F67 (ebook) | DDC 346.729/08215—dc23
LC record available at https://lccn.loc.gov/2021002953
LC ebook record available at https://lccn.loc.gov/2021002954

ISBN: 978-0-367-65109-1 (hbk)
ISBN: 978-0-367-65110-7 (pbk)
ISBN: 978-1-003-12786-4 (ebk)

Typeset in Galliard
by Apex CoVantage, LLC

To Sarah and Rupert

Contents

Foreword

I am delighted to provide a foreword to this excellent analysis and discussion of a topic which, although dear to my professional heart for the last 40 years, has recently become of real significance to many others. These days, when we think of islands in the Caribbean and increasingly the Pacific, a good many of us picture not just the allure of beautiful blue seas, waving palms and drinks on the beach, but also the more sinister shadow of money launderers, their cronies and politicians who have cashed in on their countries' legal sovereignty. Of course, the picture is a caricature – which even in the heyday of the so-called offshore financial centres would, in the main, have been misleading and unfair. On the other hand, in times when governments are strapped for money – whether as a result of mismanagement of their own financial and banking systems, increased longevity and the desire to appeal to aging voters whose welfare is increasingly supported by a narrowing tax base, or just the odd pandemic – it is not surprising that they look to ways of maximising tax revenues. Obvious and in some cases deserved targets will be those who have made it their business to reduce for others exposure to tax laws, or at least hold themselves out as being willing to do so – whether in fact they succeed or not. It is also the case that society has always liked to identify and then focus blame on scapegoats, particularly those outside the fold. So with the increasing awareness that we have failed in the so-called war on drugs and identifying terrorist finance is akin to draining the oceans to find one kind of fish – to slightly misquote the US congressional inquiry into the 9/11 outrages – it is hardly surprising that more attention has been given to those who claim or appear to be hiding wealth. Indeed, some societies, particularly those in the cold climes of Scandinavia, have become very sanguine in pursuing transparency of other people's wealth as a social end in itself – and this approach is catching! Then there are those who really do believe that criminals should not be allowed to benefit from their wrongdoing, whether this involves fraud, corruption or complicated things like insider dealing – and the law can actually achieve this. Consequently, those who mind other people's wealth now find themselves in the front line in the 'war' on everything and everyone we don't like and wish to subject sanction.

There was a time when islands in the sun – notwithstanding their convenience for the odd pirate or patriot operating under letters of marque – had modest financial aspirations which could be met, albeit often with the benefit of slaves and indentured labour. These times passed in a world that became more interdependent not just in trade, but also in social and perhaps moral expectations. Not all islands have the potential for tourism, and there are limits on how many bananas you can persuade the European Commission (EC) to purchase. Therefore, some of us in the 1970s became increasingly convinced that there was a very real potential for many of these smaller countries to develop legal, banking and general financial services for those in other countries. This financial entrepôt business resulted for some in considerable revenue from chartering banks and registering companies, providing support for such and generally fostering development not just economically but also educationally through the greater empowerment of their citizens. This was seen as positive by many, including Western governments and development agencies. Indeed, some gave technical assistance to these states in refining their laws and getting their acts together.

Competition developed between countries, particularly in the Caribbean, and additional incentives to attract foreign, largely put-through finance were found – often with assistance from overseas governments and professionals. As most of the wealth they attracted was on its way to somewhere else, it soon became sensible for these jurisdictions to offer no or substantially reduced tax deals – becoming essentially tax havens. Those within the common law tradition already had bank and professional confidentiality, but this was often enhanced by legislation to provide bank secrecy. Some, particularly in the Pacific, went a good deal further by enacting laws making it a criminal offence to give any assistance in the investigation of financial affairs other than pursuant to a court order. All this was little different to a number of European jurisdictions – albeit pressure, largely from the US and Italy, was then already beginning to weaken Switzerland's impenetrability. It is also the case that many, including some governments, extolled the virtues of discreet banking services, particularly in the face of what they saw as state-sponsored confiscation dressed up as indigenization. One or two jurisdictions went a good deal further and advertised for suspect funds which they offered to 'cleanse' for a percentage. At much the same time, the US woke up to the fact that reducing the supply and/or demand for drugs through traditional criminal justice mechanisms was not working sufficiently. Realising that traffickers do what they do to make money, it made sense to 'hit them in their wallets', undermining not just the motive for their criminal enterprise but its financial lifeblood. These interventions depended, as they do today, on intelligence and in particular the identification and tracing of wealth.

Therefore, criminal organisations had an economic incentive to hide their wealth and in particular sever the evidential connection between the rewarding of predicate crimes and their ill-gotten gains. Not surprisingly, although it did take some time for governments to wake up to the realities, in the same way that multinationals and high-tax payers found the facilities offered by these financial centres attractive, so did the criminals who tended also to be less scrupulous about observing other laws and being good citizens. In some places, the criminals introduced their lifestyle in others to assure the cooperation of governments, and such rudimentary supervisory authorities as were mustered or parachuted in resorted to bribery and corruption. Some societies were willingly 'penetrated'; others didn't see the risks until it was too late!

If this sounds familiar, like a gangster novel, this is not surprising, as this was where authors found their plots and international law enforcement their nemesis. Organised crime groups, sometimes with terrorist connections, exploited the opportunities that those who were willing to prostitute their sovereignty jostled to offer them. Politicians – some at the highest level, including judges and police officers – were corrupted and conventional attempts by other governments and international agencies to obtain cooperation were thwarted. ICPO-Interpol identified these developments as the greatest hurdle to fighting international crime, and Commonwealth Law Ministers were so concerned that they established a special intelligence network operating within diplomatic privilege – something that has never been wholly replicated. Nonetheless, no matter how much the informed concern, the abuse continued and those who did stand up were easily brushed aside – some permanently. In a few instances, states became arguably captured and almost wholly attentive to criminal interests. Governments – most notably the US, the UK, Canada and Italy – lacking access to traditional mechanisms for mutual legal assistance, relied on intelligence gathering and in some cases extrajudicial interventions.

Nevertheless, despite determined attempts by bodies as diverse as the Commonwealth Secretariat, ICPO-Interpol, the IMF and OECD to promote greater accountability, often alongside initiatives from the US, the UK and other interested parties, the most dramatic turning point came as a result of 9/11. While there is some evidence that terrorists indirectly availed themselves of these dark financial facilities, the priority before 9/11 – particularly for the US – was the illicit trade in narcotics. Indeed, the then General Counsel of the US Treasury was delivering a paper explaining why American agencies did not consider focusing on the financial aspects of terror a priority at exactly the same time as the planes flew into the Twin Towers. While Britain and especially the Northern Ireland office had a different perspective on its own, it did not have the muscle. The immediate and then considered response to the attacks was in part adopting a similar approach as US federal agencies had for its 'war' on drugs. The Patriot Act, initially designed to address the Colombian drug cartels, was the vehicle for a raft of measures and initiatives to effectively undermine financial privacy and facilitate the gleaning of financial intelligence, enabling the disruption of terrorist networks. Whether the Bush administration's assertions (that financial privacy was dead and that you are either with us or against us) were really a justified response to Bin Laden's atrocities is problematic, but this opened the doors to those who were as concerned about the laundering of criminal funds, escaping tax and frustrating economic sanctions. As a result, parts of the Caribbean are very different places today than what they were.

Dr Dominic Thomas-James, a member of the Bar of England and Wales with both a criminological and international relations background, is exceptionally well placed to chart a course through this sea of intrigue and often obscuration. While setting his unique analysis within the broader context of the development of smaller jurisdictions, he focuses on three British Overseas Territories that to a greater or lesser degree became embroiled, if not in the problem-making, at least the problem-solving: Turks and Caicos, Anguilla and Bermuda. Each of these island states has a very different history with quite different traditions. Indeed, Bermuda is not in the Caribbean and has always seen itself to be in a somewhat different sea than its southern cousins. Dr Thomas-James analyses the law, its background and development across a broad spectrum of issues in these three jurisdictions, addressing in particular the interplay with the UK Government, which retains a considerable amount of responsibility for matters relating to security and foreign policy – and therefore stability and development. The tensions that have emerged between the UK (together with the EU) and a number of smaller jurisdictions in regard to transparency of beneficial ownership of corporations and trusts are fairly, expertly and constructively presented. Indeed, as a good Welshman would, Dr Thomas-James explores and invariably explodes many myths as to the infamy of those in the region and the perfidiousness of Whitehall! Misunderstandings – often the result of ignorance, but occasionally self interest and other agendas – are exposed for what they are.

Those who wish to find webs of conspiracy and intrigue involving vested interests at the heart of capitalism compounded by grasping corrupt officials and politicians will search in vain in this scholarly and suitably dispassionate study. As a specialist in development, Dr Thomas-James is well aware of the importance of stability and security (if perhaps not always integrity) in promoting sustainable development. He is clearly aware of and alludes to the problems that some countries have faced. What this book is not is the usual polemical attack on jurisdictions which have as much complicity in money laundering as has (arguably) the City of London. Indeed, in recent times a senior British minister accepted that London was one of the world's leading money laundering centres! Of course, there are degrees of culpability, and perhaps the time has now come to extend the approach of anti-corruption and anti–tax fraud laws criminalising the failure to prevent in the course of business money laundering. However, the reality is as the US Presidential Commission on Organised Crime reported 40 years ago: all institutions that handle wealth are at risk from being embroiled – willingly or otherwise – in the laundering process.

The more we concentrate on interdicting wealth associated with crime, the more likely it is that those with suspect wealth will try and hide it. Indeed, the emphasis that was placed back in the early 1980s on assertions that the authorities would deprive criminals – particularly drug traffickers – of their ill-gotten gains, the more incentive there was for enterprise criminals to go to the time, trouble and risks of hiding their wealth and sever the nexus with specific criminal activity: to launder their wealth. A confidential report prepared by a senior police officer in the Special Branch in the UK in 1985 expressed concern that without effective measures to actually deprive criminals of their illicit wealth – something we have yet to achieve in Britain in common with most other countries – we were actually encouraging them to engage in laundering.

While many authors have been eager to chronicle the failures of these island countries to meet international standards – which are not universally appropriate or realistic – there has always been a degree of concern, even in the most corrupted jurisdictions, to address issues of compliance. Even criminal organisations need to have regard to the reputation of the place where they seek to wash their dirty money. Depending upon where one is in the laundering cycle, a reputation for sound compliance has clear commercial value. Consequently, attempts have been made and continue to be made to improve not just substantive law and regulation but also its administration. Given the history of many of these places, what is problematic is that resentment can soon arise where there is a perception (particularly in the media) that they are being told what to do; for example, to put additional costs towards the benefit of those who want to experiment with drugs (such as US high school kids). This is, of course, an overly simplistic analysis, but it has always been unfair to disregard the attempts that have been made to improve compliance and to varying degrees provide assistance to other countries, even when it is not always reciprocated. Having engaged in comprehensive field work, Dr Thomas-James tests the desire of governments and the majority of players in these three jurisdictions to clean up their reputations. None relishes remaining in a barrel where a few rotten apples have tainted all.

The intense external pressure on some jurisdictions has resulted in political concerns over their sovereignty, particularly within the Caribbean. This has been exacerbated by the feeling, albeit largely misconceived, that the measures they are being bullied into accepting are for the benefit of others. Indeed, in a recent case in Jamaica, senior judges questioned the cost benefit of requiring lawyers to disclose to the authorities their suspicions relating to criminal property on the basis that the amount of wealth interdicted as a result of such information was minuscule – in the vast majority of jurisdictions. Of course, the justification for such laws (in the minds of law enforcement officers, at least) is the potential for such information to be refined into intelligence and then utilised in the disruption of criminal and subversive activities. The problem with this, however, is that the results may well not be obvious or accountable, and therefore relatively unpersuasive for those placed in the front line, like banks and their advisers. While sovereignty is 'qualified' in the case of dependent territories, as the recent history of Turks and Caicos shows, it is no less a sensitive issue. The UK Government's interventions have been controversial and have had significant repercussions.

Therefore, in what has become a storm of indignation regarding the requirement that beneficial ownership of companies and trusts is made more transparent and there is ever-increasing pressure for more cooperation in tax and criminal matters, this book's sober and informed analysis is most timely and appreciated by those most involved. It is candid about the implications of the revelations resulting from leaked papers, and about what puts this in context. The work focuses on three dependent territories and, as I have indicated the issues thrown up by this status, both make more complex and in some respects simplify the measures that have been taken to bolster confidence and promote responsibility. Comparative lawyers have long recognised that laws for their effectiveness depend upon so many factors and not least the environment within which they operate. As Lord Denning once remarked in the context of legal colonial heritage, the

English oak fares well in Kent, less so in the jungles of Malaysia. In importing, let alone imposing, laws without sufficient regard to the realities can be problematic. This work takes these concerns and addresses them with relevance to other jurisdictions across the world. It therefore contributes to the discussion far more widely than the three jurisdictions upon which it focuses. Much of the discussion and analysis would be identified by someone familiar with what has gone on in, for example, Vanuatu as they would in the Bahamas and certainly the Cayman Islands. In this regard it is important to note that Dr Thomas-James uses the three territories as exemplars of the issues, which are therefore of relevance to other countries that have gone down the same track or are currently doing so.

This book will be of interest to a wide range of readers. Most obviously, those involved in the financial services industry in the Caribbean and Bermuda will find it unusually well informed and – while not patronising – constructive and helpful. Those involved in law enforcement and protecting the financial sector will find it helpful and supportive of their values and objectives, albeit perhaps taking a too independent and unbiased approach for some! Lawyers and professional advisers will also benefit from the book's detailed examination of the law and discussion of new approaches, such as focusing rather more on unexplained rather than tainted wealth. Those who actually do mind other people's wealth will benefit not only from an authoritative statement and explanation of the compliance obligations and costs imposed upon them, but also by presenting the discussion in the round – taking account of their concerns and the practicalities of conducting business often without the depth and breadth of support than would be found on shore. Academics may well be taken aback that the book refrains from castigating what many persist in believing are states that long ago put the 'for sale' notice up, but in the best traditions of scholarship the book sees things also from the perspective of those living and working in the countries concerned.

This is certainly not a book simply about financial crime; it is much more and should therefore interest all those in public policy, development studies, international relations, politics, economics and business studies. It suitably addresses the wide canvas of concerns and avoids sinking into subject silos. It is also a good read written by an author whose insightful comments and observations deserve respect.

Professor Barry Rider OBE
Professorial Fellow, Centre of Development Studies
University of Cambridge

Preface

This book examines offshore financial centres and their relationship with suspect wealth and economic crime. In particular, it focuses on a category of jurisdictions which are under-researched yet critically important: the British Overseas Territories. For some time, these jurisdictions have been perceived to be injudicious, harmful actors with their wilful, or inadvertent, receipt of international suspect wealth through the provision of offshore financial services. Economic crime and other misconduct is inimical to economic prosperity and sustainable development, and any country which is perceived, or shown, to harbour illicit wealth – or facilitate aggressive fiscal planning, even if permissible by law – is increasingly subject to scrutiny and challenge in securing its place in the international community. The relevance of offshore jurisdictions in the world's financial machine is inescapable and unlikely to diminish so long as globalism and the ease of doing international business persists. While researching for this book, two important events occurred which exacerbated negative sentiments towards the Overseas Territories, namely the Panama and Paradise papers. These reignited the anti–tax haven campaign and influenced both policy and legislation which have consequently been imposed on the territories. This has impacted negatively upon the relationship between the UK government and its Overseas Territories.

This book sets out to question whether the degree of criticism such jurisdictions receive is warranted in light of their apparent willingness to engage in internationally advocated standards to tackle economic crime and prevent the receipt of suspect wealth. Those British Overseas Territories which have developed sophisticated financial centres as a means of economic and sustainable development have become firm targets of governments and transparency campaigners alike. While it is long established that countries have no obligation to collect taxes for other countries, these jurisdictions are increasingly working to be perceived as valued international cooperation partners.

Understanding that economic crimes like corruption, money laundering, fraud, terrorism financing and tax offences are inimical to legal, economic and sustainable development, the book aims to signpost why we should be concerned about the role played by offshore financial centres in a less caricatured way. The book focuses on three selected island jurisdictions: Bermuda, the Turks and Caicos Islands, and Anguilla. Its main aim is to address three questions. First, are international standards regarding suspect wealth viable and prevalent in these three jurisdictions? Second, are the territories complying with these standards? And finally, how can these jurisdictions better safeguard their economies and prevent suspect wealth entering their financial centres? The book provides a comparative analysis of the legal framework, regulatory environment and compliance records across each of the three jurisdictions on key areas including bribery, money laundering, terrorism financing, economic substance, tax and beneficial ownership transparency. In brief summary of answers to these questions, international standards are viable, although an indiscriminate, one-size-fits-all approach to the territories in question is inappropriate and eschews important contextual nuances which help explain the different extents of compliance. For any country interested in securing its place in the international community, avoiding blacklists, financial de-risking and other reputational harm, it would be shocking to conclude that there is an absence of adherence or will in complying with standards. Each territory exhibits willingness and ability to comply with international standards, although the extent of their abilities and capacities vary. The book provides observations as to how the territories can better protect themselves and their financial centres from receiving suspect wealth while ensuring a reasonable balance is struck between safeguarding on the one hand and prosperity on the other, acknowledging that financial services are a mainstay of these economies and the lifeblood of their citizens. This work hopes to provide greater understanding about these under-researched jurisdictions, to contextualise their roles and to provide an assessment as to their true levels of compliance with international standards, not solely by reference to rankings but by a more holistic view of the individual territories' legal, regulatory and compliance frameworks – set against a backdrop of important contextual knowledge often omitted in scholarly discussion. This is not a defence of tax havens, however it is also not an impetuous caving to so many of those normative criticisms which we are all too familiar with, which often lack substance. In this vein, it is hoped that this book facilitates a more meaningful, sensitive discussion about these important jurisdictions.

This book draws in large part upon my doctoral research conducted at the University of Cambridge between 2015 and 2019. The materials are, with best endeavours, up to date at the time of writing, although doubtless there will be developments between finishing this book and its publication. There are many individuals, throughout this time and since, who have been of significant encouragement and support and whose assistance has contributed greatly to the writing of this book.

I first wish to thank my doctoral supervisor, Professor Barry Rider OBE LLD, of Jesus College, Cambridge, for his unstinting support and supervisory guidance throughout the research and writing of my Ph.D. and other professional activities. His vision for facilitating more meaningful international cooperation in the field of economic crime has greatly inspired this work. I am most grateful for his mentorship, belief and friendship.

I wish to acknowledge the support of my Ph.D. *viva voce* examiners, Professor Jason Sharman FBA of King's College, Cambridge, and Dr Peter German QC of the International Centre for Criminal Justice Reform, British Columbia, for their invaluable feedback on my doctoral thesis, which contributed significantly in the consequent writing of this book. I am also grateful to Professor Sir Ivan Lawrence QC, Master of the Bench of the Inner Temple, who has been a source of great encouragement and who called me to the Bar of England and Wales in 2016.

I wish to thank my dear parents, Sarah Thomas-James and Raymond Rupert Thomas-James, of the Gower Peninsula, to whom this book is dedicated. I am deeply grateful to them for giving me the profound gift of education and the encouraging wisdom to pursue my Ph.D. up at Cambridge. I am ever thankful to have shared this journey with them. Their endless motivation has made the writing of this book not only possible but an enjoyable experience, and their unwavering love and support is truly appreciated. Further, I am extremely thankful to my partner, Margarita, whose companionship, love and steadfast support has resolutely motivated me in researching and writing this book.

This book would not have been possible without the insights of many professional colleagues I have met while serving as a Secretariat Member of the Cambridge International Symposium on Economic Crime at Jesus College. This significant forum has not only served as a valued research resource but has enabled me to gather significant insights during my research, and I am grateful to my Secretariat colleagues for their support. I am further appreciative to the many colleagues and friends I have made at the University of Cambridge including at Queens' College, Faculty of Law and Centre for Criminal Justice, Centre of Development Studies, Institute of Criminology, Institute of Continuing Education, and Cambridge Tax Discussion Group. I am appreciative to colleagues at Yale University's Global Justice Program, where I am presently a Fellow. Further, I owe thanks to many at the Bar and the Inner Temple for their continued support.

I wish to acknowledge and thank those individuals who have given so generously of their time and experience in discussing my work and helping me understand important background information and developments as they have arisen. These include Professor Barry Rider OBE; Saul Froomkin OBE QC; Premier of Bermuda Hon. David Burt JP MP; Hon. Trevor Moniz JP MP; Hon. Bob Richards JP MP; Larry Mussenden; Detective Chief Inspector Nicholas Pedro; Rosemary Jones; Richard Ambrosio; William Cooper; Sheelagh Cooper; Rory Field; H.E. Dr John Freeman CMG; Hon. Rhondalee Braithwaite-Knowles OBE; H.E. Richard Tauwhare; Hon. Akierra Missick MP; Angela Brooks; Denise Samuels-Dingwall; Paul Coleman; H.E. Christina Scott; John McKendrick QC; Rupert Jones; Hon. Pam Webster; Helen Hatton; Marisa Harding-Hodge; Don Mitchell CBE QC; Gary Youinou; Howard Sharp QC; Professor Philip Rutledge; Robin Sykes; Dr Shazeeda Ali; Hon. Justice David Hayton; Benito Wheatley; Professor Rose Marie Belle-Antoine; Hon. Judith Jones-Morgan; Dr May Hen; Dr Frank Madsen; Dr Henry Balani; Tom Withyman; and Professor Chizu Nakajima.

Finally, this book would not be possible without the support of my publishers, Routledge, and my series editor, Professor Nicholas Ryder of the University of the West of England. Their belief in the book, and the support of the broader editorial team, has been gratefully received and I am proud to contribute this work to Routledge's Law of Financial Crime series.

Cases

Australia

Trio Capital Limited (Admin App) v ACT Superannuation Management Pty Ltd & Others [2010] NSWSC 286.

Bahamas

Pindling v Douglas [1994] 318, Sup Ct.
Securities and Exchange Commissioners of the USA v Guaranty Trusts Ltd [1985] SC 423.

Belize

Securities and Exchange Commission v Banner Fund International [1996] 54 WIR 123 (SC).

Bermuda

Guardian Ltd v Bermuda Trust Co Ltd [2009] SC (Bda), 54 (Civ).
X Limited v Y [2019] SC (Bda) 58 (Civ).

Jamaica

Jamaica Bar Association v The Attorney General & The General Law Council [2017] JMFC Full 02.

Jersey

Macdoel Investments Ltd v Federal Republic of Brazil [2007] JLR 201.

UK England and Wales

Akhmedova v Akhmedov and others [2018] EWFC 23 (Fam).
Akita Holdings Limited (Appellant) v Honourable Attorney General of the TCI (Respondent) [2017] UKPC 7.
Bullivant v Attorney General for Victoria [1900] 2 QB 163; [1901] AC 196.

Commissioners of Inland Revenue v Willoughby (*1st and 2nd Appeals*) (*Consolidated*) [1997] *Opinions.*

Inland Revenue Commissioners v Duke of Westminster [1936] AC 1; 19 TC 490.

Lion Laboratories Ltd v Evans [1985] QB 526.

The Lords of Appeal for Judgment in the Case (*10 July 1997*); *IRC v Willoughby* [1997] 1 W.L.R., 1071, HL; [1997] S.T.C., 995.

MacNiven v Westmoreland Investments [2001] UKHL 6.

Madzimbamuto v Lardner-Burke [1968] UKPC 18.

Misick and others (*Appellants*) *v The Queen* (*Respondent*) (*TCI*) [2015] UKPC 31.

Mosley v News Group Newspapers Limited (*No 3*) [2008] EWHC 1777 QB; [2008] EMLR 20.

NCA v *Baker and ors* [2020] EWHC 822 (Admin).

Phillips v Eyre [1870] LR 6 QB.

Prudential PLC and Prudential (*Gibraltar*) *Limited v Special Commissioner of Income Tax and Philip Pandolfo* (*HM Inspector of Taxes*) [2009] EWHC 2494. Admin.

R v Inhabitants of the Country of Bedfordshire [1855] 24 LJBQ 81.

R v Michael McInerney [2009] EWCA Crime 1941.

R v Sweett Group Plc [2016] (unreported), see SFO: Sweett Group at http://www.sfo.gov.uk/cases/sweett-group/ (Accessed on 12 August 2017).

R v Tom Hayes [2015] EWCA Crim 1944.

Richardson Anthony Arthur (*Appellant*) *v The Attorney General of the TCI* (*Respondent*) [2012] UKPC 30.

Silken v Beaverbrook Newspapers Ltd [1958] 1 WLR 743.

Three Rivers District Council and Others v The Governor and Company of the Bank of England [2004] UKHL 48.

Tournier v National Provincial Bank [1924] 1 KB 461 CA, at 473.

Young v Young [2013] EWCA 3637 Fam.

US

Bullen v Wisconsin, 240 U.S. 625 (1916).

Hilton v Guyot, 159 U.S. 113 (1894).

Peterson v Idaho First Nat'l Bank, 367 P.2d 824 (Idaho 1961).

Sec. & Exch. Comm'n v Gordon, H-03-5772 (S.D. Tx. 2003).

State v Simpson, No. BA097211 (Cal. Super. Ct. L.A. County 1995).

United States v Bognaes, 2:16-mj-06194 (D. Ariz. 2016).

United States v Chapman (E.D. Va. 2013) 326 F. Supp. 3d 228 (E.D. Va. 2018).

United States v Currin 3:06CR74-3-BR, 3:06CR403-BR (W.D.N.C. Jul. 26, 2007)

United States v Dandong Hongxiang Indus. Dev. Co. et al., 2:16-MJ-06602 (D.N.J. 2016).

United States v Dreier, S1 09 Cr. 085 (JSR) (S.D.N.Y. 2009).

United States v Hall 3:18-cv-147-J-32PDB (M.D. Fla. 2013).

United States v Inniss, CR18-00134 (E.D.N.Y. 2018).

United States v Jones, 565 U.S. 400 (2012).

United States v Lopez, 12-CR-5236 (S.D. Cal. 2013).
United States v Mebiame, 16-627 (E.D.N.Y. 2016).
United States v Meyer, 3:16-cr-62-MOC (W.D.N.C. 2016).
United States v Perez-Ceballos 2:17-CR-245-3 (2017).
United States v Sarao 1:15-cr-00075 (N.D. Ill. 2015).
United States v Sutherland, CR17 4427 (W.D.N.C. 2017).

Legislation, regulations and treaties

Anguilla

Anti–Money Laundering and Terrorist Financing Code 2009
Anti–Money Laundering and Terrorist Financing Regulations
Companies (Amendment) Act 2018
Companies (Amendment) Act 2019
Companies Act 2000
Companies Registry Act
Company Management Act
Company Management Regulations
Criminal Justice Reform Bill 2018
Draft Constitution 2016
Draft Constitution 2019
Drug Trafficking Offences Act (Designated Countries and Territories) Regulations 2004
Financial Services Commission Act 2003
House of Assembly (Powers and Privileges) Act 2000
International Business Companies (Amendment) Act 2018
Justice Protection Act 2016
Legislative Assembly (Procedure) Rules 1976
Mutual Legal Assistance (Tax Matters) Act 2010
Mutual Legal Assistance (USA) Act 2000
Police (Amendment) Act 2016
Proceeds of Crime Act 2014
Tax Information Exchange (International Cooperation) Act 2016

Argentina

Penal Code, Argentina

Bermuda

Bribery Act 2016
Constitution Order 1986

Domestic Partnership Act 2018
Economic Substance Act 2018
Financial Intelligence Agency Act 2007
Investment Business Act 2003
Proceeds of Crime (Amendment) Act 2007
Proceeds of Crime (Anti–Money Laundering and Anti–Terrorist Financing) Regulations 2008
Proceeds of Crime (Anti–Money Laundering and Anti–Terrorist Financing Supervision and Enforcement) Act 2008
Proceeds of Crime Act 1997
Public Treasury (Administration and Payments) Act 1969
Registrar of Companies (Compliance Measures) Act 2017
Revenues Act 1898
Supreme Court Act 1905

Canada

Integrity Commission Act 2017

EU

Charter of Fundamental Rights of the European Union 2000
EC 4th Anti–Money Laundering Directive (2015) 2015/849
EC 5th Anti–Money Laundering Directive (2018) (EU) 2018/843 amending Directive 2015/849
European Convention on Human Rights 1950

India

Prevention of Corruption Act 1988

Jamaica

Charter of Fundamental Rights and Freedoms (Constitutional Amendment) Act 2011

Lithuania

Criminal Code of the Republic of Lithuania

Portugal

Law 89/2017

Romania

Criminal Code of the Republic of Romania

Turks and Caicos Islands

AML/PFT Regulations and Code 2011
Bribery Bill 2017
Bribery Ordinance 2017
Companies and Limited Partnerships (Economic Substance) Ordinance 2018
Companies Ordinance 2017
Confidential Relationships Ordinance 1979
Constitution 2011
Constitution (Interim Amendment) Order 2009
Financial Services Commission Ordinance 2001/2007
Integrity Commission Ordinance 2009
Non-Profit Regulations 2014
Political Activities (Amendment) Ordinance 2016
Prevention of Terrorism Ordinance 2014
Proceeds of Crime Ordinance 2007

UK

Anguilla Constitution Order 1982
Bermuda Constitution Act 1967
Bribery Act 2010
British Nationality Act 1981
Cayman Islands and Turks and Caicos Islands Act 1958
Commercial Agents (Council Directive) Regulations 1993
Companies (Disclosure of Address) (Amendment) Regulations 2018
Companies Act 2006
Counter-Terrorism Act 2008
Criminal Finances Act 2017
Financial Services Act 2012
Human Rights Act 1998
Income Tax Act 1842
Interpretation Act 1978
Money Laundering Regulations 2007
Proceeds of Crime Act 2002
Sanctions and Anti–Money Laundering Act 2018
Serious Crime Act 2007
West Indies Act 1962

US

Corporate Transparency Act 2019
Foreign Account Tax Compliance Act 2010
Privacy Act 1974
Right to Financial Privacy Act 1978

Other instruments

FATF Recommendations 2012
Lima Declaration on Tax Justice and Human Rights 2015
OECD Convention on Combating Bribery of Foreign Public Officials in International Business Transactions 1997
UN Convention Against Corruption 2004
UN Convention on the Rights of the Child 1989
UN International Declaration for the Suppression of the Financing of Terrorism 1999
Universal Declaration on Human Rights 1948

Abbreviations

AML	anti–money laundering
BEPS	base erosion and profit shifting
BMA	Bermuda Monetary Authority
BVI	British Virgin Islands
CDD	Customer Due Diligence
CFATF	Caribbean Financial Action Task Force
CFT	counter financing of terrorism
CRS	Common Reporting Standard
CSP	corporate service provider
DD	due diligence
Deb	Debate (UK Houses of Parliament)
DfID	Department for International Development (UK)
DNFBP	designated non-financial businesses and professions
DPA	deferred prosecution agreement
DPP	Director of Public Prosecutions
DTC	double taxation convention
EC	European Commission
ECCB	Eastern Caribbean Central Bank
ECHR	European Convention on Human Rights
EOI	exchange of information
EU	European Union
FAC	Foreign Affairs Committee (UK)
FATF	Financial Action Task Force
FCO	Foreign and Commonwealth Office (UK)
FCPA	Foreign Corrupt Practices Act (US)
FIA	financial intelligence agency
FIU	Financial Intelligence Unit
FinCEN	US Financial Crimes Enforcement Network
FSC	Financial Services Commission
FSI	Financial Secrecy Index
GDP	gross domestic product
GDPR	General Data Protection Regulation
HC	House of Commons

HL	House of Lords
HMRC	Her Majesty's Revenue and Customs (UK)
IBC	international business company
ICIJ	International Consortium of Investigative Journalists
IMF	International Monetary Fund
IO	Immediate Outcome
MER	Mutual Evaluation Report (FATF)
MLA	mutual legal assistance
MOSSFON	Mossack Fonseca
MP	Member of Parliament
NCA	National Crime Agency (UK)
NGO	non-governmental organisation
NRA	national risk assessment
OAD	Overseas Association Decision
OECD	Organisation for Economic Co-operation and Development
OFC	offshore financial centre
OT	Overseas Territory
PAC	Public Accounts Committee (Anguilla)
PEP	politically exposed person
POCA	Proceeds of Crime Act
PSC	persons with significant control
SAMLA	Sanctions and Anti–Money Laundering Act
SAR	suspicious activity reporting
SDG	Sustainable Development Goal(s)
SFO	Serious Fraud Office (UK)
SIPT	Special Investigation and Prosecution Team (TCI)
STEP	Society of Trust and Estate Practitioners
TCI	Turks and Caicos Islands
TI	Transparency International
TIEA	Tax Information Exchange Agreement
TJN	Tax Justice Network
UK	United Kingdom
UKPC	United Kingdom Privy Council
UNCAC	United Nations Convention Against Corruption
UNODC	United Nations Office on Drugs and Crime
US	United States of America
UWO	unexplained wealth order
1MDB	1Malaysia Development Berhad

1 Introduction and conceptual framework

1.1 Overview

In the global financial architecture, British Overseas Territories in the Caribbean and North Atlantic are of material significance. Post-colonialism, these relatively homogenous, archipelagic territories with financial centres have been the recipients of soft domination, and more recently legislative intervention, by metropolitan interests. Through their inalienable right to self-determination and pursuit of autonomous governance and financial independence, many developed offshore financial centres to achieve sustainable development, with encouragement from the UK. Recently, and exacerbated by the Panama and Paradise papers – two unprecedented breaches and publications of confidential data from law firms in Bermuda and Panama – the Overseas Territories are subject to increased pressure and ongoing perception that their financial centres facilitate criminality by harbouring suspect wealth, due to lack of transparency.

This book concerns suspect wealth as a product of economic misconduct like corruption, money laundering, terrorism financing, tax evasion, fraud and securities violations, and the increasingly controversial tax avoidance. This includes suspect wealth derived from overseas or domestic misconduct, given law enforcement's response is typically the same irrespective of origin. The book focuses on offshore financial centres and, in particular, systematically examines the legal, regulatory and compliance frameworks of three very different Overseas Territories: Bermuda, the Turks and Caicos Islands (TCI) and Anguilla. It sets out to examine their legal, regulatory and compliance regimes and explores three questions relating to such. First, how viable are international standards on suspect wealth and economic crime in the context of these three jurisdictions? Second, how willing and able are these jurisdictions to comply with international standards on suspect wealth? Third, how can they better protect the integrity of their financial centres from the risks of, and receiving, suspect wealth? Given how the global anti-economic crime framework is envisaged at international levels, the book also considers whether a one-size-fits-all approach to the Overseas Territories is appropriate.

In short, the research finds that while universalism is a desirable aspect of the modern approach for tackling suspect wealth, some standards are unviable or existing frameworks may present viable alternatives. On a critical evaluation of their legislation, international cooperation and reviews, the research indicates that all the territories demonstrate willingness to comply with international standards – contrary to the conception that they are pariah states. However, for reasons identified in this book, their ability and levels of compliance vary greatly. The book also tackles important issues arising from increasingly developing standards, namely the status of fundamental legal protections and whether these are at times eschewed in favour of the silver bullet purportedly afforded by transparency. Proceeding on the basis that receipt of suspect wealth is inimical to development, the book discusses its impact on development for both countries from which the wealth transits and the Overseas Territories themselves, with many having fundamental development concerns. In acknowledging the facilitatively harmful role that can be played by these territories, this work draws upon evidence of implication in international cases which indicate a less positive view of the territories. Notwithstanding this, a purpose of the book is to call into question whether the degree of criticism that these and other small jurisdictions have encountered is warranted in light of their apparent willingness to engage in the enactment and administration of internationally accepted standards and legislation and to cooperate with international mechanisms and institutions. In this regard, the book approaches a series of important issues for law, international relations and development, and hopes to facilitate a more constructive, meaningful discussion about offshore financial centres and the British Overseas Territories.

1.2 Approach and chapter structure

The book begins by exploring the concerns which relate to economic crime which have manifested at international and supranational levels and have provided the basis for the inception and development of the global rules-based anti-economic crime framework, such as various international treaties and conventions, and the emerging influence of soft-law standards propagated by the Financial Action Task Force and others. The book also contextualises the problem associated with the offshore world and provides important background knowledge about the development of offshore financial centres, their utility and role in the global financial machine. Through extensive primary and secondary research, material background information on the Overseas Territories will be presented both as a collective group of jurisdictions and, importantly, as individual ones. The analysis of the selected territories' legal, regulatory and compliance frameworks is approached systematically, addressing the following themes which are widely acknowledged to be constituent elements of a country's toolkit to tackle economic crime and mitigate against the risks of suspect wealth: bribery and corruption; anti–money laundering and counter-terrorism financing; beneficial ownership, company law, and transparency; economic substance requirements; and tax information exchange and international cooperation.

One of the book's principal concerns relates to the ability of small jurisdictions to meet the expectations of the international community in addressing the threats presented both to themselves and others by their innocent, or otherwise, facilitating of laundering the proceeds of economic misconduct. It discusses the extent to which actual, or perceived, involvement in these processes harms the stability and development of the countries concerned but also the wider international community. The backdrop to this discussion takes the proposition in the preamble to the United Nations Convention Against Corruption (UNCAC), which underlines the damage to stability, development and security threatened by corruption, money laundering and other serious crimes. In order to address the aforementioned research questions, the book's methodological approach is a qualitative one, involving the analysis of primary and secondary materials including case law, legislation, treaties and other legal instruments in the international and domestic law contexts. Soft-law resources are also evaluated. This approach is complemented by informal discussions which have been conducted with a range of present and former officials, experts and practitioners in the Overseas Territories; participants of the Annual International Symposium on Economic Crime at Jesus College, Cambridge; and through professional associations such as the Inner Temple. These discussions were conducted on a non-attributable basis and informed the points made in this book.

The book comprises 8 chapters. Following a functional overview and guidance on structural approach, Chapter 1 introduces the reader to background concepts. These include economic crime, offshore financial centres, defining 'suspect wealth', and the relevance of this research within the broader field of financial crime, set against increasingly high-profile and intensifying interest in this topic.

Chapter 2 considers the impact of suspect wealth on development together with the concerns about corruption, money laundering, fraud, tax evasion and the increasingly stigmatic tax avoidance. It identifies and explores the concerns which have manifested at international and supranational levels and how suspect wealth threatens the stability of financial markets and institutions, with reference to cases. In the development context, concerns about the impact on countries losing public revenue through economic crime will be considered. Along with concerns, the chapter acknowledges and explores some of the ambivalences in the way certain types of misconduct are viewed. It also sets out for the reader the international anti-economic crime movement and its hard- and soft-law components.

In Chapter 3, offshore financial centres are discussed at greater length, as well as perceptions and cases of facilitating economic crime and harbouring suspect wealth therein. The Overseas Territories are introduced and the backdrop as to their constitutional relationship with the UK, and the legal framework, is considered. Aspects of the Panama and Paradise papers data sets are analysed by way of contextualising how the territories are increasingly becoming targets for their role as so-called tax havens. Important background is also outlined, such as capacity and development issues, putting the jurisdictions into context prior to considering three selected territories.

Chapter 4 focuses on Bermuda, one of the jurisdictions analysed. It commences with an overview of Bermuda's history, legal framework, governance and taxation system, and economic development as a financial centre. Drawing upon evidence of implication in international matters, it considers Bermuda's role as a financial centre and criticism of Bermuda's tax practices. The chapter moves to a systematic review of Bermuda's response to suspect wealth and economic crime, and levels of compliance with international standards. It also considers Bermuda's social and developmental concerns as well as evidence of implication in criminal cases overseas. In summary, the findings indicate that Bermuda's compliance and response to suspect wealth and economic crime is the most advanced of the three territories considered.

Chapter 5 focuses on the Turks and Caicos Islands, a jurisdiction which in 35 years has had periods of substantial economic growth yet also development-hindering circumstances such as allegations of systemic domestic corruption and ministerial criminality causing direct rule. The same systemic analytical approach is followed in reviewing TCI's response and compliance with suspect wealth and anti-economic crime standards. In summary, this chapter's analysis indicates TCI's increasing willingness to implement international standards, while several areas display considerable room for improvement.

Chapter 6 focuses on Anguilla and follows the same systemic analytical approach to reviewing its response to economic crime and suspect wealth. The chapter identifies Anguilla's fundamental development concerns, such as connectivity, capacity and need for legal reform. It also examines Anguilla's implication in recent data breaches, cases and reports of serious misconduct overseas, and receiving suspect wealth. In summary, this chapter indicates that Anguilla has shown some willingness to adhere to international standards, but implementation remains affected by capacity issues and a lack of progress with regards to institutional development, legal and constitutional reform.

In Chapter 7, the concept of transparency in corporate ownership is examined. The chapter considers this issue manifesting through public and central beneficial ownership register laws and policies. It also analyses the role of privacy and confidentiality and questions whether these legal protections are gradually diminishing in favour of increased transparency. It considers whether the general right to privacy extends to financial affairs and whether the utility of confidentiality and the offshore confidentiality norm stands reconcilable with recent legislation compelling public registers in the Overseas Territories. Given the importance placed on misappropriated data in the Panama and Paradise papers (and more recently in the FinCEN files) and its impact on reforming law and contributing to policy discussions, some remaining paradoxes are considered.

In Chapter 8, the main arguments raised in this book are summarised and conclusions are provided in relation to the research questions. A pertinent issue in law, development and international relations is whether it is reasonable to expect small states to be able to shoulder the same kinds of responsibilities as large, better-resourced jurisdictions. It is in this context that this book has examined the ability and willingness of three Overseas Territories with regards to the various standards and laws that have been internationally advanced relating to financial crime and the receipt of suspect wealth. It is hoped that conclusions reached through the analyses provide a research resource at a time where research and deeper thinking is lacking.

1.3 Background, topicality and contribution to research

For any society interested in upholding the rule of law, it is imperative that there remains a clear demarcation between conduct which is legal and conduct which is illegal. A long-standing principle of jurisprudential positivism is that a law 'properly so called' and the corresponding duty to obey it stands, irrespective of whether the law is morally justified or a good law (Hart 1958). Of course, law is not the single normative domain in society, given the influence of religion and ethics on behaviour (Kelsen 1934). With this, there is an increasing perception that jurisdictions which have established themselves as sophisticated business (and even offshore finance) centres are actively harming the world's economy and otherwise serve no useful economic purpose (Oxfam 2016). In other words, there is an intensifying, fervent perception that offshore finance is at the heart of so many of the problems faced today – particularly those relating to the poorest. There is, rightly or wrongly, a perceived underhandedness and iniquity in one jurisdiction facilitating 'dangerous opportunity' for those in other jurisdictions seeking to abuse and undermine their offerings, or obviate legal or other obligations. The charge is simple: that offshore financial centres knowingly, or inadvertently, facilitate economic crime, widen countries' tax gaps, and contribute to growing inequalities, however so defined. Therein lies a very interesting problem, one which is as argumentatively divisive as it is necessary to address. That is, what do we do about 'offshore'?

Part of contributing some answers in relation to this highly complex question involves understanding what the problem actually is, and parameterising it accordingly. Much has been written about offshore financial centres (e.g. Antoine 2013; Sharman 2006; Hampton and Abbott 1999; Shaxson 2011; Hendry and Dickson 2018). Yet, the discourse seems to settle at extremes: support at the one end (often found in the legal discourse) and negativity at the other (often in social science discourse). Offshore jurisdictions have traditionally been referred to as 'tax havens' and they evoke perceptions akin to author W. Somerset Maugham's famous formulation of the "sunny place for shady people". Since the OECD-led campaigns against tax havens going as far back as the 1990s (Sharman 2006), and perhaps more recently dominated by global tax justice advocates, these jurisdictions are increasingly under legislative, regulatory and popular scrutiny. Such has been compounded by recent data breaches emanating from Bermuda, the Bahamas and Panama. Notwithstanding the inimical relationship between economic crime and facilitative misconduct which harbours suspect wealth, the picture about the role of international and offshore financial centres is far more complex than the charges typically laid, and assisting in the understanding of this is a foundational aim of this book.

While much has been written on economic crime itself, particularly in legal and criminological discourse, the concept of suspect wealth is under-researched. Suspect wealth is wider in scope than proceeds of crime, and is arguably where the complexity arises when assessing the role played by offshore financial centres. The Panama and Paradise papers – two unprecedented breaches of confidential information from law firms Mossack Fonseca's (MOSSFON) office in Panama and Appleby's office in Bermuda – showed that the problem was not confined to nefarious actors and corruptibility, but rather the function of jurisdictions in enabling permissible conduct under law to be exploited for financial gain, the most notable being tax avoidance. Suspect wealth is defined in this book as wealth attributable to criminality or to controversial, yet perhaps legal conduct. Therefore, it can derive from the proceeds of criminality such as money laundering, fraud, corruption, narcotics trafficking and others defined at Schedule 1, Serious Crime Act 2007. It can also relate to wealth fleeing some type of civil, societal, legal or matrimonial injunction. Or, it could be monies which States have an interest in, insofar as its ability to be structured offshore may lead to less taxable income in a particular jurisdiction. While fiscal planning, for example, is permissible by law, aggressive forms are increasingly perceived as immoral and treated similarly to tax evasion. The fallout from the Panama and Paradise papers were as much to do with wealth emanating illicitly as legally, although the common theme was inarguably the adverse role played by offshore financial centres.

This book examines offshore financial centres and their legal and regulatory responses to suspect wealth. These jurisdictions, commonly known as tax havens, are significant in the global financial architecture but are also perceived to be the destinations, or facilitators, of suspect wealth. There is corpus evidence suggesting many are facilitators or recipients of illicit wealth transiting from foreign jurisdictions. Within many academic disciplines, there is a level of prejudice which is directed indiscriminately towards all offshore centres, which does not account for whether their flaws are deliberate acts, innate stubbornness, wilful blindness, or unintended consequences. In this book, the concept of offshore will be discussed at length, as even London and New York are commonly considered tax havens because historically these financial centres have offered fiscal incentives to non-residents in a similar way to those offshore centres offering privacy or ring-fencing (Antoine 2013, 122). Tax havens bear the impression that wealth there, or clients which use their services, is either innately criminal or the product of 'tax dodging'. It is an inescapable fact that anonymous shell companies, nominee services, trusts and foundations, lack of beneficial ownership registers or exchange frameworks, limited commercial activity requirements, and lack of regulatory controls can facilitate international criminality and the laundering of its proceeds. Offerings in the offshore world can be used by criminals, corrupt officials or other individuals or corporates to conceal or invest wealth. Moreover, structuring one's assets offshore to conceal them from spouses is being increasingly seen in high-value divorce cases (*Young v Young* [2013]). In *Akhmedova v Akhmedov and others* [2018], the UK's highest-value divorce case, Haddon-Cave J at 20 averred that the respondent was engaging in a "continuing campaign to defeat [the applicant] by concealing his assets in a web of offshore companies".

Suspect wealth is closely aligned to the concept of unexplained wealth, the inference being that the wealth is somehow suspicious and should be explained. This transcends to an important philosophical debate surrounding proprietary rights, the right to privacy and other notions of freedom to maximise wealth and protect assets. In 2017, the UK enacted the Criminal Finances Act 2017 containing extended civil asset recovery powers in the form of unexplained wealth orders (Thomas-James 2017). Interestingly, in *NCA v Baker and ors* [2020], the first major unexplained wealth order case in the High Court, Lang J at 97 emphasised: "The use of complex offshore corporate structures or trusts *is not, without more, a ground for believing that they have been set up, or are being used, for wrongful purposes*, such as money laundering" (emphasis added). Lang J went on to say:

> There are lawful reasons – privacy, security, tax mitigation – why very wealthy people invest their capital in complex offshore corporate structures or trusts. Of course, such structures may also be used to disguise money laundering, but there must be some additional evidential basis for such a belief, going beyond the complex structures used.

Such dicta re-emphasises legitimate uses of offshore structures and, importantly, the high evidential hurdle which must be passed regarding suspicion.

There is significant evidence pointing to the harmful role played by tax havens, which will be acknowledged and explored in this work. However, the book will also consider some of the mischaracterisations and conflations which confuse, rather than clarify, thinking in this area. A good example is that there tends to be conflation between indirect taxation models and referring to a country with such a system as a 'zero-tax' jurisdiction. Moreover, negative sentiments might be based on misplaced issues. For example, while attention on money laundering is correct, emphasis should also be placed on combatting the underlying predicate criminality of despotic regimes stealing money from their citizens, keeping them in abject poverty. Similar is seen in the tax evasion-avoidance debate. Sole focus on fiscally advantageous products on offer in tax havens often omits considering whether tax policy or legislative reform is needed 'onshore' as a means of addressing the issue. In other words, there is often greater emphasis on offshore facilitation, rather than onshore predicate criminality. Often is the case that onshore jurisdictions have both greater influence in the international community and greater resources than offshore jurisdictions.

This book considers an important group of under-researched offshore financial centres. These are the British Overseas Territories. There are 14 Overseas Territories which span the globe, although the ones which operate sophisticated financial services sectors are Anguilla, Bermuda, the British Virgin Islands (BVI), the Cayman Islands, Gibraltar, Montserrat, and the Turks and Caicos Islands. Within this group of jurisdictions, this book focuses on three selected territories: Bermuda, TCI and Anguilla. Various explanations could account for the lack of research in respect of the Overseas Territories, such as their relatively small share of the global offshore financial sector, or that many are micro-populated, or that many do not have universities or research institutions therein to conduct such studies. Much original scholarly writing on certain Overseas Territories pertains to their initial formation as offshore centres and challenges in transitioning from barter-based economies to world-leading financial service providers (Freyer and

Morriss 2013), much like similar timely research on Commonwealth Caribbean countries entering the same markets (Ali 2003). Such works often suggest that these jurisdictions did not enter the offshore market for nefarious purposes, but rather as a means of achieving sustainable development. Financial independence and economic prosperity are the mainstays of Overseas Territories which have been reliant on tourism and financial services.

The islands are strategically important in their own ways. Bermuda is one of the world's largest and most important (re)insurance markets, while TCI is among the fast-growing tourism destinations in the Caribbean, and Anguilla occupies an under-utilised geographical location in a shipping superhighway. What are often neglected, or perhaps omitted, in the discourse relating to economic crime, are the development stages and challenges of these jurisdictions which are in stark contrast to their fiscal paradise imagery, seen in some commentaries (Shaxson 2011). For example, Anguilla is a significant captive insurance domicile and is commonly considered a tax haven and middle-income country. However, it has significant development issues ranging from an outdated constitution to reliance on neighbouring islands for healthcare and connectivity. Various economic crises, including the collapse of its two indigenous banks, have hindered development. Similarly, TCI faces profound development concerns, including the ongoing civil recovery programme of mis-sold Crown land and, like many of the Overseas Territories, proneness to natural disasters yet too wealthy to qualify for UK development aid. Many are small, micro-population, archipelagic islands which rely largely on tourism, financial services, and property development. As the 2017 hurricanes which devasted BVI, Anguilla and TCI demonstrated, disasters of this kind can temporarily eradicate large aspects of the islands' economies. Lack of research on the challenges faced by Overseas Territories risks too much emphasis placed on them as financial centres, which paves the way for almost exclusively negative perceptions about the jurisdictions as a whole. This book aims to provide this context, upon which more meaningful cooperation, understanding and exchange can be harnessed with these jurisdictions at bilateral and international levels.

International attention is placed on the territories, in part, based on the fact that the UK brands itself as a global leader in the fight against corruption and economic crime (Sharman 2017), with its notable international Anti-Corruption Summit in 2016. However, one of the clear problems identified in this book is that some Overseas Territories have traded in a culture of unaccountability. With this, the nexus between international suspect wealth and its ability to enter OTs via corruption and lack of controls manifests. This has not only harmed (and continues to harm) others but significantly stints the territories own development of institutions of governance and law. Promoting and achieving integrity is not only an essential development strategy but also underpins compliance with international obligations. A balance between enhancing international reputation to attract legitimate business, and not being overly burdened in a way that disproportionately affects sustainability, is a constant concern for the Overseas Territories. A good example are suspicious activity reporting (SAR) requirements, the low number of which represents significant risk-areas in many of the territories' national risk assessments (NRA). However, when drugs, homicides and gang crimes have been prevalent in some territories, it is perhaps understandable why certain resource-intense international standards might be under-resourced or otherwise a lower priority. Law enforcement resource challenges are not problems confined to OFCs, but equally (perhaps more problematic) in larger metropolitan states which struggle to properly fund modern policing.

Therefore, the book contributes to an important present discussion. Since April 2016, when the first news stories were published regarding the Panama papers, rarely a week goes by without some adverse press relating to the Overseas Territories, or at least offshore financial centres generally. Not only are the territories subject to soft and hard domination by larger economies, but they are recipients of ever-changing international standards and externally dictated controls. Moreover, they are obliged to address, or implement, the standards set by increasingly influential soft-law bodies – lack of compliance giving rise to various forms of sanctions. In analysing three very different jurisdictions, the case will be made for more nuanced thinking about the Overseas Territories. While many criticisms against them are warranted, and evidence supporting these will be included as part of the analysis, many criticisms are not and bring the phrase "physician, heal thyself"[1] to mind.

To this effect, it is important to initially address some common misconceptions. The narrative against offshore financial centres often presents the proceeds of crime and fiscal matters indiscriminately. No matter how morally questionable tax avoidance may be, it is manifestly not the same as dishonestly evading it. When public services in the UK and other similar jurisdictions are subject to austerity, and other countries are dependent upon foreign aid budgets, it is unsurprising that any conduct perceived as greed-driven is scrutinised. However, there are many government-encouraged tax avoidance schemes, like individual savings accounts with increased allowances not incurring any income or capital gains tax, or tax incentives or deferrals for businesses locating in under-developed areas. What one pays in tax is a matter of law rather than morals, and legitimate fiscal planning is a well-established legal doctrine (*IRC v Duke of Westminster* [1936], Lord Tomlin, 19). It is interesting that the concept of wealth maximisation through tax structuring attracts so much revulsion, as was seen in the revelations from the Panama and Paradise papers. Saving money in a climate of record-low interest rates squarely undermines many basic taught principles of the importance of saving, which gives rise to the incentive of investments.

In a similar vein, the Overseas Territories are often viewed indiscriminately. The Panama and Paradise papers occurred during the research for this book and, since then, formidable sentiment has been directed at the territories. The publications shone an indefatigably bright spotlight on the scope and scale of offshore business and the extent to which offshore services can be used to hide

1 A proverb found in the Gospel according to Luke 4:23, which urges attending to one's own defects before criticising those of others.

or maximise wealth. If raising awareness of these issues was the objective, then the perpetrator of the Panama papers succeeded. Governmental and international interventions have accelerated and criticism towards the jurisdictions has intensified – not least with the exclusively negative tonality in the media, with major news broadcasters such as *BBC Panorama* (2017) and the *Guardian* in the UK acting as major platforms for related stories. The sacrosanct function of the media to scrutinise is enabled under the fundamental freedoms of the press. A good example was seen with the Pentagon Papers – an unprecedented leak of a US government–classified Vietnam War report. The report's effect was to discredit the government's public account of the conflict by demonstrating that Congress had been manipulated into supporting it (Quint 1981, 9; McGovern and Roche 1972). The media's role in publishing this was one of holding government accountable over a specific event. However, the Pentagon leak differs to that of the Panama and Paradise papers because the latter were as much to do with holding governments to account as they were about exposing the fiscal activities of wealthy businessmen, actors, athletes and musicians – not accountable to anyone other than law enforcement if they have committed crimes. With the media's critical role, in order for the rule of law to be upheld, there has to be a line drawn with regards to the media's objective in publishing misappropriated, confidential information and its ultimate purpose. In law, there has to be a clear demarcation between information we have an 'interest in' and that which is simply 'interesting'. Public interest justification and holding governments accountable are sensible justifications, whereas to expose fiscal dealings of the wealthy descends to a more hazardous function and one where press freedom risks operating superiorly to legitimately held legal safeguards, such as the right to private and family life, or the doctrine of confidentiality. As Leveson LJ observed in the Leveson Inquiry (2012, para 5.10), while certain modifications exist in law which give the press greater latitude within the law than is afforded to others, it "does not mean recognition within the law that, as a matter of general principle, the press possesses any entitlement or expectation to be indulged, in the national interest, in special exemption from observing the requirements of the law".

The Panama and Paradise papers data was relatively untargeted and the public databases contain legitimate, confidential information – which the International Consortium of Investigative Journalists (ICIJ) concedes. As such, those tasked with exposing and publishing it have come into contact with confidential information of innocent people that have, effectively, had their private data stolen. Concerningly, there have been reports of government and enforcement bodies not wishing to review the data due to evidential and ethical implications relating to confidentiality and prosecutorial conduct.

With a growing deference toward transparency and a reshaping of rules influenced by those who think nothing of the misappropriation of confidential data – even if it means causing problems for investigators and prosecutors – it is necessary to re-examine values and principles of law which today seem under attack, justified almost on utilitarian grounds. Rights protected by law, such as privacy, are often not given due consideration in light of political pressure. As Nakajima (2017, 114) observes, "a fundamental question we might ask ourselves is that even if we have nothing to hide, do we not wish to retain a certain level of confidentiality . . . the global move for transparency might be infringing our 'right to privacy' which is one of the fundamental human rights". This is all the more pertinent in the context of increasing surveillance seen in the push towards global financial market regulation.

However, there is the issue of whether suspect wealth is actually a problem for the selected Overseas Territories. In competitively striving for financial independence, are the territories accepting of the realities that criminals use their services? Or, does the legitimate activity therein outweigh the illegitimate activity, the former of which these jurisdictions rely upon for their development. If this is correct, then this intensifies the need to examine the viability of global anti-economic misconduct standards in the context of these small offshore jurisdictions, and the extent to which these standards are prevalent and visible within them. This requires a thoughtful and comprehensive analysis into their willingness and levels of compliance, but also their successes and challenges in tackling financial crime and the risks presented by suspect wealth.

The purpose of this book is not to present a defence of offshore centres, but rather to contribute more meaningful understanding of them and their levels of compliance with international standards. However, where law and policy regarding these jurisdictions is influenced by misconceptions, ignorance or other agendas that erode what ought to be clear demarcations between conduct prohibited or permitted under law, these will be exposed. Given this work sits within both legal and developmental discourse, it is necessary to examine the position of fundamental rights such as privacy and confidentiality, which appear increasingly at risk or dispensable. Given offshore jurisdictions have long been perceived as harmful actors, there is a considerable challenge that lies ahead in lawmaking, policy and international relations. Many critics would disavow any contention that offshore jurisdictions are compliant with international standards. However, on achieving a deeper understanding of the territories and their challenges, but importantly their levels of legal and regulatory compliance, less heedless attacks on their reputation may result, and more meaningful international cooperation achieved. It is hoped this book facilitates this important aim.

References

Ali, S. (2003) *Money Laundering Control in the Caribbean*, Netherlands: Springer.

Antoine, R.-M. (2013) *Offshore Financial Law: Trusts and Related Tax Issues* (2nd ed.), Oxford: Oxford University Press.

BBC Panorama (10.11.2017) 'Offshore Secrets of the Rich Exposed'. Available: www.bbc.co.uk/programmes/b09fgcz3

Freyer, T. A., and Morriss, P. A. (2013) 'Creating Cayman as an Offshore Financial Centre: Structure and Strategy Since 1960', *Arizona State Law Journal*, 45: 1297–1398.

Hampton, M. P., and Abbott, J. P. (1999) *Offshore Finance Centres and Tax Havens*, London: Palgrave Macmillan.

Hart, H. L. A. (1958) 'Positivism and the Separation of Law and Morals', *Harvard Law Review*, 71(4): 593–629.

Hendry, I., and Dickson, S. (2018) *British Overseas Territories Law* (2nd ed.), Oxford: Hart Publishing.

Kelsen, H. (1934/2009) *Pure Theory of Law* (2nd ed.), Clark, NJ: Lawbook Exchange.

Lord Justice Leveson (2012) 'An Inquiry into the Culture, Practices and Ethics of the Press', UK Government, Department for Digital, Culture, Media and Sport. Available: https://www.gov.uk/government/publications/leveson-inquiry-report-into-the-culture-practices-and-ethics-of-the-press

McGovern, G., and Roche, J. P. (1972) 'The Pentagon Papers – A Discussion', *Political Science Quarterly*, 87(2): 174–177.

Nakajima, C. (2017) 'Editorial: "Panama Papers" Conference in Madrid: "Transparency vs Confidentiality" – A Conflict?', *Journal of Financial Crime*, 20(4): 322–324.

Oxfam (9.5.2016) 'Tax Havens "Serve No Useful Economic Purpose": 300 Economists Tell World Leaders'. Available: https://www.oxfam.org/en/press-releases/tax-havens-serve-no-useful-economic-purpose-300-economists-tell-world-leaders

Quint, P. E. (1981) 'The Separation of Powers under Nixon: Reflections on Constitutional Liberties and the Rule of Law', *Duke Law Journal*, 1981(1): 1–70, [9].

Sharman, J. C. (2006) *Havens in a Storm*, Ithaca, NY: Cornell University Press.

Sharman, J. C. (2017) *Despots Guide to Wealth Management*, Ithaca, NY: Cornell University Press.

Shaxson, N. (2011) *Treasure Islands: Tax Havens and the Men Who Stole the World*, London: Bodley Head.

Thomas-James, D. (2017) 'Does the UK Need to Create a Criminal Offence of Illicit Enrichment – Or Is the Unexplained Wealth Order Provision of the Criminal Finances Bill 2016 a Welcome Compromise?', in *Unexplained Wealth Orders: Thoughts on Scope and Effect in the UK*, London: The White Collar Crime Centre, 18–22.

2 Concerns about economic crime and suspect wealth

2.1 Introduction

Economic crime is arguably one of the more concerning inhibitors and barriers to the development of the world's poorest countries. It threatens institutional development, stability, sustainability and reputation of developed and developing jurisdictions alike. Contrary to misconception, it is not simply an issue confined to corrupt kleptocracies, nor to high-rise offices in financial centres. Rather, it is an unfortunate inevitability of the human conditions of greed, desire, temptation and deviance (Rider 1997, 1). As such, it is persistent in all countries and is something we shall endure so long as humanity gives effect to human tendency. Short of complete cultural overhaul, or reinstatement of moral elements of religious teachings – such as Christ's refusal of Satan's temptations of hedonism, egoism and materialism while fasting in the Judean Desert[1] – it is likely that while we occupy a world filled with humanity's mad inhuman noise, we shall never rid ourselves of acquisitive crimes like corruption. Likewise, we are also unlikely to eradicate actions which reside in a grey area, like legally trying to pay less tax – notwithstanding increasing legislative and regulatory momentum targeting aggressive avoidance schemes like the 'double Irish, Dutch sandwich'[2] and so-called tax havens themselves. Any scholar conducting research which seeks to end corruption or money laundering will face insurmountable challenge (Saleh 2014). Globalisation has produced constantly evolving technologies encompassing cryptocurrency and complex software by which international financial activity is increasingly easy to conduct (Bryans 2014). This makes the challenge more laborious. For example, until recently with the enactment of economic substance laws, companies have been able to establish viable offices in low-tax jurisdictions with the help of modern communications, sufficient to comply with tax laws which have seen only protracted reform. Failures in the fight against economic

1 For account of this, see the Gospels of Matthew 4:1–11, Mark 1:12–13 and Luke 4:1–13.

2 The double Irish, Dutch sandwich is a tax avoidance technique used by large corporations for transferring profits to low or no-tax jurisdictions via Irish and Dutch subsidiary (or shell) companies.

crime are not necessarily always due to lacklustre political will, or enforcement efforts.

As the FATF Mutual Evaluation Reports demonstrate, sound progress is being made in respect of engagement with evaluation processes, acceptance of internationally prescribed rules, and adherence to best AML/CFT practises. With adoption of multi-stakeholder initiatives, like NRAs, jurisdictions are increasingly required to apply a risk-based approach to AML compliance, advocated by international monitoring bodies. While FATF is arguably the universally accepted soft-law standard bearer (Sharman 2016, 4), their methodology has incurred some criticism. For instance, Halliday, Levi, and Reuter (2014, 5) suggest the 3rd Round MER "does not articulate its objectives sufficiently precisely for reliable evaluations . . . instead reliance was placed on the prima facie plausibility of the claim that adherence to the Standards would help reduce money laundering". It is interesting to consider the increasing prevalence and legitimacy of soft-law standards which do not hold the same status as domestic or international law. Lack of engagement or compliance with them promotes adverse reputational harm and could lead to various sanctions for which there is no legal recourse.

It is axiomatic that no matter how well-regulated an environment is, criminal proceeds will find where it is darkest. While the temptations of wealth exist, traditional methods of criminal justice and civil enforcement will be acting retrospectively, not preventatively. Crime is a profit-driven enterprise, and 'getting ahead' remains a socially desirable construct – perhaps even more so in an age of social media, exacerbated by the financially volatile landscape caused by the global coronavirus health pandemic, whereby fraud has manifestly increased.

While the stereotype palm-tree island paradise is often associated with economic misconduct, the reality is larger developed countries also facilitate industrial-scale financial crime which is, perhaps, more of a pressing issue for their stability and the development of other jurisdictions. Three examples spring to mind. First, the extent of money laundering in British Columbia casinos was researched by German (2018), who found that for some time establishments served as laundromats for proceeds of organised crime, exacerbated by a sense of denial in the industry. Similarly, Sharman (2017) noted the attractiveness for corrupt Papua New Guinea politicians to launder money into Australia through its real estate market. Sharman avers the importance of a lack of motivation, rather than capacity in Australia's response. Third, as Global Witness (2017) and Transparency International (2015) reported, London's luxury real estate market is widely acknowledged to be a vehicle for laundering or concealing suspicious wealth, as was the subject of the first wave of UWOs in the UK (*NCA v Baker and ors* [2020]).

2.2 Why is economic crime an international concern?

As Benjamin Franklin (1739) famously espoused, tricks and treachery are the practice of fools who have not wit enough to be honest. Trickery and treachery, deviance and dishonesty, covetousness and skulduggery are all characteristics of misconduct for which the sole purpose is wealth acquisition. However, many modern perpetrators are increasingly sophisticated rather than injudicious. Transgressors tend to use more complex, hard-to-monitor methods to effectuate and conceal their wrongdoing. The costs of implementing AML/CFT controls, for example, are significant yet yield little results relative to suspect flows. Some scholars perceive such initiatives as an "ideological vision of the regulators which is often not accompanied by identifying criminal activity – just vague weaknesses in systems" (Saperstein, Sant, and Ng 2015, 2). Interventions of the kind required by AML regimes presuppose a significant element of compliance. This is problematic if both financial and human resources are lacking, most pertinently in micro-population jurisdictions. While technology has invariably assisted people to reintegrate illicit wealth into the international financial system, the fact remains that many types of serious crime require little resources (Levi and Reuter 2006, 289). However, for more complex misconducts, such as money laundering or tax evasion, the assistance of professional facilitators is often needed, which makes regulating professions increasingly crucial.

Despite the notion that economic crime knows no borders and often involves multiple parties, jurisdictions and complex transaction chains, the underlying motivation perhaps remains the same. Imagine parking in a carpark but not paying. While deviant, the harm caused may be minimal. However, you have at least committed civil wrongs of breach of contract and the tort of trespass. The motivation could be explained by you not having, or wanting to spend, money. Or, on a rational choice exercise, operating on a likelihood that you will not get caught; or, that the fine is a weak deterrent. This is paradigmatically similar to tax evasion. The dishonest evader uses public services like roads and healthcare, yet does not contribute to their cost through paying tax. This is contrary to Socrates and later thinkers like Hobbes (1651) and Rousseau's (1762) theoretical work on social contracts, which implies that in choosing to live in a society, one accepts its burdens and benefits. The transgressors in these examples breached the social contract, disregarded rules and got ahead by unlawful means. As Rider (1997) eloquently puts it, misconduct like this has flawed humans ever since Eve took the bite of the serpent's apple.

Economic misconduct has a dark side. It facilitates wars, fuels rebel groups, funds terrorist organisations, sustains human and narcotics trafficking and the dark economy. It furthers the amount of unexplained wealth in the world, which has been linked to growing inequality. While there is consensus about the effects of economic crime on development, there is difficulty in measuring its truest extent or cost. This is not helped by the fact there is no official taxonomy of economic crimes despite overlap between predicate and facilitative offences. Perhaps the most evident example of economic crime's impact on development comes from kleptocracies.

The scope and interrelatedness of economic crime is significant. For example: A public official of an oil-rich country accepts a $500,000 bribe for a school building contract not to be publicly tendered. He launders this bribe through a series of transactions, including property purchases in three jurisdictions through complex networks of anonymous shell companies incorporated in separate offshore financial centres. He re-mortgages one property, charges a loan to one of his companies to release capital and rents out the properties. He evades tax on rental income and fails to disclose his investments. The bribe giver, his brother, was awarded the development contract. The construction was delayed, overbudget and substandard. In this example, the public official has committed several serious offences including abuse of office, corruption, money laundering, mortgage fraud, failing to disclose financial interests and tax evasion – across several jurisdictions. Further, in undermining legitimate competition through bribery, the development was poorly built. This example shows that many types of economic misconduct operate transnationally and in tandem, as well as some costs.

While there is increasing international consensus on criminalising economic crimes, such as modern bribery offences and money laundering, there is also ambivalence in certain types of conducts. Conflating legitimate practises that are perceived to be wrong (such as tax avoidance) with conduct which is inherently criminal (like tax evasion) does not help to clarify thinking in the field. This practice is noticeable in the context of recent transparency legislation. The Hodge-Mitchell Amendment (section 51) of the UK Sanctions and Anti–Money Laundering Act 2018 (SAMLA) characterised the necessity of opening beneficial ownership registers to tackle corruption and tax avoidance. When the ICIJ engaged in exposing offshore activity with the Panama and Paradise papers, a visible outcome was to shine a bright light on the world of offshore business wholly, rather than pure criminality, and to further negative connotations surrounding tax avoidance. If the ICIJs motivation stemmed from an increasing emphasis on tax justice, then it is quite easy to see why offshore financial centres were targeted as the publications demonstrated widespread tax avoidance. There is a growing prevalence of social arguments about tax fairness. The social contract formulation provides a compelling prism through which to view taxation, given the collegial nature of paying tax. However, it is difficult to see what the correct standard would be if determining levels of taxation was a moral exercise. While the idea of citizenship presupposes a society where there are contributory obligations, this is not the case in many developing countries and is more pertinent in countries with high social welfare.

The revelations from the Panama papers reputationally damaged the offshore world. The targeted firm, Mossack Fonseca (MOSSFON), ceased trading due to reputational damage and there have been criminal cases, political scandals and intensified blacklisting campaigns since. This demonstrated the scale of offshore business, the implication being that company incorporation and associated corporate services are big business to the offshore community (Chaikin 2018, 109), something which they would not refute. It might be the case that suspect wealth entering an offshore centre through vehicles like shell companies may not produce visible harm to the jurisdiction itself, despite clear evidence that this can harm jurisdictions where the wealth therein originates. However, for offshore jurisdictions, damage can manifest in several forms. For example, TCI lost its sovereignty over economic misconduct allegations. Further, damage can manifest from the consequent reputational harm to their business sectors from published revelations. Or, negative attention as a result of legal actions implicating the jurisdiction's services or lack of controls. Moreover, damage can ensue when international AML monitoring bodies produce negative reviews if standards are lacking. Sanctions may follow or provide the basis upon which other organisations or countries blacklist states found to have deficiencies. In circumstances where financial institutions are increasingly de-risking, this presents a serious threat to offshore jurisdictions and their economic futures.

Notwithstanding the difficulty in measuring the extent of economic crime, some reported figures illustrate its global scale, thereby contextualising international interest in disrupting it. The UN Office on Drugs and Crime (UNODC) estimates that between $800 billion and $2 trillion is laundered annually. Despite this gaping range, even the *mean* value at $1.4 trillion exemplifies the significant magnitude of money laundering. As I have alluded to, it facilitates other serious crime such as corruption, fraud, terrorism and tax evasion. The figure certainly places money laundering in an industrial context, epitomising the acquisitive, profit-driven motivations behind it and its necessity in sustaining criminal enterprise. The range represents between 2% and 5% of world GDP – which is the cumulative GDP of Hong Kong, Sweden and Belgium.

Other noteworthy figures include those estimating tax evasion and avoidance. Notwithstanding the difficulty in measuring these to any degree of certainty, a study by Cobham and Jansky (2017) reported that multinational corporations' tax avoidance is $500 billion annually. In the UK, Her Majesty's Revenue and Customs (HMRC; 2018, 5) estimate a tax loss of £5.3 billion from tax evasion and £1.7 billion from avoidance. While this seems relatively small, compared to the overall tax gap in 2016–17 being £33 billion, which is 5.7% of UK tax liability, it is still a sizeable sum as it is over half the annual UK police budget in 2018–19. The US Internal Revenue Service (2016) estimated the annual gross tax gap as $458 billion between 2008 and 2010. Similarly, in 2012, the European Commission referenced a study by Murphy (2012, 23) which estimated 1 trillion in public money is lost due to evasion and avoidance each year. TJN (2020) reported $427 billion lost to tax havens annually. Notwithstanding the debate about the legality or morality of tax avoidance, these figures represent a serious issue suggesting tax authorities are losing significant income due to avoidance mechanisms and illegal evasion. The statistics on tax gaps include other matters contributing to broader tax losses, such as genuine errors, failing to take reasonable care and criminal attacks on the system such as VAT repayment fraud. In the context of the UK's tax gap, more tax is lost through errors (£3.2 billion) than through avoidance. HMRC observes: "There has been a steady downward trend in the avoidance tax gap, from £4.9bn in 2005–06 to £1.7bn in 2016–17".

In the context of suspect wealth, tax gap statistics demonstrate a problem in terms of tax revenue losses via hidden economies – where entire income is unknown to authorities. In the UK, the tax gap loss from the hidden economy was estimated at £3.2 billion. With regard to underground economies, according to Schneider and Enste (2002) their size as a portion of GDP has been suggested to range between 14% and 16% in developed economies and between 25% and 45% in developing ones. India has a substantial underground economy and, while there appears to be consensus that it is decreasing, scholars like Sharma (2016) estimated in 2013 the underground economy represented 52% of India's GDP. Interestingly, Italy has developed a reputation as having one of Europe's largest underground economies. While hidden, or underground, economies are not the same as criminal ones, they present problems given the large amounts of unaccounted wealth.

The general concerns about economic misconduct, suspect wealth and its effects on development are largely self-evident. Many social scientists and criminologists, most notably Sutherland, have engaged in work explaining white-collar criminality. Its commission can be explained by reference to various mainstream theories including strain theory (Merton 1938), rational choice theory (Cornish and Clarke 1986) and differential association theory (Sutherland 1949). It has been advanced in previous work (Thomas-James 2015) that transgressors of market abuse could operate in temporary autonomous zones, a concept developed by Bey (1991). Scholarly work on the causes of offending is important for understanding motivations behind the generation of suspect wealth. In many crimes under English law, it is not only necessary to demonstrate the accused had the *actus reus* (guilty act) but also *mens rea* (guilty mind). Despite its importance, there still remains a relatively sparse amount of scholarly work in this area.

There is demonstrable concern about flight capital, whereby money flees a jurisdiction through misconduct like tax evasion or its rulers stealing public funds. It is estimated that some $1.1 trillion flowed illicitly out of developing nations in 2013 as a result of misconduct like corruption and tax evasion (Kar and Spanjers 2015). Many NGOs have published reports detailing serious cases. For example, Oxfam (2016) found that Malawi's development is being significantly harmed by flight capital and, with those in power utilising tax havens to conceal ill-gotten gains, Malawians are deprived of public services. Similarly, Global Witness (2009) reported that the ruling family of Congo utilised shell companies in tax havens to funnel public oil revenue for personal gain. Sharman (2017) gives many examples of kleptocrats transiting illicit wealth through financial centres. While it is not disputed that tax havens, or any financial centres for that matter, can facilitate the transiting or concealment of suspect wealth, countries like Malawi have also faced many governance challenges which have undermined its development (Tambulasi 2010). Corruption became so problematic that the UK suspended aid in 2012–13, concluding that public money was unsafe in the government's hands. Focusing solely on the facilitative role tax havens can play ignores the reality that people of such jurisdictions are first and foremost victims of theft and, while theft necessitates a place to conceal stolen gains, the proverb "Once a thief, always a thief" should be borne in mind when considering solutions.

While figures paint a compelling picture, statistics containing the words 'billions' and 'trillions' often inflate arguments inaccurately. So much of the true picture relies upon information we do not, and cannot, know. The NCA (2016) estimated that some £90 billion is laundered through the UK each year. While this invites sensationalism, the fact remains that the real figure is unknown and estimates should be treated indicatively. Forstater (2016) observes the need to attribute caution when considering large figures which shape perceptions about the problem's scale, because many are mistakes or misunderstandings. There are also claims surrounding mismatches in trade pricing and invoicing, specifically under errors and omissions allowances in the context of trading and balance of payments. This is often regarded as a platform for money laundering and illicit financial flows (Altinkaya and Yucel 2013). As Sharman has observed, while it might be attractive to view trade errors and omissions as an economic crime conspiracy, the likely explanation in most cases is simply an issue of different accounting processes between countries.[3]

The impact of economic crime on development is firmly espoused in the UN Sustainable Development Goals (SDGs). SDG 16, titled "Peace, Justice and Strong Institutions", references that corruption, bribery, theft and tax evasion costs developing countries $1.26 trillion per year. It also refers to the importance of strong institutions, including the rule of law, as without them sustainable development cannot be achieved.

An important recent example demonstrating both the international nature of economic crime and the impact of suspect wealth on development is the scandal over 1Malaysia Development Berhad (1MDB), an insolvent Malaysian state-owned sovereign wealth fund. The case concerned allegations of embezzlement and findings of billions of dollars in irregular transactions which led to international investigations (Wright and Hope 2018). US authorities alleged that between 2009 and 2014, billions of dollars were misappropriated and fraudulently diverted from 1MDB. It resulted in the former Malaysian Prime Minister being charged with corruption, criminal breach of trust and money laundering. He was later convicted in respect of misconduct involving 42 million ringgit ($10 million) transferred from the fund to his private account. He was found guilty and sentenced to 12 years' imprisonment and fines of nearly $50 million. At the time of writing, this is pending an appeal against conviction to be heard in 2021 (*Reuters* 1.10.2020). There are also further proceedings underway relating to money laundering with regards to 2.28 billion ringgit ($535 million). The allegations are that he received and covered up illegal transfers between 2011 and 2014 (*BBC* 28.8.2019). Allegations were also made against the financial institution Goldman Sachs regarding raising money for 1MDB through, and advising on, bond offerings, and against employees in relation to bribing officials to win business. One employee pleaded guilty to conspiring to launder money and violating the Foreign Corrupt Practices Act, forfeiting $43.7 million proceeds of crime.[4] In acknowledging "institutional failings" regarding 1MDB, Goldman Sachs agreed to pay nearly $3 billion in disposal of its involvement in the 1MDB scandal and violations of US foreign bribery laws. Goldman was investigated by

3 Panel discussion at a screening of *The Spider's Web: Britain's Second Empire* (2017), produced by Michael Oswald and John Christensen, at Jesus College, Cambridge, (13.07.2018).

4 US Department of Justice (1.11.2018), 'Former Banker Tim Leissner Pleaded Guilty to Conspiring to Launder Money and to Violate the Foreign Corrupt Practices Act Related to 1MDB'.

numerous regulators and has agreed a settlement sum of $3.9 billion to Malaysian authorities. Several other individuals, including Jho Low, have been charged in the US with conspiring to launder billions and to commit bribery.[5] Reports of Low's ill-gotten lavish lifestyle, including a mega-yacht which US authorities have seized, as well as reports that he financed the film *The Wolf of Wall Street*, have attracted international attention (Wright and Hope 2018). This case demonstrates economic crime at a magnificent scale. It is important given the complex network of transnational players, companies and transactions, as well as the troubling extent of professional enabling. Politically, the scandal contributed to the Prime Minister's election defeat. Economically, billions in embezzled public money were diverted from job-creation and green-energy initiatives.

2.3 Concerns about corruption

Concerns about the effects of economic crime are perhaps most visible by reference to corruption. Corruption gives rise to suspect wealth because the functional side of the transaction (i.e. the bribe) is a proceed of crime and often remains unaccounted. Whether it remains in hard cash in a safe, immediately spent or converted to an asset, or whether it needs to be laundered through complex transaction chains to conceal the source and the beneficiary, corruption can occur in various circumstances. Modern bribery legislation acknowledges this and has developed accordingly in terms of offences of giving and receiving bribes, failing to prevent or report bribery, and foreign bribery including bribing public officials. Corruption can also include kleptocracies, civil servant corruption, rent-seeking activities, grand corruption, price fixing and corporate bribery. Conceptually, it could involve conduct by which no transaction takes place, such as recruiting an ill-suited associate to a publicly funded position or abusing one's office or power for non-financial favours or loyalty. Abuses could also involve straightforward embezzlement of public funds. The OECD (2014) report 'The Rationale for Fighting Corruption' highlights some further examples, such as a multinational company paying a bribe to win a public contract to build a highway despite proposing a substandard offer, or a local official demanding bribes from people to access a new water pipe. Their report notes that those hurt most by corruption are the world's weakest. In the case of financial corruption, the problem of it does not end with the giving or receiving of a bribe, but extends to the ability and necessity for corrupt monies to be consequently concealed and moved. Responding to corruption through law and regulatory initiatives is not a simple case of targeting one element of the transaction or the other. Corruption and associated misconduct has been seen at the highest levels. Prominent examples include the 2015 FIFA corruption scandal and money laundering investigations;

5 US Department of Justice (1.11.2018) 'Malaysian Financier Low Taek Jho, also known as "Jho Low", and former banker Ng Chong Hwa, also known as "Roger Ng", indicted for conspiring to launder billions of dollars in illegal proceeds and to pay hundreds of millions of dollars in bribes'.

the recent conviction of the former French President Nicolas Sarkozy for corruption; and the Watergate scandal which led to the resignation of US President Richard Nixon in 1974.

Problematically for lawyers and regulators, as well as policymakers and researchers, there is no universally accepted definition of corruption – something conceded in the UK Government's Anti-Corruption Plan (2014, 9). The World Bank defines it as the abuse of public office for private gain, while Transparency International suggests it is the abuse of entrusted power for private gain. It is paradoxical that something which appears to have consensus still lacks a settled definition. This could be explained by the ever-evolving nature of bribery which legislative reform continuously seeks to address; for example, section 6 of the Bribery Act 2010 introduced the offence of bribing a foreign official. Another possibility is that different cultures view corruption differently or place different emphasis on the nature of gifts, favours and loyalty. Corruption is particularly concerning in the private sector. It would be naïve to conclude that corruption is confined to the public sector. A common, less obvious example may be a commercial agent bribing customers and taking commissions to secure business for his principal, thus breaching his obligations under the Commercial Agents (Council Directive) Regulations 1993 and common law fiduciary duties not to make private kickbacks. Private gain is a vague concept unclearly considered in normative definitions. It assumes an enrichment element, which is all too often thought of as monetary. However, it could include favours, indebtedness, influence, gifts and even corporate hospitality which is increasingly under the regulatory spotlight. If corruption is culturally nuanced or a series of evolving behaviours depending on circumstance, perhaps a lack of definition is unsurprising. The lack thereof has itself become normative.

It is easy to frame corruption as being 'well understood' with reliance on narrow definitions and the inevitable likening of it to cancer. Consequently, we see united, high-level commitments to eradicate it at international and supranational levels. However, the picture is far more complex and culturally nuanced. For example, civil servants in a country where corruption is systemic may turn a blind eye in order to keep their jobs on the one hand, and may perhaps engage in it on the other in order to subsidise low wages. If those occupying powerful positions portray high standards of living as a result of the same behaviour, is it surprising that ordinary civil servants may accept this in order to safeguard their livelihoods? Another example is endemic police corruption in some countries (Lee 2018), where officers may regularly take bribes for not reporting crimes like drug dealing, or legally demanding business rents. While ostensibly reprehensible, it might be normative in a particular jurisdiction. Such conduct reverberates through institutions and government departments, making the entire system less efficient and uneven for users. Associated forms of corruption have been witnessed in offshore financial centres, particularly during their key stages of development.

Corruption is also closely associated with kleptocracy and embezzlement (theft of trusted property; Green 1993, 95). Embezzlement is a criminal violation of trust, rather than a strict breach which might ordinarily be seen in a civil law context. The example of the former President of Zaire (Democratic Republic of Congo), Mobutu Sese Seko, has shaped thinking and policy in this area (Sharman 2017, 26). At one stage, it was reported that Seko's personal and family allocation of the national budget was 17% – in real terms, more than he spent on his citizens' education, healthcare and welfare (Hartman 1997, 159). The impact of this on development is self-evident and demonstrates the problematic interrelationship of corruption, kleptocracy and embezzlement. It also evidences the concerns raised at the international level through instruments like UNCAC and the 2016 Global Anti-Corruption Summit declaration. Further, when development aid is stolen by corrupt governments, the contentious domestic debate about foreign aid commitments reignites.

Corruption's consequences do not end there, as the wealth often needs to transit somewhere. An elaborate illustration of this was the spending spree of Equatorial Guinea's Vice President, Teodorin Obiang. Despite an official salary of $80,000, between 2004 and 2011 he spent $314 million including on an $80 million Parisian property, a $30 million Californian property, a $38.5 million jet, luxury cars and $5 million of wine (Sharman 2017, 4). This evidences a two-sided problem: a government run by thieves and the Vice President's ability to internationally move and access ill-gotten gains over long duration.

The foremost international treaty instrument for fighting corruption and associated misconduct is UNCAC. Its foreword describes corruption as an "insidious plague that has a wide range of corrosive effects on society". It points to it inhibiting development and sustaining poverty. Given that corruption facilitates organised crime, wars and terrorism, it is charged as being the cause of many global problems. In the UNCAC General Assembly Resolution, the impact of corruption is clearly emphasised and states that parties are "concerned about the seriousness of problems and threats posed by corruption to the stability and security of societies, undermining the institutions and values of democracy, ethical values and justice and jeopardizing sustainable development and the rule of law". As former World Bank President James Wolfensöhn noted (1999): "The causes of financial crisis and poverty are one and the same. . . . [If countries] do not have good governance [and] if they do not confront the issue of corruption . . . their development is fundamentally flawed and will not last".[6]

2.4 Concerns about money laundering and terrorism financing

As the aforementioned examples relating to despotic regimes show, money laundering is intrinsically linked to corruption. Like the ability to evade tax for fiscal benefit or the ability to set up anonymous shell companies to conceal wealth, money laundering is a facilitative type of economic crime which ensures crime's

6 Address to the Board of Governors, World Bank Group, Joint Annual Discussion, 28–30 September 1999, Press Release No. 2, [5].

profitability. As well as providing a vehicle to conceal or use ill-gotten gains, it finances future criminality. Money laundering is further considered a predicate offence for tax evasion. Like corruption, the concerns about money laundering are self-evident and have become an international priority due to the levels of risk and harm it presents to institutions, economies, societies and development. The IMF (2016) note its ability to threaten the stability of financial sectors. At a basic level, it has become internationally accepted that in order for enforcement efforts to effectively disrupt acquisitively motivated criminality, the wealth gained from it needs to be targeted. If the profit can be taken out of crime, then the opportunity cost exercise which criminals engage in, explained by various theories such as 'rational choice' or 'expected value', becomes weighted against action. This is the underlying rationale for the new UWO provisions and account freezing orders under the UK Criminal Finances Act 2017. However, laundering serves to thwart investigative efforts, thereby sustaining crime as an enterprise and maintaining the acquisitive component of their motivations.

The principal organisation tasked with international AML regulation is FATF and its regional affiliates. Their 40 AML and 9 CFT recommendations have become unparalleled and unchallenged global soft-law rules.[7] While money laundering can be complex, particularly in its use of the legitimate financial architecture, it is a straightforward concept defined by FATF as "the processing of criminal proceeds to disguise their illegal origin". The International Compliance Association (2018) define it as "[the] process by which criminals disguise original ownership and control of the proceeds of criminal conduct by making such appear to have derived from a legitimate source". Concerns about money laundering at the EU level have resulted in a series of AML/CFT Directives under which domestic lectures are required to implement minimum standards. These endeavour to create a standardised regulatory landscape across the Union and close gaps identified in compliance.

Due to its depiction in popular culture, film and television as a recurring theme (e.g. *The Wolf of Wall Street* [2013]; *Riviera* [2017–]; and *Ozark* [2017–]), money laundering is possibly one of the more well-known economic crimes yet not always easily recognisable. Often, legitimate businesses are used as laundering fronts. A well-known example was the US Pizza Connection trial in the 1980s, whereby a Mafia-run drug trafficking operation utilised independent pizza restaurants to launder money to Italy, resulting in 21 convictions (Kelly 1999). The principal objective of a launderer, or facilitator, is to create the perception the wealth was legitimately acquired. Restaurants are popular choices, as one can utilise their quiet periods to absorb criminal money into legitimate trade. Unless investigators laboriously survey the restaurant, this is an effective laundering strategy.

Whether it is industrial-scale laundering allegations or AML breaches levelled at financial institutions causing market instability, or the fact that more crack cocaine and heroin are on the streets due to it facilitating organised crime, the

7 See FATF Recommendations 2012 for a complete list.

consequences of money laundering are as significant as they are broad. In July 2018, reports of money laundering allegations totalling $8.3 billion involving Denmark's largest bank, Danske, caused their share price to fall 3% (*FT* 4.7.2018). Elsewhere, Deutsche Bank were reported as being involved in this scandal, with their share price falling 3.4% (*CityAM* 6.12.2018). In 2012, allegations were made by the New York Department of Financial Services that Standard Chartered bank had breached US sanctions in scheming to hide thousands of Iranian government transactions. The allegation, involving $250 billion illegally moved money in the financial system, risked the bank losing its ability to trade in the US. Its shares immediately fell 6% following the initial report and 24% the following day (*Guardian* 7.8.2012). In real terms, £11.5 billion was wiped off the bank's market value. In 2016, following HSBC's significant $1.9 billion enforcement fine for violations of AML controls and sanctions and for assisting "drug kingpins and rogue nations", the US House Committee on Financial Services published a report detailing the extent to which HSBC was, effectively, 'too big to jail'. This showed that US officials did not prosecute HSBC due to concerns that enforcement would cause a "global financial disaster" (*BBC* 12.7.2016). Interestingly, given HSBC is headquartered in London, a US House of Representatives (2016, 43) report detailed that the then UK Chancellor, George Osborne, "intervened in the HSBC matter by sending a letter to Federal Reserve Chairman . . . to express the UK's concerns regarding US enforcement actions against British banks", and that prosecuting HSBC could have "very serious implications for financial and economic stability, particularly in Europe and Asia".

While it may be difficult to determine the impact dirty money has on a financial system once it has been integrated therein, it is clear from these examples that the reputational harm caused by money laundering allegations against institutions can cause financial market instability as well as collateral damage to innocent third parties like shareholders, employees or consumers. The 'too big to jail' reality is concerning given the revocation of trust in banking following breaches of AML controls and allegations of facilitating criminality. In a US Senate investigation (US Permanent Subcommittee on Investigations 2012), it was found that HSBC and its US affiliate exposed the US financial system to a "wide array of money laundering, drug trafficking, and terrorist financing risks due to poor anti–money laundering controls". The investigation averred that HSBC serviced high-risk affiliates, disregarded terrorist financing links, offered bearer share accounts and cleared suspicious bulk traveller's cheques. It was alleged that HSBC's US bank, HBUS, offered:

> correspondent banking services to HSBC Bank Mexico, and treated it as a low-risk client, despite its location in a country facing money laundering and drug trafficking challenges, high risk clients, high risk products like U.S. dollar accounts in the Cayman Islands, a secrecy jurisdiction, and weak AML controls. The Mexican affiliate transported $7billion in physical U.S. dollars to HBUS from 2007 to 2008, outstripping other Mexican banks, even one twice its size, raising red flags that the volume of dollars include proceeds from illegal drug sales in the US.

This demonstrates that lack of implementation of AML controls can be seen in renowned financial institutions. Mere reports of their involvement in laundering may be enough to cause financial instability, let alone any meaningful enforcement action involving the criminal justice system which, based on the HSBC example, carries the risk that financial turmoil may ensue. For offshore centres, the occurrence of money laundering through its financial institutions or of controls being assessed as lacking adversely affects their financial sectors, leading to reputational stigma, sanctions from failing assessments, blacklisting or de-risking by institutions.

Enforcing against financial institutions has become increasingly visible, including under the relatively new deferred prosecution agreement (DPA) framework. In the UK, DPAs came into force under Schedule 17, Crime and Courts Act 2013. This applies to entities which may be charged with criminal offences, yet the prosecution becomes suspended under the agreement subject to the DPA's terms. It requires judicial approval that the agreement is fair, reasonable and proportionate and that the interests of justice are served. They are available for use by statutory bodies and apply only to organisations. The recipient must have cooperated with the investigation. The rationale for DPAs includes enforcement efficiency, given the complexity and resource-intense nature of money laundering and economic crime cases. They enable organisations to make reparations, including financial penalties, and engage in operational and organisational changes while avoiding the risk of collateral damage to third parties by criminal convictions. Recent examples of DPAs include the US case against HSBC Holdings Plc and HSBC Bank USA N.A. for AML and sanctions violations, which resulted in the organisation forfeiting $1.256 billion (US Department of Justice 11.12.2012); and the Airbus case, whereby the UK SFO entered into a €991 million DPA with it as part of a global resolution stemming from investigations involving bribery (SFO 31.1.2020).

The IMF view combatting money laundering as a moral imperative and economic necessity. They aver that the adversities are not simply domestic but global and that those seeking to abuse the complexity of the global financial system are often attracted to countries with lesser, ineffective controls to operate undetected. While money laundering victims are hard to ascertain (in that there might not be a direct nexus between the process itself and the harm it causes), it is nonetheless a serious crime as defined under Schedule 1, Serious Crime Act 2007, and warrants a like response. Holistically, there are victims further down the chain – like the teenager buying illicit drugs and developing a life-changing dependency at the ruin of all else around him, or the societies with neglected public transport or underserved communities due to embezzlement. These types of victims are certainly imaginable. More specifically, the aforementioned banking fines evidence the point that it undermines financial institutions.

With a remit of promoting transparency, Transparency International has raised concerns about the relationship between lack of transparency and money laundering. In an open letter to the G20 in 2010, they stated the need to address the problem of the global financial system allowing billions of dollars of corrupt or stolen money to flow internationally unchecked. They emphasised the realities of the world's poorest seeing the wealth of their countries slip beyond their borders. They called on the G20 to ensure that multinational corporations publish country-by-country profits, revenue and taxes to ensure effective scrutiny about where money is earned and where it may be missing. While this resembles a 'control first' theory of regulation (Gordon and Morriss 2014), it demonstrates the seriousness of thought attached to the question of suspect wealth and its impact on development. Increased public scrutiny is being advocated by both campaigners and governments, doubtless exacerbated by the effects of the Panama and Paradise papers exposing widespread use of offshore centres, and the 2020 FinCEN files which demonstrated the levels of financial suspicion being seen at the institutional level and challenges with the reporting regime.

The facilitation of laundering by professional enablers and financial institutions is of concern. Professionals hiding in plain sight who know the law (or rather the law's wiggle room) represent a serious issue in terms of enabling crime, and in terms of frustrating investigations. It may involve making use of bank secrecy laws, hiding behind legal privilege or using anonymous shell companies. The latter are legal entities commonly used as transaction vehicles (Nefsky 1977) without creating value or other typical commercial activity. The ability to conceal the identity of beneficial owners or controllers means they are an effective laundering or concealing tool. It is widely accepted that shell companies can facilitate the laundering of the proceeds of grand corruption, tax offending, terrorism and corporate crime (Sharman 2010, 127). A common excuse seen for money flowing in and out of a shell company is 'consultancy fees' (Gordon 2009, 18).

There is significant literature on shell companies, with prominent work by Findley, Nielson and Sharman (2014), who conducted a study about the willingness of corporate service providers (CSPs) to incorporate shell companies under certain circumstances such as anonymity, or by providing fictitious and typically 'red flag' information. Laundering is not exclusively facilitated by offshore jurisdictions like those mentioned in the Panama and Paradise papers. Rather, laundering can be achieved equally, if not more effectively, through major financial markets. Findley et al. (2014, 170) clearly evidence this. One of their findings, after soliciting 3,700 CSPs, was that "tax havens that have long been suspected to be weak links in the global financial system are among the most law-abiding countries anywhere in the world when it comes to beneficial ownership standards". They found that CSPs in tax havens were significantly more likely to comply with rules than providers in OECD countries, and suggest the latter are the least compliant compared to poorer, developing countries. This supports the idea that in larger institutions or jurisdictions, control deficiencies might be more vulnerable – particularly for small, illicit transactions which may go undetected.

It has long been recognised that even highly developed jurisdictions face difficulty bringing economic crime prosecutions. In terms of corporate liability for tax misconduct facilitation, there have been significant developments recently. The Law Commission (2010, 5.84) traditionally branded corporate liability laws "inappropriate and ineffective". Prior to the new corporate liability legislation in the UK, in 2015 the government stated that under the existing law it was extremely difficult to hold corporations to account for the criminal actions of their agents. The UK government has implemented legislation aimed at failing to prevent criminal facilitation of tax evasion – aimed at the facilitative chain, such as professional enablers, under Part 3, Criminal Finances Act 2017. This not only epitomises the concern about tax evasion but recognises increasing instances where liability can reside with professionals, or in larger corporations for control deficiencies or lacking good corporate governance. HMRC (2017, 3) emphasised: "The new corporate offence therefore aims to overcome the difficulties in attributing criminal liability to relevant bodies for the criminal acts of employers, agents or those that provide services for or on their behalf".

As part of the global AML regime, efforts to combat terrorism financing have become an international priority, particularly given the ever-emerging threats of terror and its different manifestations. Much like targeting the proceeds of crime in the 'War on Drugs', which gave rise to the modern risk-based approach to AML, the 'War on Terror' necessitated a similar approach to tackling its financing. In the aftermath of the 9/11 attacks, the same conceptual action plan was initiated, as President George W. Bush stated, "[to] starve the terrorists of funding" (US Treasury Department 2002). As with both, not only does targeting the money enable disruption of criminality, but it affords investigators greater understanding of the nature of their operations. As Thony (2000) observes, early strategies against money laundering were predicated on a realisation that narcotics trafficking represented a risk to the state and not only a public safety issue. This is clearly the rationale for the modern AML/CFT framework.

What makes terrorism financing complex is the disparity between the methods, and therefore the financing, of terror activity. The 9/11 attacks required significantly different types of resources than, for example, the lone-wolf attacks seen in central London in the late 2010s. RUSI (2020) note that in many instances of small cell attacks, perpetrators fund operations with legitimate income. In what they term 'low- or no-cost terrorism', this could mean using salaries or benefits. By contrast, sophisticated and orchestrated terror activity and serious organised crime are intrinsically linked, for example financing terrorism through illicit arms dealing, narcotics trafficking, kidnapping and ransom. These concerns are enshrined in the preamble to the International Convention for the Suppression of the Financing of Terrorism. Recognising the need to adopt a risk-based approach, FATF established CFT recommendations for criminalising terrorism financing offences in accordance with the Terrorism Financing Convention: targeted financial sanctions related to this activity and proliferation. Symbiotically, as Thony (2000) suggests, criminal organisations benefit from chaos and damage caused by terrorist organisations, and the latter benefit from the activities of the former for financing. Given that money laundering and terrorism financing can be achieved using the financial system, this gives context to how they are treated similarly when it comes to adhering to the risk-based approach.

2.5 Concerns about tax misconduct

Tax evasion, like other types of fraud, is inherently dishonest. There is deep-seated concern about tax evasion and the widespread effects it can have on development. What is less obvious, yet increasingly controversial, is the status of tax avoidance. Evasion and avoidance have become notionally conjoined. TJN regularly refers to a category of "tax cheating". Confusion has emanated, in part, due to the classification of many types of complex fiscal dealings as falling within a grey area between evasion and avoidance. In some English cases, judges have distinguished tax avoidance from tax planning and mitigation, such as in *Commissioners of Inland Revenue v Willoughby* [1997], per Lord Nolan. The problem was articulated by Devereux et al. (2012, 3), who note: "Reasonable people can take different views of which category certain transactions fall into and only the highest court can give a definitive answer". With this manifests growing disquiet towards the tax practices of the wealthy and multinational corporations. This was visibly seen during the coronavirus pandemic, where many countries advocated that companies registered in jurisdictions on the EU List of Non-Cooperative Jurisdictions for Tax Purposes should not receive financial relief.

The concept of 'fair share' of tax is an embodiment of criticism about tax misconduct (Datt 2014, 410). Tax justice advocates are gaining increasing momentum in the fight against evasion and avoidance. However, there is consensus in the literature that no theory of taxation exists that has been able to conclude what the optimal level of taxation should be (Tanzi 2011, 32).

While there are many theoretical and practical models which characterise them (Slemrod and Yitzhaki 2002, 1428), the characteristic distinguishing tax evasion and tax avoidance is illegality. A simple, yet very important, difference is that one is criminalised and the other is not. In the English case of *IRC v The Duke of Westminster* [1936], Lord Tomlin famously considered, at 19, that legitimately ordering one's affairs to pay less tax may render dissatisfaction by one's fellow taxpayers or tax authority. There is a clear rationale for criminalising tax evasion, rooted in its dishonesty element. Indeed, the *mens rea* requirement is that the evader has to deliberately and knowingly fail to disclose income or the correct level of income and thus not pay some or all tax due. It is similar to fraud and theft, as dishonesty is integral to the offence and distinguishes it from avoidance. On a philosophical level, it is a cardinal 'social contract' offence. While tax evasion is clearer to understand because it might be clearly defined as illegal under a country's criminal code, there remain no universally accepted definitions of tax evasion or avoidance which exacerbates the grey area between them. Mr Justice Holmes articulated this principle in the US case of *Bullen v Wisconsin* (1916), at 630:

> Where the law draws a line, a case is on one side of it or the other, and if on the safe side it is none the worse legally that a party has availed himself to the full of what the law permits. When an act is condemned as evasion, what is meant is that it is on the wrong side of the line.

Transparency International define tax evasion as "the illegal non-payment or under-payment of taxes usually by deliberately making a false declaration or no declaration to tax authorities".

Tax avoidance, however, uses legitimate structures, legal entities and sometimes complex financial transaction frameworks, usually for the purpose of paying less tax. In 2016, HMRC issued guidance on what tax avoidance is:

> [It] involves the bending of the rules of the tax system to gain a tax advantage that Parliament never intended. It often involves contrived, artificial transactions that serve little or no purpose other than to produce this advantage. It involves operating within the letter but not the spirit of the law.

TJN (2021) suggest that avoidance is probably the most misunderstood and misused word in tax. Trying to understand the distinction is unsurprisingly difficult, particularly given the complexity of certain actions, and the outcomes, resembling each other. The distinction question is not a new phenomenon, as the differences have been contested for the past century (Xuereb 2015). The distinction was recognised by the Royal Commission on taxation of profits and income 1955 (Radcliffe Commission):

> It is usual to draw a distinction between tax avoidance and tax evasion. The latter denotes all those activities which are responsible for a person not paying tax that the existing law charges upon. . . . Tax avoidance [is] understood as some act by which a person so arranges his affairs that he is liable to pay less tax than he would have paid.

This principle is enshrined in English law, that no one is obliged to pay more tax than is otherwise due. This was first espoused by Lord Tomlin in the *Duke of Westminster* case, at 28:

> Every man is entitled if he can to order his affairs so that the tax attaching under the appropriate Acts is less than it otherwise would be. If he succeeds in ordering them so as to secure this result, then, however unappreciative the Commissioners of Inland Revenue or his fellow taxpayers may be of his ingenuity, he cannot be compelled to pay an increased tax.

Of course, there are several elements which trigger disquiet: the fact that it is said by critics to operate against the will of Parliament or the spirit of the law; and the fact that it often comes down to capacity or otherwise. The spirit of the law is a dubious concept, because it is about perceived intention. As Garcia, Chen, and Gordon (2014, 480) observe, ordinary people will not always know the exact information and rationale behind any given law. They suggest that "even lawmakers themselves may well forget the exact intention of any given law" and that the construal and interpretation process is highly subjective. When considering legislators' perceived intention, it is not helped if they are regularly embroiled in moral scandal, such as the 2017–18 sexual harassment scandal in the UK Parliament or the 2009 MPs' expenses scandal. On the point of capacity, while the fiscal structures of a multinational corporation may involve teams of professionals and significant resources to achieve the desired goal, society also encourages various fiscally beneficial schemes which are widely available – such as the multimillion-pound duty-free retail industry at airports. Second-guessing Parliament's intention is not a prerequisite for operating within the letter of the law.

The Panama and Paradise papers exposed significant tax evasion and avoidance worldwide and have raised awareness of this global phenomenon. They have propelled the transparency issue into the forefront of government policy, an example being the transparency provisions under Clause 6 Sanctions and Anti–Money Laundering Bill. More traditionally, the evasion-avoidance debate concerned relevant professionals, such as specialist accountants and lawyers (Hearson 2017, 1). However, 'tax justice' as a subject of activism has been increasing in potency, particularly from NGOs and charities. The Lima Declaration 2015 articulates the nexus between tax justice and human rights, and there have been many recent books that address the issue of international tax justice (Kohonen and Mestrum 2009; Zucman 2015), which is indicative of the momentum in this field. As Hearson (2017) observes, the shift in the literature on tax justice appears to have graduated from a micro-level country-based approach heavily focused on the relationship between tax and development, towards a global focus given the evolving international financial architecture. The antithesis of tax justice is tax competition, which is under formidable scrutiny. Dietsch (2015, 229) highlights the concerns of NGO activists by contending that "tax evasion and the shifting of profits to low-tax jurisdictions represent egregious forms of free-riding on the part of capital owners and one of the most blatant injustices of modern economic societies". His thesis supports the moral imperative of tax justice, arguing that the current tax competition winners have a moral obligation to compensate the losers, and that tax competition undermines the fiscal self-determination of states and widens inequality. These views are not uncommon and are widely present in social science discourse.

A significant theme in tax justice literature and criticisms about tax avoidance is the status of tax havens. Many tax justice solutions over the last decade centre on globalisation and tax harmonisation, calling for tax competition to be globally regulated. TJN (2012, 5) claims that "at least $21 to $32 trillion as of 2010 have been invested virtually tax-free through the world's still expanding black hole of more than 80 offshore secrecy jurisdictions". They suggest the scale of the offshore economy is large enough to have a "major impact on estimates of inequality of wealth and income; on estimates of national income and debt ratios; and – most importantly – to have very significant negative impacts on the domestic tax bases of key 'source' countries". The impact on the developing world is well-documented. Developing countries lose at least $100 billion annually according to Oxfam (2016), through lost tax revenues from corporations and the super-rich, and at least $7.6 trillion is being hidden from tax authorities, facilitated by a network of tax havens (Zucman 2015). These concerns represent a significant problem in terms of illicit flows depriving countries of revenue opportunities to assist their development. The issue manifests not only with corrupt actors engaged in illicit capital flows but also corporations engaged in large-scale profit-shifting, intra-firm debt or transfer pricing mechanisms, combined with the use of offshore networks. This attracts concern, perhaps more so than tax evasion given multinational corporations' income and global participation. There have been several recent high-profile reports of large-scale profit shifting, such as Google's use of companies in the Netherlands and Ireland to transit billions in profits to Bermuda through the popular double Irish, Dutch sandwich avoidance mechanism (*Reuters* 3.1.2019). In these circumstances, it is unsurprising that criticism about offshore centres is gathering momentum.

With regards to the jurisdictions perceivably facilitating this, data breaches have sought to expose the offshore world and some of its offerings. Away from the media, there is prevalent scholarly work trying to unearth who actually owns the wealth offshore. There is consensus that this is increasingly difficult to measure where the financial or fiscal interests of the wealthy or large multinational corporations are complex, multi-jurisdictional and layered. Alstadsæter, Johannesen, and Zucman (2017) conducted an analysis of new macroeconomic statistics about measuring household wealth owned by offshore financial centre jurisdictions and questioned whether the wealth is owned by ultra-rich households, corrupt elites or a broader section of the population. Some of their findings were particularly interesting, that 10% of global wealth is held offshore and that in certain regions a far greater share is held offshore. They found that around 60% of the wealth of Russia's richest households is offshore. They suggest that it is likely to have major implications for the concentration of wealth in many of the world's developing countries.

2.6 Economic crime and its ambivalence

There is significant ambivalence about certain types of economic misconduct – particularly evident in the context of the tax avoidance-evasion debate, but also corruption. There are differences in how people, societies, cultures and governments view, and ultimately deal with, them. For example, while corruption is viewed by many as a cancer, it may be viewed by others as essential to obviate bureaucracy if timely project implementation is a development goal, for instance in post-conflict or disaster zones. Former leaders of Overseas Territories have engaged in such behaviour to implement projects. Some have averred a distinction in such circumstances between rule-bending and corruption (*Royal Gazette* 1.12.16).[8]

One of the responses, fast becoming a catch-all, is transparency. There seems to be increasing support for a 'control first' theory of financial market regulation

8 In remarks to the Bermuda Commission of Inquiry (2016), Jerome Lynch QC, representing former Premier Ewart Brown, submitted that if a rule or two had to be bent when awarding government contracts, then it had nothing to do with corruption and everything to do with redressing the balance.

(Gordon and Morriss 2014, 4), particularly prominent since the global financial crisis. To this effect, the compliance sector has increased to an industrial scale. Major financial markets and institutions are perceived to be at the centre of breaches and violations, like the HSBC fine demonstrates.

Many types of economic misconduct are inherently deviant and *malum in se*. For example, dishonestly persuading people to invest savings in fraudulent schemes, such as that perpetrated by the investment manager and former Chair of NASDAQ, Bernard Madoff. This type of misconduct is being increasingly seen during the coronavirus pandemic, with fraudsters targeting the human condition of fear and landscape of vulnerability. Examples of fraud which have recently increased include falsely claiming government financial relief, pressure selling, or persuading someone that a relative is unwell and requiring payment for healthcare.

However, ambivalence sets in when the conduct is less inherently deviant. For example, through the latter part of the 20th century, some types of acquisitive misconduct were viewed as victimless (Brody and Kiehl 2010, 364). Manne's (1985) work on insider dealing and market abuse observes that later in the 20th century, legal and economic scholars began to view insider dealing in a less emotively charged manner. By contrast, events of the last two decades, such as the global recession, have increased public outrage about corporate greed, corrupt elites and multinational corporations' tax avoidance. Exemplifying this were the lack of convictions of financial executives following the worst recession in recent history caused by irresponsible risk-taking and lending practices (Zales 2016). Discontent is understandable when considering the financial industry bonus pool was $30 billion in 2013 and executive pay averaged $15 million.[9] Indeed, Sutherland in his criminological work about white-collar criminals operating 'in the suites' may have well anticipated those who would contribute to cause global recessions.

While many types of behaviour firmly cross the line of illegality, many hover in the grey vacuum which many campaigners, particularly in the anti-tax avoidance space, argue operates significantly outside the spirit of the law. Legitimate questions arise across the spectrum of economic crime: When is a gift a bribe? When does corporate hospitality fall within the purview of anti-bribery legislation? Who are the victims of money laundering? At what point is aggressive fiscal planning the same as tax evasion? Is inside dealing harmful? Is rule-bending acceptable if for the greater good? Is bribery wrong if everyone does it? These questions add confusion and may explain the difference in the way certain behaviours are viewed in different jurisdictions. A good example relates to unexplained wealth and illicit enrichment. Article 20 UNCAC recommends countries to criminalise illicit enrichment – which is defined as a significant increase in the assets of a public official that they cannot reasonably explain in relation to their lawful income.

9 Attorney General Eric Holder Jr remarks on Financial Fraud Prosecutions, NY Law School, 7.9.2014.

Many countries have implemented this, including Lithuania, Romania, Argentina and India. However, other countries utilise civil asset recovery laws, rather than the criminal law, to meet the spirit of the recommendation. There are concerns that criminalisation could undermine fundamental human rights such as the presumption of innocence. Reverse burden-shifting in the criminal context is rarely seen, save for instance of certain defences like pleading diminished responsibility. Ireland, Australia and the UK have implemented UWO legislation which places a rebuttable presumption on the asset-holder (usually a PEP or someone involved in serious crime or their associates) that the asset was funded by ill-gotten gains. The recipient can obviate this by providing a factual explanation as to its legitimate source, with false statements giving rise to criminal liability. Therefore, even for something like unexplained wealth where a conviction of bribery is not necessary, there is still disparity in the way jurisdictions respond. In Ireland it has been perceived as a welcomed tool, whereas in Australia it has been perceived as less successful. Interestingly, the Estonian government recently rejected UWO-style legislation on the grounds that it was not specific enough.[10] The success or otherwise of UWOs will be specific to country, context and content (Reuters 2017), which demonstrates that for some types of economic misconduct, harmonisation of responses may be difficult depending on how the conduct itself, and the mechanisms by which a country wishes to invoke legal preventive measures, is perceived.

There is consensus that targeting criminal property removes crime's profitability and disrupts criminal activity. The global AML campaign has seen a push towards universalism. All EU member states criminalise money laundering, however there have been stark differences in legislation and case disposal, such as the *mens rea* requirement being different between states. Until recently, there had not been a EU-wide minimum or maximum penalty for those convicted of laundering offences. According to a European Commission study on Criminal Sanctions Legislation and Practice in Representative Member States (2014), this could explain the differences in the way states deal with laundering cases. For example, in the UK the maximum prison sentence for money laundering is 14 years. In Italy it is 12, and in Lithuania it is 7. This has wider ramifications for enforcement efforts and the partnership of nations vis-à-vis intelligence sharing and investigations involving multiple jurisdictions. Given that the EU calls for shared values and shared responses through the successive money laundering Directives, if there is visible disparity, then cross-border efforts may be jeopardized. Successive EU AML Directives, including the recent 6th Directive, require members to implement agreed standards such as a 4-year minimum prison sentence for money laundering, minimum standards for aggravated cases, and liability for legal entities. They also call on member states to implement public registers of beneficial ownership information relating to legal entities. The fact that this source of law comes as a Directive means individual EU states can go further, as it simply

10 KYC360 (18 January 2019) 'AML: Estonia rejects plans for 'unexplained wealth orders'.

sets the bar by minimum requirements, with the aim of increasing cooperation. The EU stated: "The lack of uniform definitions and penalties currently allows criminals to exploit these differences and commit crimes where penalties are the lowest".[11] This is concerning when faced with an EU Commission estimate that in some member states, as much as 70% of laundering cases consist of some cross-border element.

Ambiguity of economic misconduct is well-voiced in scholarship. As has been touched upon, corruption can be perceived as a facilitative tool during post-conflict redevelopment (Glanville 2016). This is particularly pertinent if bureaucracy is excessive, and exacerbated if corruption is systemic in society. The idea of obviating unnecessary bureaucracy for rebuilding efforts to help development might make corruption seem more justifiable than objectionable. This is easier to envision in circumstances of emergency, such as housing people – something developing states are far less strategically equipped for than developed ones.

The ambiguity continues in the context of tax evasion and avoidance. While many governments have unsurprisingly voiced their opposition to aggressive tax avoidance, viewing the two indiscriminately is not a habit confined to politicians or the media (Alldridge 2017, 35). Many phrases look similar, such as tax cheating, tax escaping, tax dodging, aggressive tax avoidance, estate planning, fiscal planning, and tax mitigation. Whether tax has a legal or moral basis is a question which sets many legal scholars and social scientists aside (Prebble and Prebble 2010, 745). The concept of fairness is also problematic. Is it fair that in the UK, the top 1% paid just below 27% of all UK income tax in 2016–17, yet 15% in 1991? The fairness question applies to multinational corporations like Apple, who have been reported to pay less than 1% corporation tax in Ireland (*BBC* 18.9.2018), despite the standard rate being 12.5%. Given that multinationals consider themselves among the world's largest taxpayers, perhaps they have no moral qualms about legally reducing tax liabilities if such arrangements are finally deemed legal by the courts.

There is a moral imperative to being a taxpayer. Law is not the only normative domain in society, as other things guide and influence behaviour such as religion or ethics (Kelsen 1934/2009). However, a long-standing principle of legal positivism is that one's obedience to the law is predicated on the threat of a sanction for non-compliance (Austin 1832/1995). For example, one might view abortion as reprehensible yet be obliged to pay tax despite funding abortion treatment, otherwise face a conviction for tax evasion. Tax justice, however, is predicated on the notion of fairness and is inherently anti–tax competition. Christians (2014, 39), whose work examines the policy response in light of the impact of morality-based offensives against tax avoidance, comments that it involves "creating a single tax compliance framework with which to build a single message about the integral role of morality in taxpayer behaviour". However, scholars like Freyer and Morriss

11 Council of the E.U. Press Release 320/18, 7 June 2018: 'E.U. agrees new rules to make sure money laundering criminals are punished'.

(2014) have extrapolated dissatisfaction with the way influential left-leaning organisations are trying to push ideological views of tax fairness.

Scholars have argued that tax evasion and avoidance should be considered as "one phenomenon" (Prebble and Prebble 2010, 745). There is also the conception that only the rich and well-connected can engage in tax avoidance. While the Panama and Paradise papers exposed many wealthy and powerful people making use of offshore services, it is a flawed misconception to single out the rich as the only ones engaging in it. The argument that only elites can afford to do it indicates a prejudice towards unaffordability, rather than the purported immorality of it. This is the problem with the underlying notion of fairness as an indicator of what law is, or should be. If tax avoidance is deemed immoral or the law needs reforming to prevent it, then it should not matter who can or cannot afford to engage in it. Given the social desirability of wealth maximisation, it would be interesting to measure whether more people would avoid tax if it was inexpensive to achieve. Many media outlets have published free advice for legally saving tax. The financial commentator, Martin Lewis, conducted an online survey receiving 16,700 responses to the question: "If a [builder] offered you a discount for cash, being pretty clear it meant they would (illegally) evade tax on it, what would you do?" Fifty-seven per cent said they would "Grab the Discount"; 31% said they would "Pay Cash, but would want an Invoice"; 5% would "Use em but not pay cash [*sic*]", and only 7% would "Refuse to use them".[12] While the poll was non-representative, it illustrates the earlier point about wealth maximisation which makes the tax avoidance issue far from clear. Tax evasion in the UK appears to be increasing, as in 2017–18 HMRC reported dealing with a record 3,809 tax evasion cases (*FT* 14.6.2018).

The unfairness argument of tax avoidance is similar to the argument some scholars have made that insider dealing is harmful because of the unfairness that most of us are outsiders (Rider and Ashe 1993, 1). Manne (1985) defended insider dealing by arguing that the opposition to it centres on unfairness. Rider has talked about whether the outrage emanates from jealousy, bitterness or something similarly base. The unfairness rationale is hardly a sound basis worthy of invocation of the criminal law.

However, the toxicity associated with it has intensified recently. Some economists have argued that tax should be paid by the wealthy because communal services helped to generate their wealth (Chang 2011). This quite easily refutes the 'tax is theft' argument, which has been widely discounted. For example, the racing driver Lewis Hamilton allegedly avoided £3 million VAT on his jet, to which Dame Margaret Hodge said he should "hold his head in shame".[13] Similarly, in the fallout of the Paradise papers, Queen Elizabeth II and her estate were found to have made offshore investments in the Cayman Islands, which was criticised heavily. As with all Overseas Territories, the Queen is Head of State.

12 Lewis, Martin (@MartinSLewis) Twitter Poll: "Today's Twitter poll: If a builder/plumber/cleaner etc offered you a discount for cash, being pretty clear it meant they would (illegally) evade tax on it. What would you do. . .". 9.11.2017, 10:58 a.m.

13 HC Deb (7 November 2017) Vol 630, Col 1441.

Notwithstanding the illogicality of suggesting there is something untoward about a country's monarch investing therein, the Duchy of Lancaster confirmed that they were not aware of any tax incentive to the investment (*BBC* 06.11.2017), which perhaps challenges the popular misconception that all offshore investments carry such advantage.

2.7 Conclusion

Suspect wealth and economic crime are at the forefront of government, international and supranational organisations' agendas. Concerns about the impact of economically acquisitive crime have manifested internationally, particularly given the risks it presents to the stability and sustainability of developed and developing jurisdictions alike. Whether it is regarding losing public revenue through corruption and flight capital, or growing tax gaps through tax misconduct or sustaining organised crime through money laundering, the effects rightly call for some degree of international standardisation in legislative and regulatory terms in order to achieve cohesive implementation and meaningful international cooperation. However, there is significant ambivalence about types of conduct, despite these concerns. This calls for a cautionary outlook when considering the extent to which international standards are viable in jurisdictions, or whether a one-size-fits-all standard is appropriate. The chapter addressed some criticisms about offshore financial centres, which will be discussed at length in the coming chapter.

References

Alldridge, P. (2017) *Criminal Justice and Taxation*, Oxford: Oxford University Press.

Alstadsæter, A., Johannesen, N., and Zucman, G. (2017) 'Who Owns the Wealth in Tax Havens? Macroevidence and Implications for Global Inequality', NBER Working Paper 23805, 1–19.

Altinkaya, Z., and Yucel, O. (2013) 'The Effects of International Trade on International Money Laundering from the Perspectives of International Law and International Trade in Turkey', *European Scientific Journal*, 1: 116–124.

Austin, J. (1832/1995) *The Province of Jurisprudence Determined*, Cambridge: Cambridge University Press.

BBC (12.7.2016) 'HSBC Avoided US Money Laundering Charges Because of "Market Risk" Fears'. Available: www.bbc.co.uk/news/business-36768140

BBC (06.11.2017) 'Paradise Papers: Queen's Private Estate Invested £10 Million in Offshore Funds'. Available: https://www.bbc.co.uk/news/uk-41878305

BBC (18.9.2018) 'Apple Pays Disputed Irish Tax Bill'. Available: www.bbc.co.uk/news/business-45566364

BBC (28.8.2019) 'Najib Razak 1MDB: Malaysia's Former PM Faces Biggest Trial Yet'. Available: www.bbc.co.uk/news/world-asia-49492707

Bey, H. (1991) *The Temporary Autonomous Zone*, Brooklyn, NY: Autonomedia.

Brody, R. G., and Kiehl, K. A. (2010) 'From White-Collar Crime to Red-Collar Crime', *Journal of Financial Crime*, 17(3): 351–364.

Bryans, D. (2014) 'Bitcoin and Money Laundering: Mining for an Effective Solution', *Indiana Law Journal*, 89(1): 441–472.

Chaikin, D. (2018) 'The Law Enforcement Implications of the Panama Papers', in D. Chaikin and G. Hook (eds.), *Corporate and Trust Structures: Legal and Illegal Dimensions*, Melbourne: Australian Scholarly Publishing.

Chang, H.-J. (2011) *23 Things They Don't Tell You About Capitalism*, London: Penguin.

Christians, A. (2014) 'Avoidance, Evasion, and Taxpayer Morality', *Washington University Journal of Law and Policy*, 44(1): 39–59.

CityAM (6.12.2018) 'Deutsche Bank Shares Drop to New All-Time Low after Report Ties It Closer to Danske Scandal'. Available: www.cityam.com/deutsche-bank-shares-down-again-after-reports-drag-further/

Cobham, A., and Jansky, P. (2017) *Global Distribution of Revenue Loss from Tax Avoidance*. United Nations University World Institute for Development Economics Research. Available: www.wider.unu.edu/publication/global-distribution-revenue-loss-tax-avoidance

Cornish, D., and Clarke, R. (1986) 'Situational Prevention, Displacement of Crime and Rational Choice Theory', in K. Heal and G. Laycock (eds.), *Situational Crime Prevention: From Theory into Practice*, London: HMSO.

Datt, K. H. (2014) 'Paying a Fair Share of Tax and Aggressive Tax Planning – A Tale of Two Myths', *eJournal of Tax Research*, 12(2): 410–432.

Devereux, M. P., Freedman, F., and Vella, J. (2012) 'Tax Avoidance, Paper 1', Oxford University Centre for Business Taxation.

Dietsch, P. (2015) *Catching Capital: The Ethics of tax Competition*, Oxford: Oxford University Press.

European Commission (2014) 'Study on Criminal Sanction Legislation and Practice in Representative Member States'. Available: https://op.europa.eu/en/publication-detail/-/publication/35472a32-42d0-43ae-b86b-f75d0f1a1832

Findley, M. G., Nielson, D. L., and Sharman, J. C. (2014) *Global Shell Games: Experiments in Transnational Relations, Crime, and Terrorism*, Cambridge: Cambridge University Press.

Forstater, M. (2016) 'Making Sense of the Cost of Tax Avoidance', *Tax Journal*, 12–14.

Franklin,B.(7.10.1739)'PoorRichard'sAlmanac'.Available:www.unsv.com/voanews/specialenglish/scripts/2010/11/07/0040/Poor_Richard's_A lmanack_by_Franklin_Benjamin.pdf

Freyer, T. A., and Morriss, A. P. (2013) 'Creating Cayman as an Offshore Financial Centre: Structure and Strategy since 1960', *Arizona State Law Journal*, 45: 1297–1398.

FT (14.6.2018) 'HMRC Tax Evasion Cases Reach Record High'. Available: www.ftadviser.com/trade-bodies/2018/06/14/hmrc-tax-evasion-cases-reach-record-high/

FT (4.7.2018) 'Danske Bank Shares Fall on Money Laundering Allegations'. Available: www.ft.com/content/50f338fe-7f5c-11e8-bc55-50daf11b720d

Garcia, S. M., Chen, P., and Gordon, M. T. (2014) 'The Letter versus the Spirit of the Law: A Lay Perspective on Culpability', *Judgment and Decision Making*, 9(5): 479–490.

German, P. (2018) 'Dirty Money: An Independent Review of Money Laundering in Lower Mainland Casinos Conducted for the Attorney General of British Columbia', Government Report, Government of British Columbia.

Glanville, M. (2016) 'Corruption and Public Policy in Post-Conflict States', in B. A. K. Rider (ed.), *Research Handbook on International Financial Crime*, Cheltenham: Elgar.

Global Witness (2009) 'Undue Diligence: How Banks Do Business with Corrupt Regimes'. Available: https://www.globalwitness.org/en/campaigns/corruption-and-money-laundering/banks/undue-diligence/
Global Witness (2017) 'UK Property: A Safe Haven for Dirty Money'. Available: https://www.globalwitness.org/documents/19278/Briefing_Property_Market_j8h1bSb.pdf
Gordon, R. K. (2009) *Laundering the Proceeds of Public Sector Corruption*, Washington, DC: World Bank.
Gordon, R. K., and Morriss, A. P. (2014) 'Moving Money: International Financial Flows, Taxes and Money Laundering', *Hastings International and Comparative Law Review*, 37(1): 1–123.
Green, G. S. (1993) 'White-Collar Crime and the Study of Embezzlement', *Annals of the American Academy*, 525: 95–106.
Guardian (7.8.2012) 'Standard Chartered Shares Slump Amid Iran Allegations'. Available: www.theguardian.com/business/2012/aug/07/standard-chartered-shares-slump-iran
Halliday, T. C., Levi, M., and Reuter, P. (2014) 'Global Surveillance of Dirty Money: Assessing Assessments of Regimes to Control Money-Laundering and Combat the Financing of Terrorism', Centre on Law & Globalisation.
Hartman, J. M. (1997) 'Government by Thieves: Revealing the Monsters behind the Kleptocratic Masks', *Syracuse Journal of International Law and Commerce*, 24: 157–175.
Hearson, M. (2017) 'The Challenges for Developing Countries in International Tax Justice', *Journal of Development Studies*, 54(10): 1932–1938.
HMRC (2017) 'Tackling Tax Evasion: Government Guidance for the Corporate Offence of Failure to Prevent the Criminal Facilitation of Tax Evasion'. Available: https://assets.publishing.service.gov.uk/government/uploads/system/uploads/attachment_data/file/672231/Tackling-tax-evasion-corporate-offences.pdf
HMRC (14.6.2018) Measuring Tax Gaps 2018 Edition: Tax Gap Estimate for 2016–2017'. Available: https://webarchive.nationalarchives.gov.uk/20190509073425/https://www.gov.uk/government/statistics/measuring-tax-gaps
Hobbes, T. (1651/2017) *Leviathan*, London: Penguin Classics.
IMF (2016) 'The Fight Against Money Laundering and the Financing of Terrorism'. Available: https://www.imf.org/en/About/Factsheets/Sheets/2016/08/01/16/31/Fight-Against-Money-Laundering-the-Financing-of-Terrorism
International Compliance Association (2018) 'What Is Money Laundering?' Available: https://www.int-comp.org/careers/your-career-in-aml/career-in-aml/#:~:text=Money%20laundering%20is%20the%20generic,derived%20from%20a%20legitimate%20source
Kar, D., and Spanjers, J. (2015) *Illicit Financial Flows from Developing Countries: 2004–2013*, Global Financial Integrity. Available: https://www.gfintegrity.org/wp-content/uploads/2015/12/IFF-Update_2015-Final-1.pdf
Kelly, R. (1999) *The Upperworld and the Underworld: Case Studies of Racketeering and Business Infiltrations in the United States*, New York: Kluwer Academic.
Kelsen, H. (1934/2009) *Pure Theory of Law* (2nd ed.), Clark, NJ: Lawbook Exchange.
Kohonen, M., and Mestrum, F. (2009) *Tax Justice: Putting Global Inequality on the Agenda*, London: Pluto Press.
Law Commission (2010) 'Criminal Liability in Regulatory Contexts', Consultation Paper 195.

Lee, G. C. M. (2018) 'Police Corruption: A Comparison between China and India', *Journal of Financial Crime*, 25(2): 248–276.

Levi, M., and Reuter, P. (2006) 'Money Laundering', *Crime and Justice*, 34(1): 289–375.

Manne, H. (1985) 'Insider Trading and Property Rights in New Information', *Cato Journal*, 4(3): 933–957.

Merton, R. (1938) 'Social Structure and Anomie', *American Sociological Review*, 3(5): 672–682.

Murphy, R. (2012) 'Closing the European Tax Gap: A Report for Group of the Progressive Alliance of Socialists and Democrats in the European Parliament', *Tax Research LLP.*

NCA (2016) 'National Strategic Assessment of Serious and Organised Crime 2016'. Available: https://www.nationalcrimeagency.gov.uk/who-we-are/publications/353-national-strategic-assessment-of-serious-and-organised-crime-2016/file

Nefsky, R. L. (1977) 'Federal Income Taxation and Real Estate Development: Death Knell for Shell Corporations?' *Nebraska Law Review*, 56(3): 659–675.

OECD (2014) 'The Rationale for Fighting Corruption'. Available: https://maritimecyprus.files.wordpress.com/2017/09/oecd.pdf

Oxfam (2016) 'Tax Battles: The Dangerous Global Race to the Bottom on Corporate Tax'. Available: https://www.oxfam.org/en/research/tax-battles-dangerous-global-race-bottom-corporate-tax

Prebble, Z., and Prebble, J. (2010) 'The Morality of Tax Avoidance', *Creighton Law Review*, 43: 693–746.

Reuters (3.1.2019) 'Google Shifted $23bn to Tax Haven Bermuda in 2017: Filing'. Available: www.reuters.com/article/us-google-taxes-netherlands/google-shifted-23-billion-to-tax-haven-bermuda-in-2017-filing-idUSKCN1OX1G9?utm_source=reddit.com

Reuters (1.10.2020) 'Malaysian Court to Hear ex-PM Najib's 1MDB Appeal from Feb 15'. Available: www.reuters.com/article/us-malaysia-politics-najib/malaysian-court-to-hear-ex-pm-najibs-1mdb-appeal-from-february-15-idUSKBN26M53V

Rider, B. A. K. (ed.) (1997) *Corruption: The Enemy Within*, Netherlands: Kluwer Law International.

Rider, B. A. K., and Ashe, M. (1993) *Insider Crime*, Bristol: Jordans.

Rousseau, J. J. (1762/1998) *The Social Contract*, London: Wordsworth.

Royal Commission on the Taxation of Profits and Income: Final Report (Chair: Lord Radcliffe) (Cmd. 9474; 1955). Available: https://discovery.nationalarchives.gov.uk/details/r/C3903821

Royal Gazette (1.12.2016) 'Brown's Lawyers: Rules Were "Bent"'. Available: www.royalgazette.com/event/news/article/20161130/browns-lawyer-rules-were-bent/

RUSI (9.3.2020) 'A Sharper Image: Advancing a Risk-Based Response to Terrorist Financing', Occasional Papers.

Saleh, S. (2014) 'Challenges in Combatting Corruption and Fixing Accountability: In Iraq's Perspective', *International Journal of Business and Social Science*, 5(13): 64–70.

Saperstein, L., Sant, G., and Ng, M. (2015) 'The Failure of Anti–Money Laundering Regulation: Where is the Cost-Benefit Analysis?', *Notre Dame Law Review Online*, 91(1): 1–11.

Schneider, F., and Enste, D. H. (2002) *The Shadow Economy: Theoretical Approaches, Empirical Studies and Policy Implications*, Cambridge: Cambridge University Press.

SFO (31.1.2020) 'SFO Enters into €991m DPA with Airbus as Part of a €3.6bn Global Resolution'. Available: https://www.sfo.gov.uk/2020/01/31/sfo-enters-into-e991m-deferred-prosecution-agreement-with-airbus-as-part-of-a-e3-6bn-global-resolution/

Sharma, C. (2016) 'Estimating the Size of the Black Economy in India', Indian Institute of Management Lucknow, MPRA Paper No 75211.

Sharman, J. C. (2010) 'Shopping for Anonymous Shell Companies: An Audit Study of Anonymity and Crime in the International Financial System', *Journal of Economic Perspectives*, 24(4): 127–140.

Sharman, J. C. (2016) 'Solving the Beneficial Ownership Conundrum: Central Registries and Licenced Intermediaries', Report for Jersey Finance.

Sharman, J. C. (2017) *Despots Guide to Wealth Management*, New York: Cornell University Press.

Slemrod, J., and Yitzhaki, S. (2002) 'Tax Avoidance, Evasion, and Administration', in A. J. Auerbach and M. Feldstein (eds.), *Handbook of Public Economics* (Vol. 3), Amsterdam: Elsevier Science B.V. [1425–1442].

Sutherland, E. H. (1949/1985) *White Collar Crime*, New Haven: Yale University Press.

Tambulasi, R. I. C. (2010) 'The Public Sector Corruption and Organised Crime Nexus: The Case of the Fertiliser Subsidy Programme in Malawi', *African Security Review*, 18(4): 19–31.

Tanzi, V. (2011) 'Tax Systems in the OECD: Recent Evolution, Competition, and Convergence' [11–37], in E. Albi and J. Martinez-Vasquez (eds.), *Elgar Guide to Tax Systems*, Cheltenham: Elgar.

Thomas-James, D. (2015) 'The Prosecution of Insider Dealing in the UK: Is There a Need for Criminal Justice Reform?', Dissertation for the Degree of Master of Philosophy, University of Cambridge.

Thony, J. (2000) 'Money Laundering and Terrorism Financing: An Overview', IMF Repository.

TJN (2012) 'The Price of Offshore Revisited'. Available: https://www.taxjustice.net/cms/upload/pdf/Price_of_Offshore_Revisited_120722.pdf

TJN (20.11.2020) '$427bn Lost to Tax Havens Every Year: Landmark Study Reveals Countries' Losses and Worst Offenders'. Available: https://www.taxjustice.net/2020/11/20/427bn-lost-to-tax-havens-every-year-landmark-study-reveals-countries-losses-and-worst-offenders/

TJN (2021) 'Tax Avoidance and Tax Evasion'. Available: https://www.taxjustice.net/topics/tax-avoidance-and-tax-evasion/

Transparency International (2015) 'Corruption on Your Doorstep: How Corrupt Capital is Used to Buy Property in the U.K.' Available: https://www.transparency.org.uk/publications/corruption-on-your-doorstep

UK Government (2014) 'Anti-Corruption Plan'. Available: https://www.gov.uk/government/publications/uk-anti-corruption-plan

UK Government (2015) 'Consultation on a New Corporate Offence of Failure to Prevent Tax Evasion'. Available: https://www.gov.uk/government/consultations/tackling-tax-evasion-a-new-corporate-offence-of-failure-to-prevent-the-criminal-facilitation-of-tax-evasion

UK Government 2017–2022 Anti-Corruption Strategy. Available: https://www.gov.uk/government/publications/uk-anti-corruption-strategy-2017-to-2022

United Nations Sustainable Development Goals. Available: https://sdgs.un.org/goals

US Department of Justice (11.12.2012) 'HSBC Holdings Plc. And HSBC Bank USA N.A Admit to AML and Sanctions Violations, Forfeit $1.256 Billion in DPA'. Available: https://www.justice.gov/opa/pr/hsbc-holdings-plc-and-hsbc-bank-usa-na-admit-anti-money-laundering-and-sanctions-violations

US Department of Justice (1.11.2018) 'Malaysian Financier Low Taek Jho, Also Known as "Jho Low", and Former Banker Ng Chong Hwa, also Known as "Roger Ng", Indicted for Conspiring to Launder Billions of Dollars in Illegal Proceeds and to Pay Hundreds of Millions of Dollars in Bribes', Press Release; and, *Ibid* (1.11.2018) 'Former Banker Tim Leissner Pleaded Guilty to Conspiring to Launder Money and to Violate the Foreign Corrupt Practices Act Related to 1MDB'. Available: https://www.justice.gov/opa/pr/malaysian-financier-low-taek-jho-also-known-jho-low-and-former-banker-ng-chong-hwa-also-known

US House of Representatives (11.7.2016) 'Too Big to Jail: Inside the Obama Justice Department's Decision not to Hold Wall Street Accountable', Report Prepared by the Republican Staff of the Committee on Financial Services.

US Internal Revenue Service (4.2016) 'Report: Tax Gap Estimates for Tax Years 2008–2010'. Available: https://www.irs.gov/pub/newsroom/tax%20gap%20estimates%20for%202008%20through%202010.pdf

US Permanent Subcommittee on Investigations (16.7.2012) 'HSBC Exposed U.S. Financial System to Money Laundering, Drug, Terrorist Financing Risks', Press Release. Available: https://www.hsgac.senate.gov/subcommittees/investigations/media/hsbc-exposed-us-finacial-system-to-money-laundering-drug-terrorist-financing-risks

US Treasury Department (9.2002) 'Contributions by the Department of the Treasury to the Financial War on Terrorism: Fact Sheet'. Available: https://www.treasury.gov/press-center/press-releases/documents/2002910184556291211.pdf

World Bank Group (28–30.9.1999) 'Joint Annual Discussion', Press Release No. 2.

Wright, T., and Hope, B. (2018) *Billion Dollar Whale: The Man Who Fooled Wall Street, Hollywood, and the World*, New York: Hachette Books.

Xuereb, A. (2015) 'Tax Avoidance or Tax Evasion?', *Symposium Melitensia*, 10: 217–229.

Zales, J. L. (2016) '$22 Trillion Lost, Zero Wall Street Executives Jailed: Prosecutors Should Utilize Whistle-blowers to Establish Criminal Intent', *Notre Dame Journal of International and Comparative Law*, 6(1):167–188.

Zucman, G. (2015) *The Hidden Wealth of Nations: The Scourge of Tax Havens*, Chicago: University of Chicago Press.

3 Offshore financial centres and the British Overseas Territories

3.1 Introduction to 'offshore'

The concept of 'offshore' seems both indefensible and irresistible. The former manifests through the agendas of global tax justice organisations and international investigative reporters whose sole purpose appears to be aimed at engendering global tax harmony and the consequent eradication of offshore financial centres through increased pressure and externally dictated controls. This is based on long-held views as to their harmful role in the global economy through abuse of their offshore products and services to facilitate crime, conceal or launder its proceeds, or evade fiscal obligations in other jurisdictions. Their influence on policy and lawmaking is irrefutable and clearly evidenced in the passage of the public register amendment to the UK Sanctions and Anti–Money Laundering Act. The latter, the irresistibility, materialises through popular depiction of offshore centres, the types we see in Fleming's James Bond stories, which frequently mention numbered bank accounts, Swiss vaults to conceal wealth, or fiscal paradise Caribbean tax havens. This book does not set out in defence of offshore, nor does it flailingly adopt those predictable sentiments which often lack substance in dissent of them. It proceeds on the unpopular basis that offshore financial centres are not going to go away because the lion's share of the world's economists suggest they serve no useful purpose. And, why should they? This book is not concerned with the morality of tax havens, but rather the extent to which their regulation and participation in global financial transacting is cooperative and compliant with international standards designed to suppress and obviate the risks posed to their financial centres, and others, by suspect wealth and its origins. The morality debate which tends to result in offshore centres being presented internationally as 'pariah states' often clouds sensible, practical solutions to achieving more meaningful cooperation with these jurisdictions.

Many tax havens and offshore financial centres have been labelled as "sunny places for shady people". Prince Albert II of Monaco, the sovereign microstate in southern France, recently acknowledged that this formulation accurately described how the Principality was prior to adopting international standards on information exchange, AML regulation and compliance (*CBS* 17.3.2019). Taken against a backdrop of island nation financial centres being implicated in cases of narcotics trafficking in previous decades, right through to perceptions about multinational tax avoidance using offshore structures highlighted by offshore data leaks, has meant that the 'sunny place' idiom that has become indiscriminately synonymous with offshore and international financial centres has endured.

While many criticisms of offshore centres are justified, such as the fact that if a shell company can be incorporated without there being any record anywhere of its ultimate ownership then this gives rise to a serious money laundering risk, many arguments against offshore centres often lack substance. The concerns about international economic crime and suspect wealth discussed in the previous chapter demonstrate the problems with both predicate and facilitative criminality. There is an increasingly important emphasis placed on where suspicious wealth ends up – whether by means of concealment, regeneration into the legitimate economy, evading civil or legal obligations, or financing of future misconduct. Case law discussed later in this work demonstrates that offshore centres are often used to conceal and dispose of criminal proceeds, enabling the sustainment of lavish lifestyles – for example through purchasing luxury property. As Sharman (2017) avers, seldom is public money looted from archipelagic islands in the Caribbean and stashed in developing Africa – rather, the other way around. As a result of sustained interest in tax havens following the Bahamas leaks and the Panama and Paradise papers, such jurisdictions face increasing pressure about their perceivably harmful role in the world economy. For the international community, it seems not to matter that such jurisdictions are, in fact, different. This is nothing new, and all offshore jurisdictions have been subject to long-standing perceptions of harm. There have also been recent attempts to impose changes as to how they operate, in some cases by unilateral legislative intervention and in others by way of blacklisting.

So, what are these jurisdictions? A useful starting point is to consider some phrases – popularly understood, and incorrectly interchangeable. The term 'tax haven' is perhaps the most common phrase for offshore financial centre. As Sharman (2006) notes, no two lists of tax havens contain the same countries and no clear definition exists as to what a tax haven is. Two examples evidencing the inconsistency in approach are the EU List of Non-Cooperative Jurisdictions for Tax Purposes (the blacklist and greylist), and the subsequent 2018 Netherlands blacklist of low-tax jurisdictions.

These jurisdictions are often stereotyped as fiscal island paradises located in the Caribbean. There are also those which existed as tax havens in some form long before the establishment of Caribbean or Middle Eastern tax havens. Sharman (2006, 21) gives examples of European tax havens which exist in association with larger neighbouring countries such as Andorra to France and San Marino to Italy. For example, Switzerland is a country that has been identified by many as being active in offshore finance longer than any other (Zucman 2015, 8). Another example of an offshore centre not geographically offshore to anything is the Principality of Monaco, which commands a fervent tax haven reputation and has been placed on various blacklists in its history. Additionally, there is Liechtenstein, nestled between Switzerland and Austria. TJN's list of the world's tax havens and offshore financial centres shows that many are either landlocked or attached to land, which debunks somewhat the island fiscal paradise imagery we have become familiar with in tax haven discourse. Of course, there are many within these lists that happen to be islands. Further, municipal areas like the City of London, or the US states of Delaware and Nevada, have been labelled 'tax havens' by different organisations, such as the TJN.

These jurisdictions are subject to interchangeable phrases normatively used to describe them. As well as tax haven and offshore financial centre, the phrase 'secrecy jurisdiction' has become common. Indiscriminate use of these phrases is problematic for various reasons. 'Offshore' has become something of a misnomer, traditionally denoting something not connected to land. It has become an industry in and of itself which provides financial and business services in an alternative jurisdiction. Services typically available include company incorporation, offshore banking, trusts and management services. Some features which have negatively characterised offshore centres include respect for confidentiality, bank secrecy, issuance of bearer shares, and establishment of anonymous shell companies. Other features may include limited regulation, fiscal benefits and incentives for non-residents and entities, and closed registers of ultimate ownership and control of legal persons. It is important to distinguish fundamental legal protections, such as confidentiality, from its abuses. There is a plethora of legitimate uses of offshore services which could relate to privacy, asset protection or wealth-increasing transactions. Gordon and Morriss (2014, 7) talk about the importance of increasing the volume of legitimate wealth-maximising transactions which may utilise the offshore world due to the internationality of money movements. This can be a complex phenomenon involving a variety of interrelated, interlinked, overlapping and sometimes interdependent products and vehicles.

Whatever one's scepticism about offshore business, the provision thereof has become a major source of economic activity and sustainability, particularly so in the case of the islands this books focuses on. While some scholars such as Russell and Graham (2016, 481) claim these jurisdictions are in denial about how problematic their offerings are, it is an inescapable fact that metropolitan jurisdictions like the UK were instrumental and encouraging of islands, to which they bore responsibility, to become self-sufficient by establishing offshore financial centres.[1] Interestingly, many larger economies regularly use offshore jurisdictions to invest public money – an example being the investment of some UK public sector pensions (*FT* 7.11.2017). The UK government has utilised offshore funds to invest public sector pensions such as those of MPs. Recognising the general strength in equities markets, the Parliamentary Contributory Pension Fund lists investments in multinationals like Apple which have been embroiled in offshore tax avoidance allegations, or HSBC which have been found to have breached money laundering controls. Of its total £641 million assets, 49% were overseas equities. Similar companies also make up the BBC's pension scheme.[2] Without questioning the morality issues of where pensions are

1 See HC Deb (4.3.1994), Vol 238, cc25–8W (re. Anguilla).
2 *BBC*: 'My Pension: About the Scheme, Top Investments'.

invested, the fact is that half of MPs' pensions are invested outside the UK. At times of volatility, the benefits of diversification are evident. However, while MPs' pensions are invested in top-performing, stable multinationals, their investment therein maintains the commercial imperatives of those companies to their shareholders to increase profits. This has been notably achieved by some of these companies using offshore vehicles and jurisdictions to minimise fiscal obligations (*Guardian* 18.9.2018), the very thing Parliamentarians are legislating to prevent.

Freyer and Morriss (2013, 1297), in their appraisal of the Cayman Islands' development as an offshore financial centre, emphasise that its journey was one of collaborative policymaking and highlight the important role played by British officials. The combination of tax policy and economic development in the 1950s and 1960s in the UK, together with the post-war decolonialisation campaign, enabled various jurisdictions under British control to establish themselves to take advantage of fiscal and economic opportunities emanating from increased taxes and capital controls in the UK. In doing so, they could move towards securing futures with less control asserted upon them (Kudrle 2016, 1155; Freyer and Morriss 2013, 1296).

There are fundamental differences in the journeys various countries have taken in becoming offshore centres. Former British colonies in the Caribbean entered the industry due to various factors including reliance on being consumption or barter-based economies, or encouragement from the UK to become financially sustainable by providing offshore services. By contrast, as Palan (1998) observes, the European-based tax havens did not set out to become tax havens, rather they were sufficiently autonomous to resist pressure from their neighbours, who themselves were substantially increasing their taxation and regulations.

The perceived problems about these jurisdictions are well-documented. Many are evidenced by findings in case law, assessments from monitoring bodies, or illustratively in NGO reports. The problematic nature of the offshore centres in Overseas Territories was emphasised by the UK International Development Committee's 2016 report 'Tackling Corruption Overseas', which states, at 16: "Enabling money to be held or hidden in offshore tax havens too often deprives developing countries of essential tax revenues, which can have a devastating impact on the provision of public services". In evidence to the Committee at 17, Transparency International stated that:

> secrecy and corruption in the Overseas Territories and Crown Dependencies make a significant contribution to the UK's role as a safe haven for corrupt funds. The secrecy offered by the offshore company structure enables corrupt individuals to hide the source of their funds and use them to buy property, luxury goods and education in the UK.

They called for public beneficial ownership registers as a necessity for accountability. Similarly, Heywood at 13 reminded the Committee of the facilitative role the UK plays with the significant financial flows going through the City of

London. The Committee captured at 9 the common issue taken with the Overseas Territories:

> The Government's efforts have recently come under question, particularly with relation to the continued tax haven status of many of the Overseas Territories and Crown Dependencies and the release of leaked papers from Panama firm MOSSFON which revealed the major role which some individuals and companies based in the UK and the Overseas Territories and Crown Dependencies have played in global tax evasion and aggressive tax avoidance.

These sentiments identify a clearly perceived problem, the spirit of which was seen in the concerns already discussed about economic crime and suspect wealth in Chapter 2. The charge is clear: that the Overseas Territories, Crown Dependencies (and by extension, the UK) play a significant role in facilitative subversive activity abroad. The general idea seems *prima facie* difficult to dispute given the overwhelming amount of information relevant to the territories in the Panama and Paradise papers. Such a conclusion needs to be balanced against important features and distinctions relating to their domestic anti–economic crime frameworks and levels of compliance with international standards. Other important nuances also add ambivalence in identifying where the problems precisely lie – such as collectively grouping the Overseas Territories and Crown Dependencies together. While negative attention from the Panama papers seemed to rest heavily at the UK's door, 7 of the 10 most featured offshore centres in the Panama papers were neither Overseas Territories nor Crown Dependencies. BVI was significantly named, as were the Seychelles and the Bahamas. Bermuda and TCI were absent from this list.

This book focuses on jurisdictions which have, to different extents, embarked upon establishing sophisticated financial and offshore services centres. These are the UK Overseas Territories. Of the 14 territories in total, those relevant to this book are the ones with financial centres: Anguilla, Bermuda, the British Virgin Islands, the Cayman Islands, Gibraltar, Montserrat and the Turks and Caicos Islands. What is not very well understood is that the territories are fundamentally contrasting jurisdictions despite their *prima facie* similarities. They have different economies, cultures and histories with varying nuances in their relationship with the UK, as well as relationship and reliance with other jurisdictions like the US, France, the Netherlands and Spain. They are also at significantly different stages of development. They attract stigma for being tax havens and any use of them attracts stigma to the user.

The blacklisting exercise of labelling harmful tax jurisdictions has existed for decades, with the OECD undergoing campaigns against them in the 1990s and 2000s. In 1999, the OECD started compiling a list to name and shame tax havens on the basis of harmful tax practices (Sharman 2006, 15). Ahead of the OECD's 2000 report, Bermuda and Cayman (among others) committed to reforming its laws in line with OECD standards, such as information exchange with OECD member states. In the report, 35 jurisdictions were named including

Anguilla, BVI, Gibraltar, Montserrat, TCI, Guernsey, Isle of Man and Jersey. Since then, blacklists and greylists have been produced by many organisations based on secrecy, transparency, cooperation and tax practices.

There are well-founded concerns about the phrase 'tax haven', and not simply coming from those subject to this label. The phrase is almost always used negatively. While officials in countries labelled with this name unsurprisingly denounce it, there are also few scholars who have written positively about tax havens (Mitchell 2008). The phrase itself is stigmatic, exacerbated by the agendas of transparency groups and data breaches highlighting controversial activity therein. There is concern that tax havens adversely impact development through facilitation of certain types of misconduct – not simply in their own jurisdictions but in jurisdictions from which suspect wealth originates. Scholars such as Zucman (2015) and Shaxson (2011) highlight the impact tax havens have on the development of other countries. The phrase 'tax haven' conjures imagery of shadiness, dishonesty and cheating – all characteristics of economic crime. Moreover, tax havens can facilitate the financing of terrorism and other forms of serious organised crime and can be used to evade fiscal obligations (Workman 1982). Negative use of the phrase is unsurprising and even justified, at times. However, while some tax havens are culpable of misconduct, as the Panama and Paradise papers sought to demonstrate, the phrase in its negative connotation cannot be equally applied to all offshore financial centres.

Many negative arguments surrounding tax havens, unsurprisingly, point to taxation, including the perception that they are no- or low-tax jurisdictions. Parameterisation of the concerns about tax havens often become convoluted at this juncture. While it is expedient to view the no- or low-tax point in the same negative category as various services such as secrecy or non-disclosure of beneficial ownership, clearer lines in the sand should be drawn. Whereas, just because a jurisdiction is a no- or low-tax jurisdiction – or more accurately stated, operates an indirect taxation model – does not mean it is a tax haven or secrecy jurisdiction. On that argument, given that Hong Kong is often referred to as a tax haven, surely the UK is one given corporation tax is only a few per cent higher than in Hong Kong. Compared to the US, in which corporation tax was 35% until recently lowered under the President Trump administration, it would have been fiscally beneficial to locate corporate affairs in the UK rather than the US if fiscal factors were a commercial priority. The indirect taxation model is common among many offshore centres, including the Overseas Territories, who collect significant public revenue through payroll tax, import duties and other levies. These taxes might be as arduous for their citizens, who have to pay $12 for a box of cereal, as traditional direct taxes are for people in countries like the UK. For island jurisdictions that have to import everything, from basic to luxury items, indirect taxation often represents an expedient, efficient revenue-building method. Of course, there are practices within offshore centres which offer preferential tax rates to certain people such as non-residents or foreign companies. This perhaps more suitably triggers the tax haven label. It should be borne in mind that this practice is by no means confined to small offshore jurisdictions. Many offshore centres, including Overseas Territories, actively exchange information on tax matters and do not operate preferential tax practices like ring-fencing.

The third interchangeable phrase is 'secrecy jurisdiction' – in other words, a jurisdiction which has practices, legislation and/or culture of anonymity and privacy at all costs. Formerly prevalent in the banking industries of many offshore centres, secrecy can also relate to ownership of entities and accounts. For example, the concept of bank secrecy as a mechanism and as a culture ensures client anonymity at all costs. Switzerland was famous for such an approach prior to radical overhaul in the previous two decades. Typically, those Overseas Territories and offshore centres which have executed TIEAs based on the OECD model framework do not have bank secrecy legislation. TJN's Financial Secrecy Index defines a secrecy jurisdiction as one which provides facilities that enable people or entities to escape laws, rules and regulation of another jurisdiction using secrecy as its main tool. On this definition, many Overseas Territories would fall short. Many are well-regulated environments which have been positively reviewed by AML monitoring organisations like CFATF. For those jurisdictions which have made commitments under the Common Reporting Standard, under which exchange of information requests are automatic, indiscriminate use of the term 'secrecy jurisdiction' to refer to all jurisdictions which offer offshore services is problematic. Given a haven presupposes something is safe, if tax havens and secrecy jurisdictions store and readily exchange information with other jurisdictions' enforcement authorities, then this clearly falls short of keeping something secret.

Tax Justice Network (2013) suggests that such jurisdictions are used to escape something such as financial regulation, criminal laws, fiscal obligations such as inheritance tax, corporate governance and responsibility. They add the concept of 'elsewhere' to the characterisation. In the Australian Supreme Court case of *Trio Capital Limited (Admin App) v ACT Superannuation Management Pty Ltd & Others* [2010], Palmer J at 22 went as far as suggesting that such jurisdictions are precisely where one goes to shelter criminality. While offshore centres have long been regarded as uncooperative and uncompliant, there is scholarship which has found them to be amongst the more compliant jurisdictions when it comes to standards regarding beneficial ownership, and that they are subject to the most stringent regulations compared to metropolitan states (Findley, Nielson, and Sharman, 2014).

3.2 The British Overseas Territories: law, governance and development as offshore financial centres

The UK is responsible for 14 Overseas Territories across the globe. Most are largely self-governing territories with their own democratically elected legislatures and constitutions which have been recognised by UK Acts of Parliament. They have a collective population of about 250,000 people, and citizens of the territories are also British. The 14 territories are Anguilla; Bermuda; British Antarctic Territory; British Indian Ocean Territory; British Virgin Islands; Cayman Islands; Falkland Islands; Gibraltar; Montserrat; Pitcairn, Henderson, Ducie and Oeno Islands (the Pitcairn Islands); Saint Helena, Ascension and Tristan da Cunha;

South Georgia and the South Sandwich Islands; Sovereign Base Areas Akrotiri and Dhekelia (on Cyprus); and Turks and Caicos Islands.

The Overseas Territories are defined under Schedule 6 British Nationality Act 1981. This legislation replaced the term 'dependent territory' as implemented in Schedule 1 Interpretation Act 1978. This manifested in the British Overseas Territories Act 2002. Notwithstanding reliance and certain levels of dependency, it is incorrect to describe them as 'dependent territories'. As Hendry and Dickson (2011, 3) observe, the important rationale for this is that it reflected "a change in nomenclature that had already occurred informally". This sentiment was also seen in the 1999 White Paper which suggested that change was necessary to reflect future partnership.

The smallest populated territory is the Pitcairn Islands with a population of 49. Most territories are archipelagos and some are military bases or research centres. Many have vibrant tourism industries, such as TCI which is renowned for having some of the world's best beaches. Others have world-leading markets, such as Bermuda's (re)insurance industry. They are home to unique biodiversity and environmental features, coral reefs and rare wildlife. Whilst many are known as tropical paradises, they are also prone to adverse weather conditions, particularly those located in the Caribbean. Many territories have suffered devastating natural disasters such as the volcano eruption in Montserrat in 1995 and Hurricanes Irma and Maria wreaking destruction on Anguilla, BVI and TCI in 2017.

Of the 14 Overseas Territories, 7 operate sophisticated financial sectors. Given their constitutional link, the UK is perceived as a facilitator of some of the problems discussed in Chapter 2. Exacerbated by the offshore data breaches, there are continued and ongoing constitutional threats to their sovereignty, such as the UK Parliament legislating for them or the threat of direct rule. In the UK, successive Labour Party leaders, including recently Jeremy Corbyn and Ed Miliband, have called for the territories to be brought under direct rule if they cannot comply with international standards. This, of course, is despite them once being encouraged to enter the offshore industry as a means of achieving financial independence. In the context of dissolving the post-war British Empire, small jurisdictions created a sustainable development strategy modelled on financial product and service offerings. As Freyer and Morriss (2013, 1300) note of the Cayman Islands:

> [They] constructed a financial regulatory system that enabled the territory to achieve more economic development and diversification than its peers, bringing it the highest per capita wealth in the Caribbean and putting Cayman on par with the prosperity of Britain.

This model has been replicated by similar jurisdictions for economic diversification and sustainability.

Scholars have long argued that these types of locations ought to be the last place one would envision or expect a financial centre (Palan 1999, 18–21). There were many reasons the Overseas Territories entered this industry. Development and bilateral aid from large developed countries declined in the 1980s and 1990s, a good example being the US, whose aid in the Caribbean fluctuated greatly during a 30-year period and declined in the 1990s following the break-up of the Soviet Union (Meyer 2016). Other pressures motivating this move included threats to trading preferences established under the African Caribbean Pacific EU programme, as well as resourcing, emigration and 'brain drain' issues for islands. Sharman (2006) notes the islands' geographical situation as a contributor to the lack of economic diversification and being situated in a natural disaster zone.

Progression towards financial independence and increased autonomy was achievable through the provision of offshore and business services. This was assisted, in part, by financial deregulation in the world's larger economies. Sharman (2006, 24) suggests that it is unsurprising that small Caribbean states were prompted to become offshore centres given the pressures they faced, together with financial deregulation and technological advancement. This innovation was not a fantasy conceived by the territories themselves. Rather, the rationale might have roots as far back as the original power struggles of former colonial structures, by which the colonial state would have the power to control the economic development of its colonial possessions (Darwin 1988). Many islands under colonial rule or dependency entered into the offshore market with encouragement and pressure from their metropolitan states (Sharman 2006, 24), an example being Vanuatu (Dwyer 2002). Pressure and a desire to limit dependent liability in faraway regions seems to have been a concern for metropolitan states. As Freyer and Morriss (2013, 1317) observe, "Given [Britain's] concerns over being left with an expensive legacy of financially dependent territories, Britain's interest in the region focused on finding a means for fiscal self-sufficiency in the Caribbean". This was also the earlier view of the Colonial Cabinet Policy Committee (1961), who were adamant that Britain should not be left with a residue of financially dependent territories.

The UK government's policy towards the Overseas Territories is based on a relationship of mutual benefits and responsibilities. The then UK Prime Minister David Cameron emphasised in the 2012 FCO White Paper that the balance of benefits and responsibilities must be respected by everyone. The relationship is rooted in shared values and appreciation of the territories' history. Particularly important is the right of each territory to choose to remain an Overseas Territory or to seek an alternative future, known as the principle of self-determination – their right of which is inalienable (UK Government 2010–2015 Policy 'U.K. Overseas Territories'). This principle was included in the government's 1999 White Paper, which acknowledged that the UK would grant independence if requested and if it is an option. It is but one recognition of their histories and a visible move away from their colonial past. However, this approach lacks any middle-ground option between the two extremes of being an Overseas Territory or completely independent, such as free association. However, the relationship does give effect to the desirability of the Overseas Territories to have, and exercise, the greatest possible autonomy across many aspects of their societies. There are prevalent independence movements throughout many of the

Overseas Territories, with examples including previous TCI governments regularly expressing longer-term independence ambition, and the Free Montserrat United Movement calling for independence as an ultimate goal. None have yet opted for independence.

The UK government's responsibilities include ensuring the territories' good governance and defence. This aspect of the relationship was reaffirmed in the 2012 White Paper, which acknowledges the territories' achievements on transparency. In 2012, the UK Foreign Secretary William Hague commented that several challenges faced by the territories and the UK are shared ones. These include cutting public sector deficits and building more diverse and resilient economies. Of course, there is the challenge to ensure financial sectors, and business activity is effectively regulated.

The UK government's duty is to assist the Overseas Territories to observe the same upholding of the rule of law, human rights and integrity as experienced in the UK. With this in mind, the UK emphasised in the 2012 White Paper that it expects high-quality public financial management and services regulation in the territories. The UK has echoed determination to tackle corruption and work closely with the territories on issues of governance. Corruption led to political and constitutional crisis in TCI, resulting in its constitution being suspended in 1986 and 2009, leading to periods of direct rule being imposed. The fact that governance in TCI was in a state of national emergency frankly questions the effectiveness of the UK's relationship with the territories and, in particular, adherence to the aforementioned responsibilities in ensuring their good governance. At the very least, it appears not enough was done to prevent national emergency until the only option was to cure it.

That said, generally the Overseas Territories have a proud tradition of good governance. While the UK government acknowledged in the 2012 White Paper that some of the territories outperform comparable states, they make the point that in the context of the smaller territories challenges are rife, such as maintaining the necessary skills to regulate their economies to meet public expectations for specialist services. For example, while the international response to economic crime is calling for greater monitoring of financial transactions through SARs, a small jurisdiction might simply lack the human, technical and financial resources to effectively implement this – despite the necessity of doing so given its activity in this market. A better-resourced, larger jurisdiction operating a financial sector can shoulder these enhanced regulatory burdens, as and when they increase, far more easily. Moreover, when resources are an issue, more pressing burdens on public services might be prioritised, such as street policing to combat gang crime.

The concept of how small jurisdictions acquire law is an important one, as are the constitutional and legal statuses of the Overseas Territories. They are separate legal jurisdictions from one another and from the UK, although they share the Judicial Committee of the UK Privy Council as their final appellate court. While not part of the UK, they do have a constitutional relationship with it. Their primary sources of law are their distinct written constitutions, recognised in UK legislation. While the legal systems in the territories are based on English common law, the respective territories place legislative emphasis on their own written constitutions. It is a well-established common law principle that the sovereign has the power to establish constitutions for, and on behalf of, its territories as espoused in the English case of *Phillips v Eyre* [1870]. This power to legislate, which is theoretically legally unlimited (*Madzimbamuto v Lardner-Burke* [1968]) is achieved through Orders in Council. Various UK Acts of Parliament created the constitutions for the respective territories (Hendry and Dickson 2011). The statutory legal basis for TCI's constitution is found in the West Indies Act 1962, Bermuda's is found in the Bermuda Constitution Act 1967, and Anguilla's is found in the Anguilla Act 1980. Convention stipulates that intervention powers ought only to be used in exceptional circumstances, such as matters concerning defence, security, judiciary, other non-devolved matters, and extraordinary circumstances such as the suspension of TCI's constitution following Commissions of Inquiry. Wheeler (2016) observes that the UK government's power creates significant political difficulty. There are conventions which clearly state that Parliament should not legislate on devolved matters except with the express agreement of the devolved legislature in question.[3] The Sewel Convention is one which appertains to devolved legislatures in the UK and applies when the UK Parliament wants to legislate on a matter within the devolved competence of the Scottish Parliament, Welsh Parliament, or Northern Ireland Assembly. Under the terms of the Convention, the UK Parliament will not normally do so without the relevant devolved institution having passed a legislative consent motion. Section 51 SAMLA, adopted in May 2018, was a move fundamentally inconsistent with Parliamentary convention, yet justified on grounds of national security. The legal landscape in the Overseas Territories has seen much development in the past decade (Hendry and Dickson 2018). Various legal instruments which represent the territories' response to economic crime and suspect wealth will be considered in greater depth in the coming chapters.

The territories are important components of the global financial architecture, given the volume of transnational finance and business which occurs therein and through them. While they account for only a small portion of the global offshore business sector, they have each developed significant markets; for example, Bermuda world's leading (re)insurance market and the Cayman Islands' major hedge-fund market. In recent years, prior to hurricane devastation, TCI was the fastest-growing Caribbean tourist destination with the highest visitor spending per capita in the region. Anguilla is a leading captive insurance domicile, and the BVI is a major incorporation centre. While some are significant financial players with highly developed professional sectors, many have micro-populations with their own development concerns. The Panama and Paradise papers, which implicated the incorporation sectors in various Overseas Territories like BVI and Bermuda, demonstrates the scale of offshore business. For example, MOSSFON's client list consisted of 14,153 intermediaries. As Chaikin (2018, 109) notes, this sheer number demonstrates "a very

3 HL Deb (17 January 2018) Vol 788. Col 689, per the Earl of Kinnoull.

large global market for offshore companies and trusts and that offshore corporate structures are an essential feature of global business and finance".

With this in mind, a major challenge in certain Overseas Territories is transparency and accountability. The confidentiality norm upon which fundamental components of offshore business are based finds itself swimming against the increasingly strong international flow of transparency. The UK acknowledged in the 2012 White Paper that the financial services industry is one of the main economic contributors to many of the territories. Indeed, the government urges that adhering to international financial regulation standards is necessary for the territories' long-term development strategy. Regulation of their financial markets needs to promote fair competition and growth while ensuring its stability and prevention of inveiglement by others. Given the adverse perception internationally that the territories facilitate economic misconduct, this is particularly important. Reputational stigma, rather than evidence-based analysis of their systems, is more commonly being seen as a basis for legal and policy intervention.

The FCO has set up a Caribbean Regional Financial Services Advisor based in Barbados, who provides regulatory training and activities in the region. Such technical assistance programmes are valuable tools for promoting integrity in the region, which is a necessary first hurdle in implementing international standards. It is clear that this type of support needs enhancing. In the 2012 White Paper, HM Treasury communicated that it will work in the international arena to ensure that there is no discrimination against well-regulated offshore financial centres. While encouraging in principle, it could be said that the UK has failed in this assurance, judging by the fallout from the Panama and Paradise papers. Particularly with the latter, Bermuda was reputationally attacked in an indiscriminate fashion despite being compliant with many international AML, anti-bribery and transparency standards. The 2012 White Paper acknowledged proactivity from several Overseas Territories, for example Anguilla and Bermuda, in their involvement with CFATF initiatives. It also acknowledged that the financial service regulators in Bermuda, Cayman and BVI are members of the International Organisation of Securities Commissions, the Group of International Financial Centre Supervisors and the International Organisation of Insurance Supervisors, among others. The White Paper, in acknowledging that all the Caribbean Overseas Territories and Bermuda are members of CFATF, stated that they have high standards of financial regulation. This points to proactivity and international engagement, rather than the converse which is often portrayed.

As mentioned, the UK is also responsible for their security and defence. This is particularly important for those located between South America and the US, not least due to the transhipment route for narcotics into the US. Some islands have a chequered history of being used to facilitate drug trafficking. Their geographical faculties – such as being a few hundred miles from Florida, or being archipelagos making it easy to land watercraft – assisted in this activity. Indeed, in some cases, trafficking has been facilitated by public officials (*New York Times* 13.3.1985).

The UK is responsible for the territories' international relations. While many territories are largely self-governing and have devolved legislative powers, they cannot be party to international conventions. Many are not seen as parties to international treaties for fighting corruption and money laundering, such as UNCAC. Rather, they can ratify conventions via extension arranged for by the UK. For example, the UN Convention Against Illicit Traffic in Narcotic Drugs and Psychotic Substances 1988 was extended to TCI in 1995, and Bermuda obtained extension of UNCAC in 2018.

Demonstrating the importance of the relationships, and the need for more contemporary review in light of recent developments, the UK Foreign Affairs Committee (FAC) carried out an inquiry into the future of the Overseas Territories in 2018–19. It had a broad remit to examine financing, human rights, governance, environment and international representation. Understanding the territories at an individual level, rather than exclusively as a collective, is both necessary and often lacking. In the context of this book's theme, the territories' response to financial crime and regulation was an issue examined by the Inquiry, particularly SAMLA. Under section 51, the UK imposed a legislative ultimatum compelling the territories to commit to going public with their registers of beneficial ownership by 2020, later extended to 2023, or face having them imposed by Orders in Council. The legal, constitutional and political ramifications of this will be analysed in respect of each territories' beneficial ownership regime later in this book. However, while acknowledging that this has put the relationship under strain, the FAC supports the proposition on the basis that it considers public accessibility to beneficial ownership information to be a matter of national security and that the public have a right to see it (House of Commons, Foreign Affairs Committee 2019, 3).

Another issue of topical relevance is the question of development aid. The UK government recently announced the intention to provide aid to the territories as part of the foreign aid budget having secured a change in rules at the OECD level (DfID 1.11.2018). When 2 Category 5 hurricanes devasted several territories in 2017, they were ineligible to requalify for aid under international rules. Reversing this graduation is a promising policy which re-emphasises the important mandate the UK has in its responsibility to its Overseas Territories' citizens. The question of aid is, however, controversial and has been widely considered in the context of tax havens. Based on DfID's criteria, many territories have been considered 'middle-income jurisdictions' and thus ineligible for aid. There is also the issue of inconsistency. Montserrat, Saint Helena and the Pitcairn Islands receive substantial monies from DfID and are the only territories supported under the aid programme (DfID 2012). It planned to spend £22.9 million on Montserrat financial aid and £28.7 million for Saint Helena in 2017–18 (DfID 2017). It is appreciated that policy is heavily influenced by the capacities of these islands. However, given some prevalent concerns raised about hurricane susceptibility, the approach may warrant re-thinking on an individual needs basis. It is interesting to note that both the 2017–18 and 2019–20 FCO Strategy for the Overseas Territories reports state:

> The main threats to the Territories are hurricanes, volcanoes, earthquakes and tsunamis. . . . As such, support to Montserrat, St Helena, Tristan da

Cunha, and the Pitcairn Islands in their disaster preparedness is necessary to ensure they can respond well in the event of a crisis or natural disaster.

Despite the hurricanes occurring between the publication of these two strategy documents, it is notable that Anguilla, BVI and TCI are not mentioned in the same context as the aforementioned territories.

Adding to the negative perceptions about offshore centres, scholars have argued that assisting territories following hurricanes should be conditional on reforming their approach to transparency, suggesting that such crises are the time to remind the Overseas Territories that just as the UK will support them, they have responsibilities as well (Murphy 2017). Contrarily, Anguilla's former Attorney General and British barrister, Rupert Jones, argued that the adverse publicity toward Overseas Territories from the Panama papers should not cause the UK government embarrassment so that they distance themselves from the islands at their time of need (*Guardian* 12.9.2017). Aid represents a difficult issue, particularly when faced with statistics on financial support given to other territories. For example, a reported £400 million has been spent in Montserrat since the 1995 volcanic eruption and there have been concerns about mismanagement of funds (*Guardian* 16.7.2013). The inconsistencies with the aid budget leads to legitimate questions in light of the fact that the remaining jurisdictions have not been aided since 2003 (UK Aid 2012, 8). Moreover, when the UK announced £32 million across all three territories devastated by Irma, it is understandable why proportionality was questioned.

The UK's decision to leave the EU through Brexit naturally impacts the territories, some of whom, like Anguilla, have borders with French and Dutch neighbours. Nine Overseas Territories are directly associated with the EU under the Overseas Association Decision enacted in 2013. These are not distinct EU members (unlike Gibraltar) and not subject to EU law. This went further than the original 1973 link by virtue of the UK joining the EU. As Clegg (2016, 7) observes, until recently the agreements between the Overseas Territories and the EU were lite versions of the arrangements in place with the African, Caribbean and Pacific countries. Of the 9 territories which have associated status, Anguilla, Bermuda and TCI are included.

Other than the OAD-associated status afforded to the territories, the past two decades have seen increasing Overseas Territories–EU links. Clegg (2016, 9) outlines the OAD benefits which include policy dialogue, access to the EU market, and developmental assistance. On the latter, the EU provides financial support, which in the period 2014–20 amounts to €80 million. In circumstances where DfID aid was lacking, this has been a beneficial feature of EU association. With the inevitable uncertainty Brexit presents, this is a growing concern for the territories. Benefits like free movement across the EU present travel, work and study opportunities for Overseas Territories' citizens. This is important for certain territories which rely on their students being educated abroad to then return to work in the jurisdiction. Indeed, many of the territories' leaders expressed great desire to maintain the mutually beneficial relationship with the EU after Brexit in the FAC Inquiry.[4] Some political figures used the issue to reignite the independence discussion. Bermuda's former Deputy Premier Bob Richards stated:

> [If] the external situation affecting Bermuda should change, so that our way of life and business and our ability to feed ourselves is threatened by U.K. policies, whether inside or outside Europe, then I would not hesitate to go for independence.
>
> (*Royal Gazette* 16.9.2016)

In a recent report by the Anguilla government (2017), the case was made as to the strategic importance of EU association given that Anguilla borders France and the Netherlands, which provide essential assistance and access to Anguilla. The EU is the most significant funder of Anguilla's capital development, and its government has been vocal about the concerns of life post-Brexit. Concerns relating to access to funding, development aid, trade and borders are serious matters for individual territories, yet there seems to have been little meaningful discussion to date on these issues, politically or academically.

As has been noted, offshore jurisdictions are subject to a confusing array of labels. The term 'Crown Dependency' is often misused in reference to the Overseas Territories, or is used indiscriminately to describe the offshore centre jurisdictions the UK has close association with. The Crown Dependencies are Jersey, Guernsey and the Isle of Man. The former two are the Channel Islands located off Normandy, and the Isle of Man sits in the Irish Sea. Crown Dependencies and Overseas Territories are visibly similar as they have established offshore centres. Unlike the territories, the Crown Dependencies are not former colonies of the British Empire. Many territories are former colonies which chose to remain British, and the UK government's policy is to respect their right to self-determination. The Crown Dependencies are dependents of the Crown. The Crown, acting through the UKPC, is ultimately responsible for their good governance. Constitutionally, they have elected Assemblies and their own courts in a similar fashion to the Overseas Territories. The Crown Dependencies can make domestic legislation although, as dependents of the Crown, these require Royal Assent as with UK law. UK legislation rarely extends to Crown Dependencies.

3.3 Perceptions about "sunny places for shady people"

As has been alluded to, the development of the territories in the Caribbean and North Atlantic as sophisticated financial centres was not for nefarious purposes. Rather, such was thought to be positive for the development of small islands. An illustrative example of this in the Commonwealth Caribbean was the establishment of the Society of Trust and Estate Practitioners (STEP) in the Bahamas in 1996. This was to provide training and qualifications to support a growing

4 UK FAC, Oral Evidence 'Future of the UK Overseas Territories' HC 1464 (5.12.2018).

professional infrastructure, set against a backdrop of phenomenal literacy increase in the Bahamas between the 1970s and 1990s. Bahamians received STEP with a sense of pride, as it afforded islanders the ability to obtain recognised qualifications of use as the islands ventured into economic diversification through the provision of sophisticated business services. This was instrumental in enabling the islands to establish themselves in the offshore market.

Recent data breaches demonstrate widespread use of offshore financial centres – a revelation which is unsurprising. What is concerning is that as well as the facilitation of obvious criminal misconduct, a significant portion of the leaks relate to either legal conduct, like legitimate company ownership, or controversial conduct, such as tax avoidance. Disregarding confidentiality to try and expose a portion of business which may be unlawful meant that the rights of many individuals and entities engaged in legitimate business were compromised without recourse. A common, if not simplistic, dissent of offshore centres recently articulated by TJN (2017) is that "no one would go offshore if they could do whatever they wanted to do onshore".

The data breaches convincingly shone an indefatigably bright spotlight on the world of offshore business. In the case of the Panama papers, the perpetrator wanted to expose wrongdoing of an offshore law firm which they averred was causing great harm to the world. The tone was therefore set to paint offshore jurisdictions and activities therein in a shady light – adding weight to the "sunny places for shady people" formulation. In terms of awareness-raising, both publications and the ensuing media reports succeeded. Both the Panama and Paradise papers targeted law firms, but they were relatively untargeted in terms of information. This is evidenced by the ICIJ's disclaimer which avers that the information in the data sets does not imply or suggest wrongdoing. The Panama papers were not concerned with, for example, a targeted list of PEPs suspected, and later confirmed, to be using offshore centres. It involved information of legitimate individuals and entities conducting normal business, which led to various civil actions being brought in respect of rights clearly infringed (e.g. *Appleby Group Global v BBC and Guardian* [2018]). It provided a line of inquiry and, as such, can be used as an investigative tool. As stated by Andrew Mitchell MP, one of the architects of the Overseas Territories' public register amendment under section 51 of SAMLA, it provided civil society, the media, NGOs and charities the ability to scrutinise offshore activity.

The information paints a different picture of the Overseas Territories than their assessed levels of compliance with various internationally advocated economic crime standards. This is particularly so for BVI and Anguilla in the Panama papers, and Bermuda in the Paradise papers. While the number of published documents were in the tens of millions, and hundreds of thousands of entities were named, cases resulting in enforcement action are relatively low. However, those which did result in cases, or general fallout including political crises, were significant matters which rightly attracted attention. Moreover, online research demonstrates reports of several ongoing investigations and concluded cases in multiple countries following the revelations. Some of note include the conviction of former

Pakistan Prime Minister, Nawaz Sharif, for corruption. He was imprisoned for 10 years and his daughter and son-in-law were also convicted. Data from the Panama papers showed that 3 of his children were linked to BVI-registered entities which owned several London properties and had purportedly been used to channel purchasing funds. These were not disclosed on his family's wealth statement. Despite the Panama papers not specifically naming Nawaz Sharif, arguably its main utility was to provide investigative lines of inquiry into individuals closely connected to him (*New York Times* 28.07.2017).

In Armenia, it was reported that authorities re-opened a criminal case into Mihran Poghosyan, a politician, for matters relating to abuse of office, failing to disclose interests, and possible money laundering (*ICIJ* 23.1.2019; *Hetq* 4.4.2016). This emanated from data published in the Panama papers alleging he had interests in 3 offshore companies, legally prohibited for government officials. Elsewhere, the singer Shakira was charged in Spain with tax evasion relating to some €14.5 million. Data from the Paradise papers purportedly demonstrated that she represented her residence as the Bahamas despite allegedly living in Spain (*Guardian* 14.12.2018). Other notable cases included the resignation of Icelandic Prime Minister Signumdur Gunnlaugsson following revelations of his interests in a BVI-registered company which owned bonds in the 3 major Icelandic banks (*ICIJ* 5.4.2016).

While publicly reported criminal cases from the Panama papers revelations appears limited or ongoing, the *ICIJ* suggests that momentum is more recently underway reporting that its investigation has helped governments recover more than $1.2 billion worldwide through fines and back taxes, based on public announcements or reports (*ICIJ* 3.4.2019). Similarly, with the Paradise papers findings, there are several ongoing investigations internationally, such as those in Canada whereby its Revenue Agency recently launched audits into approximately 100 taxpayers named in the Paradise papers (*Mondaq* 18.3.2019).

However, as evidence in the coming chapters will demonstrate, this is not the full picture. In general terms, the UK's Anti-Corruption Strategy 2017–22 acknowledges some important aspects of the territories' adherence to international standards. For example, the OECD Bribery Convention has been extended to various territories, such as BVI, Cayman and Gibraltar. The territories were also acknowledged in the Strategy to have committed to FATF AML/CFT standards and bilateral agreements on access to central registers of company beneficial ownership.

When dealing with perceptions about offshore jurisdictions, and particularly the UK given its close link with the Overseas Territories and Crown Dependencies, it is worth commenting on the City of London, which is a major global financial services hub. While different to the types of financial centres this book focuses on, the fact of its scale and location makes it hugely important in the context of perceptions about offshore. As Keatinge notes: "As a leading global financial centre, the U.K. will be dealing with dirty money" (HC Treasury Committee 2019, 5) and that light-touch regulation has contributed to the UK receiving more than a fair share of suspect wealth. With the City's global scope, some suggest that the offshore dimension of international finance is a heinous plot created by secret cabals within the City, which is the linchpin of a strategic network of jurisdictions like Jersey and Bermuda, to resurrect British financial imperialism based on some hidden power elite in British society.[5] There are two distinct sides of the City: the functional and institutional sides. The former involves the financial sector and professional support organisations. The latter is the traditional side, which is perhaps the most visible through events like the Lord Mayor's Parade, yet less understood. This consists of the City of London Corporation, Mayoralty and Livery Companies – of which there are 110 ancient companies, often styled 'Worshipful' including Vintners, Carpenters and Scriveners. Many of those involved in the City Corporation and Livery have little to do with the City's financial side. Most Livery Companies have a largely charitable function and collectively fundraise circa £40 million annually. While some Lord Mayors have financial backgrounds, a recent former Lord Mayor, Sir Andrew Parmley, is a school teacher.

While much criticism of this side of the City is rather superficial, contrastingly the financial side has provided opposition to various developments designed to strengthen the approach to certain types of economic misconduct – particularly those initiatives directed at facilitators and professionals. A few examples include historic opposition to insider dealing legislation, modern bribery legislation, and the recent failure to prevent offences. Professional firms therein have been implicated in facilitating large-scale tax avoidance, as evidenced by the UK Committee for Public Accounts in its 2013 inquiry into tax avoidance and the role of accountancy firms.

3.4 Capacity issues in the overseas territories

Building upon the above long-standing adverse perceptions about the Overseas Territories' offshore centres, exacerbated by the Panama and Paradise papers leaks, it is necessary to contextualise capacity issues in the territories. Fundamental development constraints include issues of capacity for law enforcement, personnel, financial and technical assistance. This concern is often neglected in international discourse pertaining to the abilities, or otherwise, of the territories to comply with economic crime standards. The concerns have been documented by the UK National Audit Office (2007, 19), which observed that such circumstances necessitate external assistance. Given the increasingly sophisticated nature of compliance and regulation, Overseas Territories' capacity limitations have had a fundamental effect on progress. This has been particularly so in the area of investigations, for example low numbers of SARs being reported in the territories – a framework typically requiring significant resources, recruitment and training staff and financial resources for compliance. As well as political and industry will, there are technical considerations which, at times, rebalance priorities in favour

5 A good example demonstrating sensationalism around the City of London is the documentary film *The Spider's Web: Britain's Second Empire* (2017).

of day-to-day challenges which may be perceived as more contextually pressing. Unsurprisingly, there will always be a tendency to place great capacity and emphasis on fighting street crime in jurisdictions where there is a substantial tourism business or problems with drugs and violent crime.

Small islands, including the Overseas Territories, can also suffer from 'brain drain'; the phrase was coined in the 1950s by the British Royal Society to describe the outflow to the US and Canada of scientists and technologists – in this context, the migration of skilled talent to jurisdictions with better living standards, connectivity, access to advanced technology, career-mobility and higher salaries (Dodani and LaPorte 2005, 488). For those territories which have entered the offshore financial industry, and in particular those whose centres are still developing, it is as much a challenge to recruit talent to its shores as keeping talent from migrating elsewhere for work. The World Bank in a 2003 study found that in the case of 5 countries located close to the US, migration takes a large share of the best educated. Small jurisdictions in this network share resource challenges, a finding echoed by the Foot Report (2009, 7). It will be shown in the coming chapters that jurisdictions like Bermuda, which have developed significant professional sectors, do not have the same capacity needs in this regard as Anguilla and TCI, whose limitations present greater development challenges. The coming analysis examines Bermuda, TCI and Anguilla in detail and conducts a comparative examination of their legal and regulatory frameworks regarding suspect wealth.

References

Anguilla Government London Office (2017) 'Anguilla and Brexit: Britain's Forgotten E.U. Border'. Available: https://westindiacommittee.org/anguilla-brexit-britains-forgotten-eu-border/

Ashton, S. R., and Kinningray, D. (eds.) (1999) *British Documents on the End of Empire* (Ser B. Vol. 6: The West Indies), London: The Stationary Office.

CBS News '60 Minutes' (17.3.2019) 'Prince Albert II: The Multitasking Monarch'. Available: www.cbsnews.com/video/prince-albert-ii-monacos-multitasking-monarch/

Chaikin, D. (2018) 'The Law Enforcement Implications of the Panama Papers', in D. Chaikin and G. Hook (eds.), *Corporate and Trust Structures: Legal and Illegal Dimensions*, Melbourne: Australian Scholarly Publishing.

Clegg, P. (2016) 'The United Kingdom Overseas Territories and the European Union – Part 1 – EU Benefits to the United Kingdom Overseas Territories', Report for UK Overseas Territories Association.

Darwin, J. (1988) *Britain and Decolonisation: The Retreat from Empire in the Post-War World*, Hampshire: Macmillan.

DfID (2017) 'British Overseas Territories Country Profile'. Available: https://assets.publishing.service.gov.uk/government/uploads/system/uploads/attachment_data/file/636551/Overseas-Territories1.pdf

DfID (1.11.2018) 'UK Secures Changes to International Aid Rules: Restrictions to Britain's Aid Support to Countries Affected by Crises and Natural Disasters that Severely Impact Their Economy are Lifted', Press Release.

DfID. Overseas Territories Department (2012) 'Operational Plan 2011–2015'. Available: https://assets.publishing.service.gov.uk/government/uploads/system/uploads/attachment_data/file/67360/ovseas-terr-dept-2011.pdf

Dodani, S., and LaPorte, R. E. (2005) 'Brain Drain from Developing Countries: How Can Brain Drain be Converted into Wisdom Gain?' *Journal of the Royal Society of Medicine*, 98(11): 487–491.

Dwyer, T. (2002) '"Harmful" Tax Competition and the Future of OFCs', *Journal of Money Laundering Control*, 5(4): 302–317.

FCO (1999) 'Partnership for Progress and Prosperity: Britain and the Overseas Territories', Cm 4264. Available: http://www.uniset.ca/naty/BNA_ptnr-prosperity.pdf

FCO (2012) 'The Overseas Territories: Security, Success and Sustainability', White Paper. Available: https://assets.publishing.service.gov.uk/government/uploads/system/uploads/attachment_data/file/14929/ot-wp-0612.pdf

Findley, M. G., Nielson, D. L., and Sharman, J. C. (2014) *Global Shell Games: Experiments in Transnational Relations, Crime, and Terrorism*, Cambridge: Cambridge University Press.

Foot, M. (2009) 'Final Report of the Independent Review of British Offshore Financial Centres'. Available: https://www.gov.im/media/624053/footreport.pdf

Freyer, T. A., and Morriss, P. A. (2013) 'Creating Cayman as an Offshore Financial centre: Structure and Strategy Since 1960', *Arizona State Law Journal*, 45: 1297–1398.

FT (7.11.2017) 'Westminster Pension Fund Holds Offshore Investments'. Available: www.ft.com/content/563ea65e-c314-11e7-b2bb-322b2cb39656

Gordon, R., and Morriss, A. P. (2014) 'Moving Money: International Financial Flows, Taxes and Money Laundering', *Hastings International and Comparative Law Review*, 37(1):1–123.

Guardian (16.7.2013) 'Montserrat Aid Programme Comes under Fire from UK Watchdog'. Available: www.theguardian.com/global-development/2013/jul/16/montserrat-aid-dfid-icai

Guardian (12.9.2017) 'Hurricane Irma Has Devastated British Territories – So Why Such Little Aid?'. Available: www.theguardian.com/commentisfree/2017/sep/12/hurricane-irma-british-territories-aid-anguilla

Guardian (18.9.2018) 'Ireland Collects More than €14bn in Taxes and Interest from Apple'. Available: www.theguardian.com/world/2018/sep/18/ireland-collects-more-than-14bn-disputed-taxes-from-apple

Guardian (14.12.2018) 'Shakira Charged with Tax Evasion in Spain'. Available: www.theguardian.com/music/2018/dec/14/shakira-charged-with-tax-evasion-in-spain#:~:text=Spanish%20prosecutors%20have%20charged%20the,while%20actually%20resident%20in%20Catalonia

Hendry, I., and Dickson, S. (2011) *British Overseas Territories Law* (1st ed.), Oxford: Hart Publishing.

Hendry, I., and Dickson, S. (2018) *British Overseas Territories Law* (2nd ed.), Oxford: Hart Publishing.

Hetq (4.4.2016) 'Mihran Poghosyan: The Armenian General Who Mastered the Ins and Outs of Panama's Offshore Zone'. Available: https://hetq.am/en/article/66918

House of Commons, Foreign Affairs Committee (2019) 'Inquiry: Global Britain and the Overseas Territories: Resetting the Relationship', Fifteenth Report of Session 2017–19.

House of Commons, Foreign Affairs Committee, Oral Evidence (5.12.2018) 'Future of the UK Overseas Territories', HC 1464. Available: http://data.parliament.uk/writtenevidence/committeeevidence.svc/evidencedocument/foreign-affairs-committee/the-future-of-the-uk-overseas-territories/oral/93391.html

House of Commons, International Development Committee (19.10.2016) 'Tackling Corruption Overseas'. Available: https://publications.parliament.uk/pa/cm201617/cmselect/cmintdev/111/11102.htm
House of Commons, Public Accounts Committee (2013) 'Tax Avoidance: The Role of Large Accountancy Firms', Forty-Fourth Report. Available: https://publications.parliament.uk/pa/cm201213/cmselect/cmpubacc/870/870.pdf
House of Commons, Treasury Committee (2019) 'Economic Crime – AML Supervision and Sanctions Implementation'. Available: https://publications.parliament.uk/pa/cm201719/cmselect/cmtreasy/2010/201002.htm
ICIJ (5.4.2016) 'Iceland Prime Minister Tenders Resignation Following Panama Papers Revelations'. Available: www.icij.org/investigations/panama-papers/20160405-iceland-pm-resignation/
ICIJ (23.1.2019) 'Armenia, Under New Leadership, Re-opens Panama Papers Case'. Available: www.icij.org/investigations/panama-papers/armenia-under-new-leadership-re-opens-panama-papers-case/
ICIJ (3.4.2019) 'Panama Papers Helps Recover More than $1.2bn Around the World'. Available: www.icij.org/investigations/panama-papers/panama-papers-helps-recover-more-than-1-2-billion-around-the-world/#:~:text=Panama%20Papers%20helps%20recover%20more%20than%20%241.2%20billion%20around%20the%20world,-More%20than%20%241.2&text=First%2Dtime%20gains%20in%20Panama,of%20the%20offshore%20finance%20industry
Kudrle, R. T. (2016) 'Tax Havens and the Transparency Wave of International Tax Legalization', *University of Pennsylvania Journal of International Law*, 37(4): 1153–1182.
Meyer, P. J. (2016) 'U.S. Foreign Assistance to Latin America and the Caribbean: Recent Trends and FY2016 Appropriations', Congressional Research Service.
Mitchell, D. J. (2008) 'Why Tax Havens Are a Blessing', Cato Institute.
Mondaq (18.3.2019) 'Paradise Papers, New VDP Not Government's Panacea in 2019'. Available: www.mondaq.com/canada/tax-authorities/789500/paradise-papers-new-vdp-not-government39s-panacea-in-2019
Murphy, R. (7.9.2017) 'Hurricane Irma and the UK's Caribbean Tax Havens', Tax Research UK. Available: www.taxresearch.org.uk/Blog/2017/09/07/hurricane irma-and-the-uks-caribbean-tax-havens/
New York Times (13.3.1985) 'In Old Pirate Haunt, Daunting News of Drug Trade'. Available: www.nytimes.com/1985/03/13/world/in-old-pirate-haunt-daunting-news-of-drug-trade.html
New York Times (28.7.2017) 'How the Panama Papers Changed Pakistani Politics'. Available: www.nytimes.com/2017/07/28/world/asia/panama-papers-pakistan-nawaz-sharif.html
OECD (1998) 'Harmful Tax Competition – An Emerging Global Issue'. Available: https://www.oecd-ilibrary.org/taxation/harmful-tax-competition_9789264162945-en
OECD (2000) 'Towards Global Tax Co-operation – Progress in Identifying and Eliminating Harmful Tax Practices'. Available: https://www.oecd.org/tax/harmful/2090192.pdf
OECD Observer No. 230 (2002) 'The Brain Drain: Old Myths, New Realities'. Available: https://www.oecd-ilibrary.org/economics/oecd-observer/volume-2002/issue-1_observer-v2002-1-en

Palan, R. (1998) 'Trying to Have Your Cake and Eating It', *International Studies Quarterly*, 42(4): 625–643.
Palan, R. (1999) 'Offshore and the Structural Enablement of Sovereignty', in M. Hampton and J. P. Abbott (eds.), *Offshore Finance Centers and Tax Havens: The Rise of Global Capital*, Basingstoke: Macmillan.
Royal Gazette (16.9.2016) 'Independence Idea Revived amid Brexit'. Available: www.royalgazette.com/politics/news/article/20160916/independence-idea-revived-amid-brexit/
Russell, D., and Graham, T. (2016) 'The Panama Papers', *Trusts and Trustees*, 22(5): 481–486.
Sharman, J. C. (2006) *Havens in a Storm*, Ithaca, NY: Cornell University Press.
Sharman, J. C. (2017) *Despots Guide to Wealth Management*, Ithaca, NY: Cornell University Press.
Shaxson, N. (2011) *Treasure Islands: Tax Havens and the Men Who Stole the World*, London: Bodley Head.
Tax Justice Network (2013) 'What Is a Secrecy Jurisdiction?' Available: https://fsi.taxjustice.net/en/faq/what-is-a-secrecy-jurisdiction
Tax Justice Network (2017) 'Are the Activities Uncovered in the Paradise Papers "Legal" – A Plea to Journalists'. Available: www.taxjustice.net/2017/11/06/activities-uncovered-paradise-papers-legal-plea-journalists-covering-story/
UK FAC (2019) 'Global Britain and the Overseas Territories: Resetting the Relationship', Fifteenth Report of Session 2017–2019.
UK Government. 'Anti-Corruption Strategy 2017–2022'. Available: https://www.gov.uk/government/publications/uk-anti-corruption-strategy-2017-to-2022
UK Government. 2010–2015 Policy 'U.K. Overseas Territories'. Available: https://www.gov.uk/government/publications/2010-to-2015-government-policy-uk-overseas-territories/2010-to-2015-government-policy-uk-overseas-territories
UK Government. Aid (5.2012) 'DfID's Work with the Overseas Territories'. Available: https://assets.publishing.service.gov.uk/government/uploads/system/uploads/attachment_data/file/67426/DFID-work-overseas-territories.pdf
UK National Audit Office (2007) 'Managing Risk in the Overseas Territories'. Available: https://www.nao.org.uk/wp-content/uploads/2007/11/07084.pdf
UN Convention Against Illicit Traffic in Narcotic Drugs and Psychotic Substances 1988. Available: https://www.unodc.org/pdf/convention_1988_en.pdf
Wheeler, G. J. (12.4.2016) 'The British Overseas Territories and "Direct Rule"', UK Constitutional Law Blog.
Workman, D. J. (1982) 'The Use of Offshore Tax Havens for the Purpose of Criminally Evading Income Tax', *Journal of Criminal Law and Criminology*, 73(2): 675–706.
World Bank (2003) 'International Migration, Remittances, and the Brain Drain: A Study of 24 Labor-Exporting Countries', WP3069. Available: https://openknowledge.worldbank.org/handle/10986/18161
Zucman, G. (2015) *The Hidden Wealth of Nations: The Scourge of Tax Havens*, Chicago: University of Chicago Press.

4 Bermuda

4.1 Bermuda: an overview

Bermuda's response to suspect wealth is the most advanced of the three jurisdictions this book analyses. Many aspects of its AML/CFT, anti-bribery, tax information and beneficial ownership regime have been positively reviewed by international monitoring bodies. This is further evidenced by several domestic initiatives designed to improve standards and strengthen the regulated environment. However, Bermuda has faced allegations of public misspending and has been implicated in criminal cases overseas. Its offshore sector was particularly targeted in the Paradise papers 2017. In recent years it has attracted criticism and inclusion on the EU's blacklist of non-cooperative tax jurisdictions, but later removed. While these instances present a less positive view, this chapter evaluates evidence to consider the extent to which Bermuda is willing and able to comply with international standards, and the extent of this compliance.

At the time of writing, there appear to be various measures in place in Bermuda to tackle financial crime and suspect wealth. These include a 'Just Good Business' campaign launched in 2018 on AML and integrity-related themes, and NRAs conducted by its AML Committee. Many such initiatives are not globally normative, such as NRAs which have in recent years been lacking from many jurisdictions including several G20 countries. There has been growing criticism towards Bermuda following the Paradise papers, which negatively placed it in the transparency spotlight. There are various mischaracterisations levelled at Bermuda, such as with its beneficial ownership regime, as well as negative sentiment propagated by various influential NGOs like Oxfam (2016a), which reported Bermuda as the world's "worst corporate tax haven". This chapter will consider such criticism against evidence of compliance with international standards.

Bermuda has a rich history. It was first discovered by accident in 1503 by Spanish Captain Juan de Bermudez and was officially founded in 1612 becoming the second permanent English colony in the New World (Bernhard 1985, 57). Its original discovery is mentioned in D'Angheria's *Legatio Babylonica*. The more well-known story is its 1609 discovery by Admiral George Somers and his crew of 150 sailors, who took refuge there following the wreck of *Sea Venture* in treacherous seas. There, they built new vessels for their onward journey to Jamestown

(Glover and Smith 2008). From this point on, Bermuda has been continuously inhabited. In 1612, the Virginia Company of England, a stock company chartered by King James I, sent a group to Bermuda to commence official settlement. Bermuda's position and involvement in geopolitical rivalries between metropolitan powers over the years, from the US Revolutionary War right through to the Cold War, has ensured that much money has been spent there for military purposes. In the 20th century, there was a shift in military presence from British naval bases to American ones, and an agreement between UK Prime Minister Winston Churchill and US President Franklin D. Roosevelt saw Bermuda acquire a US naval and air base, which played an important role in the Cold War. Domestically, US servicemen rented houses from Bermudians and spent money on the island, propelling the Bermudian economy. With a major airstrip built in 1942, the island's development increased extensively which facilitated the development of Bermuda's tourism industry. Economically, the US military presence created jobs for Bermudians who worked on the bases and were paid US dollars, which increased living standards. Billions of dollars were brought into the islands and invested throughout the economy, which allowed Bermuda to develop its business infrastructure, tourism and services, affecting both residents and visitors (Glover and Smith 2008, 6).

Bermuda is self-governing and a parliamentary dependency under constitutional monarchy, with a population of 62,278 as at 2020. Bermuda lies in the Atlantic Ocean off the US coast, rather than the Caribbean which is a common misconception.[1] An archipelago, although colloquially known as 'the Rock', it measures 20.5 square miles. The capital and business centre is Hamilton. Its Atlantic location is a competitive advantage for tourism and business.

The Queen appoints a Governor, who appoints a Premier capable of commanding a Parliamentary majority following a General Election. Bermuda has a House of Assembly and an Upper House. The former has 36 elected members who represent parishes (electoral constituencies) and the latter has 11 appointed members. Bermuda's political framework largely follows Westminster's. There are two major political parties: Progressive Labour Party (PLP) and One Bermuda Alliance. Hon. David Burt MP is Premier and the PLP are in government, having won considerable majorities in the 2017 and 2020 elections.

Bermuda's legal system, like its fellow Overseas Territories, is based on English law and the common law legal tradition. The country's laws are derived from the courts, sometimes known as judge-made law. Statutes are a fundamental component of a common law system, yet common law does not rely exclusively on statutes or codes as the sole source of law. Bermuda's legal system encompasses doctrines of equity and statutory instruments dating back to 1612. Justice is administered through Magistrates' courts, Supreme Court, Court of Appeal and Commercial Court, with the UKPC being its final appeals court. The presence

1 *News.com.au* (29.11.2017) 'Bermuda faced its first drop in tourism in almost 2 years because of a spelling error'.

of a legal system borne from principles of English common law is a major contributor to Bermuda's success as an international financial centre, due to the attractiveness of a legal tradition understood and respected the world over (Wood 2008). It epitomises stability and a secure place to conduct business, both in terms of facilitating and resolving disputes. Scholars have noted the importance of English law for enabling foreign investors to feel safe when conducting business in, or with, Bermuda or its companies (Stanton 2016, 13), particularly given Bermuda judges recognise the jurisprudential scholarship of their English counterparts (Jenkins 2009, 280).

4.2 Economy and development as a financial centre

Bermuda is one of the world's wealthiest jurisdictions. At 2019, its GDP per capita was $116,890 ranking it the third largest per capita economy in the world (Bermuda Government 2020), behind Monaco and Liechtenstein. Tourism and business services have fuelled spectacular economic growth; for example, 7.94% in 1980, 9.32% in 2000 and 7.22% in 2001 (World Bank Development Indicators). Its strategically important geographical positioning has been compared by some to Singapore, Gibraltar and Suez (Richards 2017, 5). Being 1,000 km from North Carolina, Bermuda is highly proximate to influential US East Coast cities like New York and Washington. Its relationship with Canada is also of importance in terms of trade, tourism and employment.

Bermuda has developed into a significant international financial and offshore centre, which contributed to 39% of GDP and accounted for 18% of its employment in 2016 (Bermuda Government 2017b, 2). Bermuda's world-leading (re)insurance market dominates the financial sector, with 15 of the world's top 40 reinsurers based there (KPMG 2017, 1). This market contributed some $35 billion over 12 years to cover US catastrophe losses and provides more than a quarter of capacity for Lloyd's of London. It has covered many natural and non-natural disaster claims globally. Two examples of Bermuda's international impact include that its reinsurance market covered 9% of total claims arising from the 9/11 terrorist attacks and 20% of claims arising from UK flooding losses after the 2016 floods (Bermuda Business Development Agency 2016). This particular market activity distinguishes Bermuda from offshore centres which mainly focus on corporate services.

Bermuda's investment sector is relatively large, while its banking sector is relatively small, comprising only 5 domestic banks. By contrast, Cayman has nearly 300 banks. There are no offshore banks licenced in Bermuda. Its banking industry focuses mainly on servicing the international business sector demands, such as the provision of financial management, trustee and investment services. It has a stock exchange, and economic growth has been created and assisted by the presence of 23 law firms, 31 fund managers, administrative services, 6 accountancy firms (including KPMG, PWC, Deloitte and EY), telecommunications and technology companies, a growing compliance function and regulators. Bermuda's technology sector, particularly FinTech, is also advancing. The international business sector in Bermuda provides some 3,894 jobs and brings business visitors to Bermuda who support the local economy (Bermuda Government 2015, 4). There are 441 collective investment schemes/investment funds and 2 money service businesses. There are 1,231 insurance companies. Bermuda's incorporation sector is relatively small compared to territories like BVI, with circa 17,000 limited companies and 1,004 limited partnerships. There are 28 trust service providers and 62 corporate service providers (CFATF 2020, 25).

Bermuda is a consumption-based economy with an indirect taxation model. As Atkinson (1977) avers, the distinction between direct and indirect taxation is one of the oldest issues of taxation policy. Bermuda, like many small island jurisdictions, is completely reliant on imports. It is a well-established principle of law that jurisdictions have the sovereign right to decide their tax system by which they build revenue.[2] As Faulhaber (2010, 177) observed in the context of the EU, no institution has the authority to regulate direct taxation without the unanimous support of all Member States. The nature of Bermuda, and other islands for that matter, requires a different taxation philosophy than that of a mixed economy. Bermuda does not collect income or corporation tax. However, this does not mean it is a 'no-tax jurisdiction'. In 2019, Bermuda's government had a total revenue of $1.1 billion, including customs duties of $226 million and payroll tax of $467.5 million (Bermuda Finance Ministry 2019, 52). Since the Revenues Act 1898, Bermuda has collected import tax, customs duties, land and property tax, premiums for foreign purchasers, licence fees, stamp duty, passenger tax and payroll tax. The latter is levied on all employers and those who are self-employed. Annual fees for operating a Bermuda company also generate revenue. This model is not uncommon for island jurisdictions, with Cayman being a similar example. Levies and taxes in Bermuda make up circa 85% of public revenue. This is proportionately similar to that in Canada and the US.

There are two things here to point out. The first is the issue as to whether an indirect taxation model provides any real opportunity for international money launderers and criminals, tax evaders or avoiders. In other words, does it benefit those seeking to abuse it? This is an important question given the frequent characterisation of such jurisdictions as tax havens simply on the basis of their indirect taxation systems. It would be principally beneficial to an overseas investor if they became ordinarily resident in Bermuda. If they remained resident elsewhere, they would not qualify for the tax benefits of Bermuda's indirect taxation model. Residency is a difficult process and Bermuda has been traditionally protectionist, such as offering jobs to Bermudians first, making it difficult to obtain residence and work permits, and with premiums on property sales to non-Bermudians. Of course, this is not to say that those seeking to abuse the system cannot do so – and may make use of a Bermuda-registered entity for the purpose of fiscal

2 For background, see Pivetti, M. 'High public debt and inflation: on the 'disciplinary' view of European Monetary Union' [292–307] in Mongiovi, G., and Petri, F. (eds) (1999) *Value, Distribution and Capital*, Routledge, [295]; and, Ring. D.M. (2009) 'Democracy, Sovereignty and Tax Competition: The Role of Tax Sovereignty in Shaping Tax Cooperation', *Florida Tax Review*, 9: 555–596.

efficiency. However, under the principles of international reporting, which Bermuda is signatory to, as well as in the case of beneficial ownership exchange, it would be difficult to utilise the jurisdiction for concealment given Bermuda's obligations with foreign competent authorities under these frameworks. Should a tax investigation into a UK company or resident involve requests being made to Bermuda authorities for information, then they are bound under the terms of their bilateral exchange agreements, to comply. The issue as to whether such a system facilitates tax avoidance, however, is more complex given that it relies wholly on the ability to utilise structures which are deemed permissible under law on both sides of the transaction.

The second issue is whether the indirect model is appropriate for Bermuda, taking account of various developmental concerns. Richards (2017) argues that the system works in Bermuda's context. Yet, there is also convincing sentiment amongst local economists that it is leaving behind the bottom 25% who have been living in relative poverty. For a country with Bermuda's GDP per capita, it is surprising that there are significant social welfare issues which some suggest require tax reform to boost public expenditure (Stubbs 2016, 22).

Tourism is the second most important industry in Bermuda, representing 5.1% of GDP in 2019. It accounts for 9.4% of direct employment. In 2016, 646,465 visitors came to Bermuda, with estimated visitor spending at $358 million (Bermuda Government 2016). In 2017, Bermuda hosted the 35th America's Cup, a global sailing competition broadcast to some 400 million viewers. A resident impact survey (DeShields and Riley 2015) predicted it would have significant economic and social impact. At the time, and largely a reverberation of the global financial crisis, Bermuda had lived through a 7-year depression whereby tourism had suffered (Stubbs 2016, 28). The America's Cup was seen by some critics of offshore centres as an extravagant platform for luxury brands, corporate sponsors and wealthy spectators (*BBC Panorama* 6.11.2017). However, Bermuda was able to demonstrate its tourism offering to a global market, something small island jurisdictions seldom have the chance to do on this scale. Hosting the event was $12.9 million under budget and contributed $336.4 million to GDP, costing $64.1 million to host (PWC 2017). Wider impact included $500,000 donations for community initiatives such as computer equipment and refurbished sail-school boats; 9 acres of land were developed, hostels were built and many existing ones were upgraded (America's Cup Bermuda Ltd 2017). It is interesting to note Bermuda's capacity and ability to host such a high-end global event and be reviewed positively with regards to spending, investment and legacy. Bermuda's significant level of development is important in the context of assessing its abilities and willingness to adopt and comply with international economic crime standards.

4.3 Implications in economic crime cases and the Paradise papers

Corruption and lack of integrity have not materialised to the same extent as in other islands, such as TCI. With the advancement of Bermuda's financial sector, particularly its (re)insurance market, there is a significant degree of regulated professional industries. This is seen in Bermuda's increasing compliance sector, harnessed by various local AML and integrity initiatives. Of course, no country is immune to corruption and misconduct, as the UNCAC emphasises. Bermuda was recently subject to a Commission of Inquiry into the Report of the Consolidated Fund of the Bermuda Government for the Financial Years 2010, 2011 and 2012. The Auditor General found significant mismanagement of Bermuda's finances during the Report period, particularly in 2010 and 2011. It was alleged that the government had failed to comply with Financial Instructions on handling public finances. It was emphasised that, as in the past, it is not the issue whether controls regarding rules exist but that they are "ignored or overridden" with those responsible "immune" to the imposition of sanctions (Commission of Inquiry 2017, 18). In the context of upholding the integrity and accountability of institutions as an essential constituent element of democracy, this presents a realisation that domestic lapses can occur in public life. While some of the language in the report was cautious, such as the use of the phrase "possible criminal activity", the fact that senior officials in Bermuda have shown appetite and have been unhindered in their examinations is a positive example of accountability, notwithstanding the original reason for the report. Several findings are worth noting. During 2010, approximately $14 million expenditure did not have the required Cabinet approvals. For example, $957,762 and $1,863,386 were spent on government building renovations, respectively. The Report flags breaches regarding monies paid for supply agreements without first signing contracts, as well as significant contracts not tendered. Further, it identified millions paid for professional services without prior approval. The report aimed to consider whether laws and regulations were satisfactory and to safeguard against violations. As a result, a Commission of Inquiry was appointed to look at whether Financial Instruction violations had occurred and whether there was evidence of possible criminality.

In summary of their findings, 7 government business dealings had evidence of possible criminal activity and were referred to the police. Under Bermuda law, the Financial Instructions only have legal backing through section 3, Public Treasury (Administration and Payments) Act 1969. Power exists for the Minister to give Financial Instructions full statutory force so that breaches become criminal matters. However, this power had not yet been exercised. The Commission took the view that breaches without reasonable excuse ought to be disposed of as crimes, although they do add that not all breaches should be criminally regarded, and thus an element of selectivity is necessary.

Bermuda was heavily implicated in the Paradise papers. This was unsurprising given Appleby's Bermuda office was targeted. Yet, in the Panama papers – a leak of comparable size and attention – Bermudian-registered legal entities were not named. This is an important point, given the influence that data breaches of this scale have on law and policy. It demonstrates that MOSSFON, whose practises have since been proven to have legally and ethically fallen short, did not appear to register or manage Bermuda entities for its clients. With respect to the Paradise papers, there were 9,450 Bermuda-registered entities named in the data. Of these, the data showed

6,059 had already been closed (*ICIJ* Offshore Leaks database, Paradise papers). Simply naming entities does not demonstrate wrongdoing, only the undisputed fact that Appleby provided corporate legal services to clients. Other than demonstrating use of Bermuda as a jurisdiction in which multinationals have fiscally benefited, the impact upon Appleby has been significantly less than on MOSSFON, which ceased operating in the aftermath of the Panama papers. Except launching and settling civil suits for breach of confidence against key media organisations, there does not appear to have been any lasting adverse impact on Appleby.

With regards to the number of entities mentioned, at the time of writing there are approximately 17,000 legal entities in Bermuda, including LLCs and LLPs. There are 25 law firms in Bermuda, and two major offshore ones – Appleby and Conyers, Dill and Pearman. It is unsurprising, therefore, that in targeting a large firm in Bermuda, some 9,450 entities were mentioned. However, the data provided by the ICIJ is incomplete as commercial activity or company status are often omitted, while the Panama papers showed many companies mentioned had been dissolved decades before the publication.

As was acknowledged in Bermuda's NRA, at 39: "The money laundering threat from predicate offences committed overseas is assessed as high, as given the nature of [its] economy, it is likely that the proceeds from such offences will be found in Bermuda's financial industry". Predicate offences include drug trafficking, fraud, insider dealing and market abuse, tax crimes and bribery. The report emphasises that the proceeds of crime which emanate from foreign criminality present a significant threat. Drawing upon several law reports of criminal cases in foreign courts, Bermuda has been implicated as a jurisdiction connected to such instances of criminality, typically through the disposal of criminal proceeds, or tax evasion through its financial system. For example, in 2017 Credit Suisse settled an Italian case which involved allegations of it helping clients to transfer undeclared funds offshore, after it was placed under investigation for money laundering. The scheme affected some 13,000 clients and related to €14 billion. The transactions allegedly took place between Liechtenstein and Bermuda in order to evade Italian tax authorities (*Reuters* 21.10.2016).

In the US case of *United States v Perez-Caballos* (2017), the wife of the former Finance Secretary of Tabasco, Mexico, was convicted for conspiracy to commit bank fraud. The crime involved the laundering of $40 million via fictitious companies and complex transactions. A total of $2 million was moved to an offshore account in Bermuda as a result of false statements made to a US banking institution (US Department of Justice 16.10.2017).

Similarly, in *United States v Sutherland* (2017), an executive was convicted for filing false tax returns and obstruction. The allegations involved concealing significant income and filing tax returns omitting $2 million in unreported income received from a bank in Bermuda. He falsely claimed the transactions were capital contributions/loans, yet most transactions were insurance commissions of money obtained from a brokerage account which he controlled in Bermuda. Using Bermuda-based companies allowed him to funnel personal and business funds to his US domestic bank accounts.

In the matter of *United States v Inniss* (2018), Bermuda was implicated in an American FCPA case. The case concerned a former Barbados Minister of Industry criminally charged in the US with laundering corrupt payments in respect of influencing lucrative insurance contracts. Such payments were received from a Barbados insurance company, the controlling shareholder of which was a Bermuda-registered company.

Finally, in the US case against former Mayor of Matamoros, Erick Santos, who is a fugitive following a conviction for accepting bribes totalling between $5.3 and $10 million, US prosecutors are engaged in asset seizure relating to his funds kept in the Bermudian bank Butterfield and Sons (*San Antonio Express* 5.8.2016).

These criminal cases demonstrate that Bermuda's financial sector has played host to the proceeds of overseas criminality. These have included using local companies and bank accounts to evade tax, launder money, and dispose of the proceeds of crime. Other than criminality, Bermuda's financial sector has been implicated in some significant instances of tax avoidance involving some of the world's largest multinational corporations. In fact, given the statistically insignificant levels of criminal proceedings following the Paradise papers, the leak was overshadowed by revelations of tax avoidance rather than allegations of criminality. For example, it was reported that Google moved €19.9 billion to Bermuda via its Netherlands-registered company in 2017 via a double Irish, Dutch sandwich vehicle. This reduces overall corporate tax by using the Netherlands subsidiary to shift global non-US profits to Google Ireland Holdings, an affiliate in Bermuda which is not subject to income tax (*Reuters* 3.1.2019). In the European Parliament, one member averred: "Firstly, the profits generated in the E.U. are transferred to a subsidiary in Ireland, where they are subject to a very low tax rate agreed with the Irish government. Then, the subsidiary transfers the money in question to a Dutch company with no employees which forwards it to a letterbox company in Bermuda" (European Parliament 9.1.2019).

Similarly, the medical corporation Abbott was reported to have made use of the double Irish structure and a series of inter-company transactions and charges to divert profits to Bermuda-registered companies. Ireland recently announced changes to its laws which gave multinationals with the structure in place until the end of 2020 to alter their subsidiaries structure. However, multinationals like Google have been implicated as stepping up their use of the double Irish framework prior to its eradication (*Irish Times* 5.1.2019), with its parent company later making a public commitment to cease its use and consolidating its intellectual property back in the US (*Tax Journal* 8.1.2020). This decision was arguably affected by the tax reforms under the Trump administration.

The Paradise papers implicated Nike's use of Bermuda for tax avoidance purposes from 2006 to 2014 (*ICIJ* 10.1.2019). An EU Commission report examining multinationals' aggressive tax strategies outlined that Nike had entered into an arrangement with Dutch authorities, allegedly enabling it to shift billions of dollars of European profits to Bermuda (E.U. Commission 21.6.2018, 6–8). It should be noted that in terms of revenue-related enforcement actions, many are either not reported or would not attract public attention, and therefore a fuller picture in this context is difficult to determine.

Bermuda was recently named in Transparency International's 2018 report *The Cost of Secrecy*. This analysed information concerning Overseas Territories which have been connected to corruption and related misconduct overseas in the Paradise papers. One of its case studies concerned the wife of a former Russian Deputy Prime Minister who was allegedly the beneficial owner of a Bermudian-registered entity that owned a private jet. The report draws an adverse inference based on the jet's value being incommensurate with the purported beneficial owner's known wealth. By implication, Bermuda's financial service sector may have facilitated suspect wealth from overseas connected to a PEP. However, the information presented is incomplete given the evidence it relies upon does not contain material information about timestamps and dates. As such, Transparency International concedes it is not known when the jet was ultimately owned by those in question. Of course, they acknowledge that some of the cases they draw upon only provide "*prima facie* evidence of corruption". Whilst the tone of the allegations are serious insofar as Bermuda is concerned, concrete conclusions cannot be drawn.

Matters which are non-disputed facts in case law, or serious reported allegations which implicate Bermuda's financial centre, give a *prima facie* case that its offshore centre has received suspect wealth, facilitated economic crime, and avoidance of tax. However, in the coming sections, Bermuda's response to suspect wealth will be critically analysed to consider the extent of its compliance.

4.4 More sinned against than sinning? Bermuda and its critics

Having considered some case law and implications from data breaches, this section identifies and considers some of the more prevalent attacks against Bermuda which have related to its harmful tax perception, its regulatory and compliance regime, and perceived lack of transparency on beneficial ownership. Where appropriate, it seeks to add context or to expose those criticisms which lack substance.

As mentioned, Oxfam's (2016a) damning assessment of Bermuda is worth exploring further. Its singling out of Bermuda as the "world's worst corporate tax haven" is unprecedented as, for example, there are jurisdictions at the very extreme ends of international rankings, such as the Financial Secrecy Index, which have not been subject to this manner of high-profile labelling. Oxfam's criteria was the same seen in historic tax haven criticisms (such as those by the OECD) which include considering corporate tax rates, incentives and commitments on international efforts to curb 'tax dodging'. One aspect of this assessment clearly hinges on Bermuda's indirect taxation model. This indicates a general bias against low-tax jurisdictions, irrespective of that jurisdiction's level of compliance on relevant, internationally advocated measures such as information exchange. Oxfam (2016a, 3) identified its 0% corporate income tax and 0% withholding tax; lack of participation in multilateral anti-abuse, exchange and transparency initiatives; and evidence of large-scale profit shifting. While some of these are accurate, such as no corporation tax, Bermuda has signed numerous bilateral information exchange agreements. The assessment came closely after the Panama papers, in which Bermuda was not implicated. It also came as 300 of the world's leading economists claimed that tax havens generally serve no useful purpose to the world economy (Oxfam 2016b). These views omit consideration of Bermuda's economic value proposition through its (re)insurance sector, such as paying out billions of dollars annually for natural disaster losses. Other similar jurisdictions under attack which simply park or conceal assets have a more difficult task demonstrating a valuable contribution (Richards 2017, 133). Oxfam's assessment is concerning given it occupies an increasingly influential policy role. While the manner in which they have singled out Bermuda may be questionable, the criticism itself is rather more representative of long-standing, repeated blacklisting attempts. Of note is the OECD's campaign against tax havens in the 1990s, which turned into a struggle between the OECD and its members and smaller jurisdictions that were the subject of it. In an attempt from larger high-tax jurisdictions to impose regulations and tax reform on smaller island jurisdictions, this struggle was not insignificant. On the side of the OECD initiative was billions of potentially taxable revenue with the inevitable benefits this would have on developed and developing countries alike. On the side of the small islands was a risk of unprecedented scale to their economic viability and consequent sustainable development. A helpful account can be found in Sharman (2006, 40–48), who observes that it was a 'David and Goliath' story with David slaying the campaign of Goliath – at least temporarily.

While obvious, not all jurisdictions' economies are the same, and it is worth remembering that all 30 OECD countries are characterised by having market-based economies and typically high tax rates. The OECD's 1998 report 'Harmful Tax Competition, an Emerging Global Issue' aimed to identify and blacklist countries they deemed harmful tax jurisdictions. The OECD's criteria included (1) no or nominal income tax in the case of tax havens and no or low effective tax rates on the relevant income in the case of preferential regimes; (2) lack of effective exchange of information; (3) lack of transparency; and (4) no substantial activities in the case of tax havens, and ring-fencing in the case of preferential regimes. Due to advance commitments, Bermuda avoided inclusion on the list (OECD 2000, 29). Many criteria do not apply to Bermuda such as ring-fencing. While bank secrecy was not an OECD criterion (bearing in mind Bermuda does not have bank secrecy legislation), lack of transparency and information exchange was – something the confidentiality norm present in offshore banking, as well as bank secrecy more generally, would otherwise facilitate. In Bermuda's case, information sharing is now fully integrated via the CRS and automatic exchange of information obligations.

The OECD defines tax havens as jurisdictions which, among other things, have "laws or administrative practices which prevent the effective exchange of relevant information with other governments or taxpayers". This is an increasingly developing area of Bermuda's regulatory infrastructure. While automatic information exchange agreements are now common practice and exist via bilateral agreements in Bermuda, there are two things to observe. First, Bermuda has had a central beneficial ownership register in relation to legal entities for some 70 years – something seldom acknowledged by critics. Second, Bermuda's framework for information exchange established and includes obligations under the CRS and TIEA frameworks. More recently, the UK government's ultimatum on the Overseas Territories represents a disregard of Bermuda's framework on beneficial ownership or the extent to which it may be viable. Richards (2017, 126) notes a meeting at the FCO where officials were astonished when Bermuda representatives explained that its register had been established for 70 years. Notwithstanding Richards' bias (as a former Deputy Premier), at that time Bermuda's register was functioning and providing the NCA with 24-hour turnaround on information requests, while the UK had not yet implemented its own PSC register.

In 2013, France blacklisted Bermuda as an uncooperative jurisdiction. This was short-lived, and Bermuda was removed by committing to cooperate with French requests for information exchange. The move was accompanied by a 75% withholding tax on all payments made from France to Bermuda. Its global insurance offering was one of the main reasons Bermuda was removed from the blacklist. France's insurance sector pressured its Finance Ministry emphasising that the withholding tax prohibited France from getting the best reinsurance rates, which were available in the Bermuda market (Richards 2017, 124).

Another blacklisting effort came in June 2017, where the EU Code of Conduct Group served a questionnaire on Bermuda about its tax system. This was viewed in Bermuda as another blacklist threat and that questions were phrased in such a way leading to the predetermined conclusion that Bermuda is a tax haven and danger to the global business sector. As has been pointed out, it is not surprising that Bermuda would reject the tax haven label, given its negative connotations. In December 2017, the EU's List of Non-Cooperative Tax Jurisdictions was established. This blacklisting exercise was based on a wide criteria including good governance, fair taxation, tax systems and adherence to Base Erosion and Profit Shifting (BEPS). It compiled a blacklist of jurisdictions which had failed to take meaningful action to address deficiencies identified by the EU, and a greylist of jurisdictions that had committed to enhancing transparency and subject to ongoing review. While Bermuda was not originally blacklisted, it was placed on the greylist. Despite acknowledging commitments of jurisdictions like Bermuda, a greylist acts as a quasi-blacklist by association in terms of reputational harm. However, in early 2019, Bermuda was transferred to the blacklist on the basis of shortcomings relating to tax and its economic substance regime. It was removed shortly thereafter following commitments made to the EU. Bermuda was included, however, as part of the 2018 Netherlands list of low-tax jurisdictions.

There is consensus that the use of jurisdictions to hide assets provides criminals with an easier framework to facilitate criminality. Aside from company executives, or the 'white-collar criminal' formulation (Sutherland 1949), it enables narcotics producers and traffickers, arms dealers, tax evaders, despots of resource-rich nations and terrorists the ability to sustain their enterprises. Notwithstanding the array of scholarly work referenced in Chapter 2 which arrives at this well-accepted conclusion, the discourse is being driven by the misconception that jurisdictions like Bermuda are disproportionately used for such purposes. In other words, as if their offshore markets were set up to engage in this type of facilitate misconduct. If it is accepted that anonymous shell companies are an essential part of the laundering and tax evasion process, as some cases implicating Bermuda indicate, then it is interesting to consider the study by Findley, Nielson, and Sharman (2014) which found that small island jurisdictions tended to be harder environments to incorporate shell companies, with the opposite being the case for larger developed countries. The study exposes a clear misconception as to the perceived facilitative role of certain jurisdictions. It found that Bermuda scored a relatively high level of compliance (higher than the US and UK), which ties in with their general thesis that tax havens are more compliant because they have been subject to more long-standing and intense pressure to improve their corporate transparency practices since the 1990s (Findley, Nielson, and Sharman 2014, 58).

A continued criticism of Bermuda relates to the impact of its tax regime on the development of other jurisdictions. This is clearly the motivation of those who point to Bermuda's tax practices as increasing inequality, poverty and harming development (Tax Justice Network 2012). Richards (2017, 129) illustrates this in a recollection of a FCO meeting in 2013: "The narrative was that multinational corporations engaged primarily in extractive industries in various African countries were . . . bribing corrupt politicians there and second, shifting the profits they were making in those countries [to countries] like Bermuda". In discourse which is critical of offshore centres, there seems to be significantly less focus on predicate criminality in source countries and more on the tax havens themselves.

In the case of the Paradise papers, information appears to have been stolen from the law firm. While whistleblowing attracts various safeguards, hacking and theft are tautologies. It is interesting that many in the international anti–economic crime community exclusively focused on the good the Paradise papers did. For example, former Chair of the UK Public Accounts Committee, Dame Margaret Hodge MP, stated: "We have the *Guardian* and *Panorama* to thank for their brilliant investigative work and for placing the data relevant to us under public scrutiny".[3] Those who justify non-targeted thefts of confidential information risk ignoring the specific costs to those whose private information has been compromised and the underlying dangers of dispensing of legal safeguards. This is not to undermine the seriousness of allegations raised in the publication; rather, in the interests of the rule of law, great caution ought to be attributed to a 'means justifying the ends' mentality. The actions of the perpetrators have been given a false sense of legitimacy, exacerbated by the media and lawmakers who have given weight to their actions. There is also the concern both public disclosure and non-disclosure can have on investigations. In the case of the latter, the Panama papers

3 HC Deb (13 November 2017) Vol 631, Col 55.

were only disclosed to HMRC for a fee and, as at May 2018, it was reported that HMRC still did not have access to the Paradise papers and that the *BBC* and *Guardian* were not responding to investigative inquiries[4] (UK Committee on Public Accounts 2016, 44–48).

Publishing misappropriated confidential information often hides under the veil of public interest. However, a fine line must be drawn on the basis that if it becomes socially normative or morally acceptable, then this has dangerous consequences for process, legal protections and the integrity of investigations. At what point does committing, or conspiring to commit, a crime to expose another crime become acceptable? This is particularly dubious when such is defined by the media and others' moral definitions of such conduct. If these values are eschewed in favour of exposing wrongdoing as some exercise in utilitarianism, then at what point does it become permissible for law enforcement to break into someone's property without a warrant or reasonable suspicion of crime taking place? The minute procedural misconduct becomes acceptable and lines start to blur comes the immovable point at which integrity is lost. Assuming that it actually solves a problem, it certainly risks creating another of epic proportion. The balance of freedoms and rights is, of course, a complex legal balancing act. This will be discussed at greater length in the context of corporate transparency in Chapter 7.

4.5 Analysis of Bermuda's legal and regulatory response to economic crime and suspect wealth

The various concerns outlined about Bermuda as a financial centre give rise to a more negative view of Bermuda, from which adverse inferences might be drawn. However, such is not indicative of Bermuda's compliance with international economic crime and financial regulatory standards. This chapter now moves to assess several key elements of Bermuda's legal and regulatory regime. In sum, the analysis shows that Bermuda's framework is compliant, cooperative and responsible across many measures. The analysis also indicates that the jurisdiction is fundamentally different to the other Overseas Territories.

4.5.1 Anti-bribery

Recognising the consensus that corruption threatens the sustainability of societies and institutions, Bermuda has recently reformed its anti-corruption legislation to address deficiencies. Bermuda's Bribery Act 2016 is largely based on the UK's Bribery Act 2010 – widely viewed as the 'gold standard' in anti-corruption legislation (Ryder 2015). Bermuda's then Attorney General Trevor Moniz (2016) commented that while Bermuda has had anti-corruption legislation since the 19th

4 See evidence of Jon Thompson, HMRC Chief Executive and Permanent Secretary: "In relation to the BBC and *The Guardian*, we would like the information and we will continue to request it. They are making a decision not to give it to us, but we would obviously like it", Q44.

century, failing to modernise it would harm Bermuda's ability to deal with future cases. This clearly points to a functional imperative of updated legislation. Otherwise, Moniz averred that Bermuda would "not stand to benefit from the developing case law through court decisions and appeals" (Bermuda Government 20.5.2016).

The modernised legislation includes offences of bribing a foreign public official and a new offence of failing to prevent bribery on the part of a corporate. These are, of course, familiar to those provisions in the UK Act. The legislation also provides for extraterritoriality, meaning that a prosecution might be brought in Bermuda for a charge of bribery committed abroad (wholly or partly) by Bermuda residents, Bermudians, and Bermuda-registered corporates. In enacting this legislation, Bermuda has demonstrated commitment to preventing the recurrence of past instances of lapsed standards in public life which prompted the Commission of Inquiry, but also the fact that bribery can take many forms including through corporate hospitality or promotional expenditure. The then Attorney General made the point that while the Act is not designed to penalise legitimate business, Bermuda needed to follow the UK's lead and recognise that possible offences of bribery are widely drawn. The government has made commitments to amend the broader anti-corruption framework, such as putting in place enhanced codes of conduct for public officials, showing that legislation alone is not enough. This acts to foster integrity through alternative initiatives which do not require significant resources to enforce. It also demonstrates a commitment to promoting high standards in public life and accountability in public finance and procurement.

The Bribery Act came into force in 2017. At the time of writing, it is not possible to measure its effectiveness – not least given there have not yet been any convictions thereunder. This is not unusual with modern bribery legislation. It is expected that some years will pass before the first prosecution is brought, due to the timescales of financial crime investigations involving bribery. These are typically complex and hinge on significant documentary evidence. Evidence-gathering procedures, as well as preparation time to bring proceedings, adds to this timescale. Doubtless, such problems are compounded by Bermuda's size. Financial crime cases take significant time from investigation to disposal regardless of jurisdiction. For example, the case emanating from the UK LIBOR-rigging scandal, *R v Tom Hayes* [2015], commenced with Hayes' arrest in December 2012 and ended with his conviction in 2015. The UK Bribery Act 2010 came into force in 2011, and the first conviction obtained by the SFO for an offence thereunder came in *R v Sweett Group plc* [2016] after an investigation commenced in 2014. Even with the UK's capabilities, the first proceedings took 5 years to bring. While this might be expected, the rate at which proceedings came under the new Act attracted criticism by anti-corruption commentators (Hawley 2014).

In 2019, it was reported that Bermuda's Police Service had announced that over 40 criminal investigations involving acts of corruption by individuals and businesses were underway (Ogletree Deakins 14.5.2019). While there have not yet been convictions, the scope of Bermuda's bribery legislation was recently considered in the Bermudian Supreme Court case of *X Limited v Y* [2019]. This case effectively concerned the extent to which proper performance of a contractual payment term could result in bribery being committed after the fact in the course of business dealings – specifically, whether an agreed payment obligation under a contract (in this case, a separation agreement) could constitute the giving or receiving of a bribe, thereby rendering it unenforceable. The Court gave effect to the Act's "surprisingly broad" scope. Kawaley J, at 3, confirmed that "payments which do not resemble popular traditional notions of a bribe are caught by the Act, which applies to private and public sector recipients alike". This decision demonstrates the wide scope of Bermuda's bribery law (Carey Olsen 6.4.2020).

Bermuda also created an offence of "failing to report bribery", modelled on sections 13–15 of the Isle of Man Bribery Act 2013. Failing to prevent bribery is seen in section 7 of the UK Act and carries a deterrent function. However, failing to *report* is not. The rationale is to give public officials a greater incentive to be more proactive with authorities vis-à-vis reporting bribery. Thus, the legislation engages the deterrent function of the law and mobilises the private sector. By modernising, Bermuda demonstrates an appetite to legislate in line with modern bribery standards, which was precisely the aim of international conventions like UNCAC and the OECD Convention. The Act essentially implements international bribery standards into domestic law equivalent to those Conventions. Bermuda is covered by UNCAC and is working to have the OECD Convention extended to it. The Act significantly updates the old legislation and goes further than the UK on areas like 'failing to report' bribery. This demonstrates progress and compliance with international standards. If Bermuda wanted to facilitate, or be wilfully blind to, corruption, attract dirty money or trade its centre on a lax attitude to controls, then it is suggested Bermuda would not implement sophisticated legislation containing provisions for extraterritoriality, bribing public officials and failure to report offences. Bermuda clearly is taking international momentum on this type of economic crime seriously by increasing legislative scope and the obligations on the public and private sectors.

However, as scholars such as Horder (2013) have argued, it might be that regulatory strategy in the first instance modelled on anti-bribery policy might have served as more of a deterrence than its legislative counterpart. It is a commonly accepted principle that while legislation can have a deterrent effect, it is little use unless accompanied by an efficacious regulatory and enforcement plan. Take, for example, the UK's adoption of UWOs. While the civil measure may be useful compared to criminalising illicit enrichment as UNCAC advocates (Thomas-James 2017), very few were predicted to be used and, even then, the assets projected to be recovered seemed relatively insignificant (Home Office 2017). If it is sparsely enforced, or investigators overemphasise the role of offshore structures as evidence of suspicion of misconduct (*R v Baker and ors*), then the deterrent function of that legislation is compromised. Empirical work by Nagin (2013) suggests that severity makes little difference and that certainty of apprehension is a guiding principle of deterrence. In its Bribery Act Guidance Note, Bermuda acknowledges that enacting legislation, while necessary, is only a first step.

There is also the emphasis in the islands of fostering principles at all levels of the community, rather than simply updating the statute book. While integrity problems have not plagued Bermuda's legal development as they have in TCI, collegial initiatives can play a significant role alongside legislation and enforcement activities. Moniz stated:

> Bermuda as a society must be prepared to take action when and where we see corruption. . . . It requires us to overcome a reluctance in the community to deal with these difficult issues [and] it is not enough to say that we are against corruption.
>
> (Ministry of Legal Affairs 2016, 1)

The failure to prevent offence is important because it communicates the need for institutional and multi-stakeholder action. As the penal philosopher Beccaria (1764) advanced in his work on deterrence theory, it is better to prevent crime than to punish it. In this vein, important initiatives have manifested in the islands including in the private sector and the media, such as workshops, seminars and briefings to assist businesses with compliance and increasing their understanding of the law and obligations thereunder. This leaves an impression that Bermuda's industries are taking note of the modernised legislation and engaging in awareness-raising. If Bermuda follows the UK's path and prosecutions and convictions take several years, then in the meantime the Beccarian view that prevention is better than cure is a purposive ethos for the island upon which to promote understanding and knowledge of the Act's scope and the importance of integrity.

In Bermuda's NRA, bribery was acknowledged to be a predicate offence which poses a high money laundering risk. There were two civil recovery cases in the review period based on foreign corruption/fraud resulting in over $5.2 million being confiscated. It also acknowledged potential bribery matters identified by the Commission of Inquiry which were then under investigation. However, the fact remains that little evidence is available, particularly with the occurrence rather than the threat of domestic money laundering emanating from overseas corruption. The NRA acknowledged the risk that private banking poses to the commission of money laundering, given its products and services are offered within a culture of confidentiality. They suggest that institutions' desire for lucrative, high-net-worth business relationships may compromise compliance officers' responsibility to persuade their institutions not to deal with dubious customers (Bermuda NRA, 34). Notwithstanding the difficulty in measuring deterrence by example, Bermuda's Act carries a penalty of a fine of up to $500,000 and/or up to 10 years' imprisonment on summary conviction, or 15 years' imprisonment and/or an unlimited fine on indictment.

4.5.2 Anti–money laundering and counter-terrorism financing, including FATF compliance and national risk assessments

Bermuda's AML/CFT regime has been reviewed positively by international peer review. As part of strengthening resilience and identifying risk, Bermuda has engaged in various initiatives at wider industry and social levels. As mentioned, in 2018 Bermuda launched the 'Just Good Business' campaign to engage stakeholders and to raise awareness and understanding of AML best practices and compliance. This was conceived by Bermuda's National AML Committee and Financial Intelligence Agency in collaboration with various professional bodies including the Monetary Authority, Business Development Agency, Banking Association and Association of Insurers and Reinsurers. The aim is to foster commitment and action from the public and private sectors in enhancing Bermuda's AML/CFT framework.

One of Bermuda's goals in recent years has been to target the compliance industry, with its Business Development Agency launching an initiative to increase awareness of the responsibilities of compliance officers, including 'Hug a Compliance Officer' to provide greater visibility to this industry which is critical to Bermuda's AML/CFT regime. Bermuda's compliance industry is growing rapidly, which demonstrates an underlying commitment to market integrity. Bermuda's number of compliance officers rose from 65 in 2013 to 110 in 2019 (Bermuda Employment Survey 2020). Of these, 73 were Bermudians demonstrating a clear ability to recruit from Bermuda's domestic labour force.

Initiatives like this cannot be underestimated, as they point to a partnership-building function, which as well as having obvious benefits for a regulated environment, enables better engagement at the multilateral level to address shared challenges. This underpins the modern risk-based approach to AML/CFT regulation. The 2016 Anti-Corruption Summit in London was a good example of this in practice, which Prime Minister David Cameron averred was the largest demonstration of political will to address corruption in many years. While some held it to be window dressing or one good event, Transparency International (2017) concluded that multilateral-level visibility of collaboration is a positive outcome and points to partnership-building. It established the International Anti-Corruption Coordination Centre, the Global Declaration Against Corruption and Global Form on Asset Recovery.

Indeed, PWC (2018) suggests that awareness-raising and increased understanding of the scope and extent of economic crime is responsible for increasing levels of reporting of economic crime. In the context of small jurisdictions, actions can manifest in various forms. It might take years to bring a successful prosecution under progressive bribery legislation, yet by placing increased importance on fostering social denunciation of economic crime, institutions can be strengthened. Motivating and incentivising stakeholders at all levels to report and denounce such behaviour is indicative of a collaborative appetite. It might be the case that while wishing to adhere to strict, sophisticated internationally driven best practices, small states cannot achieve this without first strengthening their values across sectors. Such standards have a better chance of success than simply imposing them without consideration of domestic realities and, often, differences. The fact Bermuda is showing willingness to engage in wider initiatives beyond technical compliance is positive.

There are many money laundering risks applicable to Bermuda. A lesser risk is laundering via anonymous shell companies, as Bermuda is not an incorporation-focused jurisdiction relative to some of its fellow Overseas Territories like BVI. The empirical findings by Findley et al. (2014, 76) are important as Bermuda featured high in its table of CSP compliance, ranking higher than some OECD countries which are responsible for tightening up global financial rules.

Bermuda's AML regime is robust and it has enjoyed an upwardly positive trajectory through the FATF process (Farles 2012). Possibly the most important piece of legislation is Bermuda's Proceeds of Crime Act 1997, which gives powers to the police and courts to confiscate ill-gotten criminal gains. The Act affords Bermuda Police the opportunity to obtain an order or search warrant where they can demonstrate reasonable grounds for suspecting money laundering. The Act also establishes various requirements on financial institutions to undertake certain risk-based actions including DD measures, reporting, monitoring, and creating offences which deal with failure to comply with the regulations – such as failing to comply with a production order and failing to comply with a direction, found at sections 38 and 49J POCA 1997, respectively.

With the intrinsic link between money laundering and terrorism financing, another relevant statutory instrument is the Anti-Terrorism (Financial and Other Measures) Act 2004, which established offences related to facilitation and involvement of raising or using funds for terrorist activity. It provides a framework of targeting specific entities/persons known to be involved in terrorism financing and, importantly, countries which have not addressed AML/CFT deficiencies. The Act allows directions to be issued to financial institutions in order to enhance and protect the reputational integrity of Bermuda. This is modelled on similar powers conferred upon the UK Treasury under Schedule 7, Counter-Terrorism Act 2008. Requirements under Bermuda's Act include those made via the Anti-Terrorism (Financial and Other Measures) (Businesses in Regulated Sector) Order 2008, which classifies activities within the regulated sector and creates obligations to report suspicions of terrorism financing to Bermuda's FIA.

An independent body, Bermuda's FIA is provided for under the FIA Act 2007. It is tasked with receiving and processing SARs. Under the Act, the FIA has authority to enter into exchange agreement processes with other foreign competent authorities. They can serve disclosure demands on suspicious individuals or entities to produce relevant information regarding transactions, and they also have the authority to serve freezing order notices of up to 72 hours.

While such legislation demonstrates the regime's robustness, Bermuda has also acknowledged that its professionals are at risk of inveiglement or lowering standards to facilitate money laundering. The Proceeds of Crime (Anti–Money Laundering and Anti–Terrorist Financing) Regulations 2008 accommodates this and applies to regulated financial institutions and independent professions. It is widely accepted that professional gatekeepers to complex transactions, engaged in managing securities accounts, property transactions, incorporating companies or holding client money, can facilitate wrongdoing (Lord Justice Jackson 2015). The Proceeds of Crime (Anti–Money Laundering Financing Supervision and Enforcement) Designation Order 2012 established the Bermuda Barristers and Accountants AML/CFT Board as the authority responsible for overseeing and supervising the independent professions. The Regulations require that these professions establish AML/CFT policies, for example customer DD and ascertaining identity on the basis of documents, data or information obtained from a reliable, independent source, and beneficial ownership identification (per Part 2). The Regulations also task the BMA with oversight of all wire transfers. This emphasises the partnership aspect of oversight and also measures for institutions which include retaining records for a period of 5 years and verifying accuracy and completeness of information before transferring funds.

Another statutory weapon in Bermuda's armoury is the Proceeds of Crime (Anti–Money Laundering and Anti–Terrorist Financing Supervision and Enforcement) Act 2008. This designates the BMA as the financial regulator with regards to supervising AML/CFT-regulated financial institutions. The BMA's functions under section 5 of the Act include monitoring and taking necessary measures for the purpose of securing compliance, issuing guidance regarding compliance with AML/CFT provisions, conducting public reporting and informing the FIA of suspicions of criminality. It also outlines the functions of other competent authorities such as the Bermuda Casino Gaming Commission, FIA, and Real-Estate Superintendent. Enhanced regulatory measures have been put in place with examples being in the context of commercial reinsurers and sustained compliance and implementation of Basel III measures. Competent personnel are critical in offshore environments like Bermuda and can be the distinguishing feature between compliance and non-compliance. While brain drain is more pertinent in less developed nations (Docquier, Lohest, and Marfouk 2007, 193), jurisdictions like Bermuda attract qualified personnel with technical competencies to its business sector.

As part of strengthening its regulated environment, the BMA recently announced improved policies which demonstrate not only avidity for enforcement but acknowledgment that public denunciation of enforcement actions serves a deterrent function. Pre-2016, the BMA typically limited publicity of enforcement actions. From 2016 onwards, the BMA now publishes details of any use of its enforcement powers including nature of action, size of penalty, identity of entities or persons, and circumstances of the breach. This shows a renewed focus on integrity and public accountability from the regulator and an acknowledgement of the function of public awareness of its enforcement actions.

In 2016, BMA's enforcement activity increased across all financial sectors and they issued decision notices to 5 licensed entities. At the time, large unpublished civil fines were imposed on two entities for serious breaches of AML/CFT obligations. Utilising the Business Act 2003, the BMA published its decision against Barrington Investments Ltd (a licenced entity) which involved a civil penalty of $50,000 imposed for serious breaches of corporate governance and Minimum Criteria for Licensing in the Investment Business Act 2003. There was also default enforcement regarding non-payment of business fees, totalling $105,341.

In the context of financial supervision, the IMF's 2008 follow-up from its 2003 assessment raised interesting points demonstrating Bermuda's established approach to supervision. It stated that since 2003, "Bermudian authorities had made impressive progress in developing and implementing a risk-focused approach to supervision across the range of their sectoral supervisory responsibilities". They noted that all their recommendations had been taken into account or implemented, particularly relating to supervision of the insurance industry.

This review demonstrates upward trajectory, something which is often ignored in discourse about offshore centres. There are similarities with this and the positive 2014 FATF review. Bermuda's 3rd Round MER was published in 2008, where Bermuda was assessed as Compliant with 9 recommendations; Largely Compliant with 10 recommendations; Partially Compliant with 16 recommendations and Non-Compliant with 14 recommendations. By the time of the 1st Follow-Up Report in 2009, Bermuda was found to have addressed many deficiencies particularly with regards to DD of PEPs. Since then, it has engaged in regular follow-ups and assessments. At 2014, during the 5th Follow-Up Report, CFATF (2014, 3) assessed Bermuda as Compliant or Largely Compliant with 8 of the 16 Core and Key Recommendations, and Partially Compliant or Non-Compliant in the other 8. It concluded that Bermuda's legislative actions addressed all deficiencies identified for the following Core and Key Recommendations: 13, II, IV, 3, 36 and SRIII. With regards to the remaining recommendations, it stated that

> Bermuda has progressed to the point where only Recommendation 12 can be considered to be outstanding. Recommendations 11, 14 and 24 have been significantly addressed and now have only very minor shortcomings. All the Other Recommendations that were rated as Partially Compliant and Non-Compliant have been fully rectified.
>
> (CFATF 2014, 6)

Importantly, the 5th Follow-Up Report recommended that Bermuda's request for removal from regular follow-ups to biennial updates be accepted. This demonstrates FATF's positive conclusion as to the progress made and technical compliance with implementing its recommendations and action points. The criteria for removal is that the jurisdiction has taken "significant action . . . where it has an effective AML/CFT system in force, under which it has implemented the Core and Key Recommendations at a level equivalent to a Compliant or Largely Compliant taking into consideration that there would be no re-rating".

In the OECD's 'Global Forum on Transparency and Exchange of Information for Tax Purposes: Bermuda 2017' report, Bermuda is reviewed as 'largely compliant' overall. The OECD emphasised that the number of requests for information exchange have increased, and responses from exchange partners dealing with Bermuda have been very positive.

Like many Overseas Territories, Bermuda has engaged in NRAs in furtherance of complying with FATF standards and preparing for the latest MER. FATF's Guidance Note on NRAs emphasises that once countries properly understand money laundering and terrorism financing risks, then they can apply the measures in a commensurate way in furtherance of the risk-based approach. In Bermuda, the most recent was undertaken in 2017, which was a follow-up from its 2013 money laundering risk assessment and the 2016 terrorism financing risk assessment. Having engaged in three relevant NRAs in the past decade, Bermuda has shown a willingness to engage in the risk-based approach that underpins the international AML/CFT framework. By contrast, Transparency International (2018) found that 8 G20 countries had not conducted a NRA in the past 6 years.

The NRA found that the risk of money laundering in Bermuda as at 2017 was 'medium-high' and it was 'medium-low' for terrorism financing. The latter was based on 'potential threat', as there was no evidence that terrorism financing had taken place in the jurisdiction (Bermuda NRA, 5). In considering predicate crimes giving the highest risk of money laundering, it identified drug trafficking and offences under the Misuse of Drugs Act 1972. While acknowledging that Bermuda is an end-user destination for drugs, the average annual value of Bermuda's drug market is $25 million. In the review period 2013–16, 1,365 trafficking cases were detected resulting in 364 prosecutions and 326 convictions. Fifty-one money laundering cases were investigated whereby drug trafficking was the predicate offence. Ten prosecutions resulted, with 100% convictions. From these cases, criminal proceeds totalling $2.4 million were confiscated. While fewer cases than domestic fraud, international fraud was considered as being a high money laundering threat "because of the much higher value of proceeds involved and the actual use of the financial system in Bermuda to launder those proceeds" (Bermuda NRA, 36). The NRA reported that international tax crimes did not form the predicate basis for any money laundering in Bermuda during the review period, while assessing this to represent a high money laundering risk. There were two civil asset recovery cases undertaken involving fraud and international tax evasion, resulting in $6 million being frozen and $2.8 million confiscated. Corruption was also considered to be a high threat, however, with primary activities occurring outside the jurisdiction.

On SARs, the majority came from the banking sector. Interestingly, many were low-value transactions for currency conversion relating to the drug trade, detected principally on the basis of this occurring in front of bank tellers and through ATMs. SARs in the securities sector were found to be relatively low, although there is a steadily increasing number of SARs coming from the financial sector in general, something the National AML Committee considers to be an indicator of enhanced private sector compliance. The NRA concluded that the level of SARs in the trust sector was low, with only 2 investigations and no prosecutions or convictions. Given Bermuda's trusts market is sizeable with a large international client base, including PEPs and resident and non-resident high-net-worth individuals, this puts this sector at a high money laundering risk. The assessment acknowledged that there is generally a lack of information available in this sector, and oversight for private trust companies is limited.

In 2020, CFATF published the latest MER for Bermuda. This MER measures technical compliance but also effectiveness of Bermuda's AML/CFT system. The Report concluded that Bermuda has a "high level" of understanding of its money laundering and terrorism financing risks, and noted 3 national risk assessments that had been completed. It noted that AML/CFT supervision measures are "robust", while observing that despite major financial institutions adopting the risk-based approach in terms of both implementation of standards and the provision of trainings, not all financial institutions and DNFBPs reach the same high standard. However, the report praises Bermuda and its continued significant work to bring about a high level of compliance in all sectors. It also noted significant upgrading of its beneficial ownership regime and reporting requirements, while observing that Bermuda has maintained such information for many decades.

The Report also points to active pursuance of money laundering investigations in Bermuda as well as prosecutions. They aver that the sanctions under the legislation correlate with a lack of recidivism. It also acknowledges that there have been no prosecutions or convictions for terrorism financing, as expected with Bermuda's risk profile in this regard. The report does, however, point to effectiveness challenges faced with the low levels of restraint and recovery of illicit funds, explained on the basis that restraints are typically granted prior to charges being laid. CFATF concluded that Bermuda's progress with technical compliance since the last MER has seen "significant improvement". It states that "[Bermuda's] main technical compliance strengths are in the areas of understanding ML and TF risks . . . national cooperation and coordination, customer due diligence, record keeping, internal controls, legal persons and arrangements, criminalisation . . . and responsibilities of law enforcement and investigative authorities" (CFATF 2020, 9). As to technical compliance, Bermuda was assessed as being Compliant with 28 recommendations, Largely Compliant with 11, and Partially Compliant with 1. Effectiveness was assessed by reference to Immediate Outcomes (IOs) as follows: High for IO 1; Substantial for IOs 2, 3, 5, 6, 9 and 10; Moderate for IOs 4, 7 and 11; and Low for IO 8. The report also refers to the recent implementation of various measures as having limiting ability on measuring effectiveness, with particular reference to DNFBPs.

4.5.3 Company law, beneficial ownership and transparency

The term 'beneficial owner' refers to the true owners of equity in a business or its controllers, even if the title might be in another name. While beneficial ownership transparency initiatives are generally increasing in both onshore and offshore jurisdictions, they largely pertain to ownership of companies rather than trusts which is seeing more protracted development.

In 2020, Bermuda committed to implementing a public beneficial ownership register in accordance with section 51, SAMLA 2018. FATF standards on beneficial ownership, in recommendations 24 and 25, stipulate that "countries should ensure that there is adequate, accurate and timely information on beneficial ownership and control of legal persons that can be obtained or accessed in a timely fashion by competent authorities". While silent on whether this should be in a public register, it does highlight the importance of countries being able to have access to such information in good time. The 2020 MER clearly observes Bermuda's compliance in this regard, even independently of its most recent commitments to 'go public'.

The IMF (2008, 8) noted that "incorporation of Bermuda companies requires that ultimate beneficial ownership be established twice before registration is accepted: once by the party submitting the application (normally a lawyer), and again independently by the authorities". This supports the view that Bermuda has established regulations in place on beneficial ownership due diligence. The Bermuda Government (22.5.2017) proposed legislative changes to its framework including intensified disclosure obligations on information changes for local companies, which must be filed on the register. In 2016, Bermuda and the UK executed an Exchange of Notes Agreement which made changes to the Exchange Control Act 1972 and the Exchange Control Regulations 1973. This concerns the sharing of beneficial ownership information via Bermuda's central registry and was implemented in June 2017.

As well as amendments to the Companies Act 1981 via the Companies and Limited Liability (Beneficial Ownership) Amendment Act 2017, Bermuda also introduced the Registrar of Companies (Compliance Measures) Act 2017, which confers increased powers on the Companies Registrar. These include "to monitor, inspect and enforce and otherwise regulate Bermuda registered entities to ensure compliance with their governing legislation" (Bermuda Government 14.3.2017). This was in direct response to the OECD Assessment Team's recommendations made during the peer review of Bermuda, which included enhancing the Registrar's power to inspect Bermuda-registered entities' compliance with governing legislation. In addition to this commitment, measures created under the Act include default fines and civil penalties, per sections 10–13. With respect to protecting the interests of Bermuda-registered entities, the Act also provides procedural safeguards including the provision of notice under section 6, and the right to appeal default fines and civil penalties, per section 16.

There is presently no empirical evidence suggesting that making a beneficial ownership register public carries any further deterrent than a register which is government accessible. Therefore, for would-be criminals, it is not unreasonable to suggest that information in the hands of law enforcement is as dangerous to their operations as being in the hands of the public. There is corpus opinion about increased transparency deterring illicit activity, although there is also sentiment towards striking a balance between transparency and privacy, something discussed in Chapter 7. This is particularly so with corporate ownership and how publicly accessible shareholder information might have a converse effect in deterring foreign investment from those who wish to observe privacy. For Bermuda, external business is crucial to its economic sustainability. The same debate is also occurring in the UK with regards to property and beneficial ownership, particularly luxury property. In response to the UK government's call for evidence on this issue, there was significant concern about the negative impact a public register would have on the UK property market in deterring overseas investors and making it less competitive (UK Department for Business, Energy and Industrial Strategy 2018, 6).

Given the UK's action in seeking to impose open registers on Bermuda, it seems as though the achievements of Bermuda's system have been disregarded.

The inference is that a register which is closed is non-transparent and therefore can facilitate misconduct. Such arguments are often predicated on a 'nothing to hide' view, which will be explored in Chapter 7. The Paradise papers' aims were to expose information the public were hitherto prohibited from accessing, despite this information being legally protected by confidentiality and privacy laws or professional privilege. UK legislators have gone as far as claiming that "the public . . . have a right to see beneficial ownership information" (House of Commons, Foreign Affairs Committee 2019, 3). Abrogating fundamental legal protections with the language of rights, without such being afforded by law, is jurisprudentially flawed. Prior to altering its stance, Bermuda took the view that this sort of information does not give rise to legitimate public interest, rather it is a matter for investigative authorities. This seems more aligned with FATFs position. Bermuda has traditionally made such information available to competent authorities, and recently more so via international bilateral exchange agreements. This was viewed by transparency campaigners, the media and UK politicians as inadequate and was accompanied by significant legislative reform. Baroness Stern noted: "In absence of the transparency [Amendment 73] calls for, we've had to rely on hackers and whistle-blowers to take great personal risks in order to expose this criminality".[5] Richards (2017, 129) suggests that for the UK as a large diversified economy, introducing a public register is incidental. However, for the Overseas Territories which depend on financial services, the commitment is more a matter of economic life or death. However, unlike other territories, Bermuda is not a significant incorporation jurisdiction or a typical domicile for shell companies (IMF 2008, 8). Bermuda entities were not implicated in the Panama papers. By contrast, about half the legal entities revealed were incorporated in BVI, while data clearly showed BVI and Panama as favoured jurisdictions for incorporation services (Trautman 2017, 864). Bermuda's initial resistance may have pivoted on convention relating to the manner in which the UK issued what was effectively an ultimatum to comply. Public statements from officials, and evidence submitted to the FAC, supports this view. For example, Bermuda's Premier argued in 2018 that the public register decision represented a regressive colonial mindset. This, and arguments about the fact public registers are not yet normative, may have represented a greater concern, rather than the functional impact of public registers on Bermuda's financial sector. Such a conclusion certainly fits with the fact that Bermuda has now agreed to it.

4.5.4 Economic substance

An international standard which formed part of the EU Code of Conduct Group for business taxation's investigation into the tax policies of EU and third countries, is the requirement of economic substance. Following the Conduct Group's investigation in 2017, Bermuda was named as needing to address economic

5 HL (17 January 2018) Vol 788, Col 687.

substance concerns. Under the Economic Substance Act 2018, every Bermuda-registered entity engaged in a relevant activity is required to maintain a substantial economic presence in the jurisdiction and comply with the Act's economic substance requirements. 'Registered entity' is defined under section 2 of the Act as a company, LLC or partnership. 'Relevant activity' is defined as business in the following: banking, insurance, fund management, financing, leasing, headquarters, shipping, disruption and service centre, intellectual property, and holding entity. The substance requirements are defined at section 3(1) and include if the entity is managed and directed in Bermuda; core income-generating activities are undertaken in Bermuda; entity maintains adequate physical presence in Bermuda and adequate and full-time employees in Bermuda with suitable qualifications; and adequate operating expenditure incurred in Bermuda in relation to the relevant activity. The requirements stipulate that entities must file an annual economic substance declaration with the Registrar. The purpose behind this regime is self-explanatory, given the concerns about shell and paper companies and the increasing momentum against aggressive avoidance schemes and profit shifting. 'Form over substance' has caused reputational damage to offshore centres for decades. Bermuda created this legislation in accordance with EU commitments. These requirements appear capable of rendering more meaningful presence by multinational companies accused of shifting profits to Bermuda for fiscal benefit.

Of course, given the significant obligations implicit under the Act's provisions, this will necessitate Bermuda intensifying promotional efforts aimed at foreign investors and businesses, as well as those already domiciled in Bermuda to ensure compliance. In January 2019, Bermuda's government announced the need to implement various incentives, such as with work permits and payroll tax concessions (*Royal Gazette* 10.1.2019).

4.5.5 Tax information exchange and cooperation

It is worth remarking on Bermuda's position with regards to the OECD's Multilateral Competent Authority Agreement on the Exchange of Country-by-Country Reports. Bermuda's commitments to the OECD's BEPS tax transparency regime is another important development in its framework to tackle suspect wealth. The G20 Leaders Declaration (2012, 9) explicitly addressed the need, as part of the global fight against such conduct, to prevent base erosion and profit shifting. BEPS represents an increased attitude by multinational corporations to engage in income-shifting for the purpose of fiscal efficiency. The OECD led the BEPS Project and has emphasised that while eliminating double taxation is essential to support the efficient operation of the global markets, it is also necessary to eliminate what they call "inappropriate double non-taxation". Brauner (2014, 55) suggests that while the phenomenon is not new, globalisation and the international movement of money has doubtless contributed to the framework whereby multinationals can engage in advantageous fiscal efficiency. The OECD's action plan regarding BEPS is complex and has been referred to as a "potpourri of issues" (Brauner 2014, 69). More generally, BEPS occupy a controversial position in the tax discourse. BEPS conjures up perceptions which have fuelled anti-tax competition rhetoric and transcended to criticism of Overseas Territories and their facilitation of fiscally advantageous offerings to multinational corporations.

In furtherance of international focus on this issue, Bermuda and the UK signed a Country-by-Country Authority Agreement in 2017. Bermuda has faced criticism in the past because of the practice of multinational enterprises transferring revenue to their offshore holding companies to limit fiscal liability elsewhere. This Agreement strengthens the regime of tackling tax dodging, which has become as problematic in the anti-tax haven discourse as illicit wealth. Bermuda avers that this commitment completes the OECD's BEPS tax transparency package with the UK and furthers the work already undertaken with common reporting. Bermuda was the first Overseas Territory to complete such an agreement with the UK. It intensifies Bermuda's regulatory regime and, like the other measures referred to in this chapter, demonstrates commitment to international cooperation. After signing it, Bermuda's Premier also urged other countries to meet the Bermuda standard.

Despite being on the receiving end of a long-standing blacklisting offensive by key international stakeholders, Bermuda is now classified as 'largely compliant' by the OECD in respect of tax practices. The OECD (2017, 12) announced that it was the year of the "switch-on" for automatic EOI with respect to financial accounts. Prior to making this commitment, Bermuda was screened under peer review assessment to assess compliance for EOI on request to tax authorities. Bermuda's Largely Compliant rating on this measure compares well with OECD countries.

Bermuda has entered into tax agreements with a significant number of jurisdictions. TIEAs, based on the OECD's Model Agreement on Exchange of Information on Tax Matters, are a mechanism by which signatory jurisdictions agree to cooperate in tax investigations through information exchange procedures. As a mechanism to control tax misconduct, TIEAs enable governments to enforce their own tax laws and investigate and detect crime through exchanging information on someone under tax evasion suspicion. Building upon its central register and absence of secrecy laws, Bermuda's framework enables cooperation with any competent authority in a TIEA jurisdiction. Since the development of the CRS in 2014, in accordance with the OECD's Convention on Mutual Administrative Assistance in Tax Matters, exchange frameworks are increasingly automatic.

Bermuda has entered into 67 automatic exchange relationships for CRS information, which builds upon the 41 TIEAs entered into, and develops Bermuda's exchange regime to automatic. The question of effectiveness of TIEAs is a matter of contention. They are likely to deter bad actors in utilising a jurisdiction like Bermuda to conceal wealth or evade fiscal obligations. The initiative, which is now automatic, ensures that an increasing number of countries are committing to exchange basic information. In Bermuda's case, it engages in this with major, relevant markets such as the UK and US – between whom considerable financial transacting occurs. Moreover, the information can relate to investigations of both a civil and criminal nature. Neslund (2009) highlights that the past regime was problematic because it would fail if the predicate offence requiring the information was not an offence in the receiving country – in other words, if tax evasion was not criminalised in both countries.

For legitimate investors wishing to reduce investment costs, choosing a jurisdiction which engages in automatic information exchange is inconsequential. As Kemme, Parikh, and Steigner (2017) observe, for legitimate enterprise there are list of variable considerations which are important including language, legal system, proximity, time zone and governance when making a choice of where to invest. These characteristics reduce costs for the genuine investor, yet are not desirable for tax evaders whose priority may be to increase the difficulty in being detected. As such, if more countries engage in information exchange which bear the characteristics of international cooperation and a responsible investment environment, this leads to the conclusion that deterrence will be served. Bermuda has also entered into DTCs with several jurisdictions which are bilateral agreements designed to protect against the risk of double taxation where the same income is taxable in two states. This provides certainty of treatment for cross-border trade and investment and prevents excessive foreign taxation.

Despite the developments with the CRS since 2014, Bermuda has engaged in bilateral EOI agreements for many years, including having signed one with the US in 1988, Australia in 2005 and the UK in 2007 (later replaced by the TIEA). Among the many developments is the advent of automatic exchange rather than 'by request'. Like the CRS, developed by the OECD in 2014 which calls on jurisdictions to obtain information from their financial institutions and automatically exchange it with other jurisdictions on an annual basis, TIEAs are achieving global acceptance. As PWC (2016) observe, "hiding information is not tax planning [and] working on the assumption that the tax authorities will not find out is a strategy that is very likely in its dying days".

Bermuda also has many Mutual Legal Assistance Treaties (MLATs) in place with jurisdictions internationally, a finding echoed by CFATF (2020), which noted Bermuda's comprehensive legislative framework to allow for international cooperation. CFATF (2014, 83) noted that Bermuda had reported 13 MLA requests in 2013, 3 in 2012 and 7 in 2011. It also reported on other formal requests made and received through memorandums of understanding and other instruments with foreign competent authorities. CFATF (2014) also showed that in 2013 Bermuda's Financial Intelligence Unit reported 42 outgoing and 23 incoming requests for information, with 47 outcoming and 34 incoming in 2012.

4.6 Development concerns

The research for this book found deep-rooted economic challenges in Bermuda, despite its high GDP. As Bermudian economist Stubbs (2016, 2) observed, "Everyone in Bermuda knows of the economy's weakness . . . even the most financially and economically switched-on people in Bermuda regularly cite [the] 10% decline in GDP since 2008". Stubbs also suggests that Bermuda's economy is worse than people think and that such a proposition often produces responses such as "Where's the unemployment?" or "Where are the soup lines?" Bermuda suffers from violent crime, with a murder rate at 2015 of 6.45 per 100,000. By comparison, the US is 5.35 per 100,000. It is difficult to make conclusions from statistics of this sort in small jurisdictions. Bermuda Police Service crime statistics 2016 reported a 28% decrease in crimes against the community between 2015 and 2016, yet murder statistics show there were 5 murders in 2015 and 7 in 2016, which represents a significant statistical increase. Bermuda has had well-known gang crime problems that increased significantly from the late 2000s (Bermuda Police 2012, 2), and of 2,526 arrests in 2016, 247 were drug related. Gang-related homicides accounted for 35 murders between 2009 and 2017 (Bermuda Government 17.11.2017).

Bermuda does not have many of the stereotypical development-hindering problems like sanitation, lack of education or public health concerns, so therefore might not meet traditional connotations of poverty. However, living standards, combined with relatively little in terms of social welfare, and homelessness present concerns. Many Bermudians struggle on non-professional wages. Various social initiatives, including Bermuda's Coalition for the Protection of Children providing nutritional breakfasts for school children, have been seen in recent years.

Bermuda's economic success is characterised by its financial, business, retail and tourism sectors. The incumbent government ran on a platform of 'putting Bermudians first', and there have been calls to establish a minimum wage (*Royal Gazette* 24.4.2017). There is also interest at government level at adapting Bermuda's tax structure (*Cayman Compass* 11.1.2021). The Bermuda Tax Reform Commission (2018) recommended new taxes such as an interest and dividend withholding tax, a general and managed services tax, and tax on commercial and residential rental income. However, in the context of Bermuda enhancing its compliance with international standards such as economic substance and public registers, it is conceivable that some of these concerns will have to be balanced against the need to incentivise businesses to locate to, or remain in, Bermuda.

4.7 Conclusion

Bermuda's implication in foreign cases, as well as in the Paradise papers, paints a picture of Bermuda as a harmful offshore jurisdiction. Inclusion on blacklists, despite removal, adds to this picture. It should not come as a surprise that transparency campaigners have publicly criticised Bermuda, given the improbability that the notions of offshore and transparency will ever become good bedfellows, irrespective of one's compliance records.

However, in examining evidence of Bermuda's legal and regulatory responses to suspect wealth, this analysis has shown that Bermuda complies with many international standards. Its cooperation and compliance record is evidenced by positive reviews from international monitoring bodies, including CFATF and the OECD. Across the areas measured, Bermuda demonstrates visible adherence to international standards. This is evidenced through enhanced companies register requirements, a centrally maintained beneficial ownership register with recent commitments to make it publicly accessible, TIEAs, CRS and other international cooperation agreements. Its economic substance laws and modernised, far-reaching bribery legislation demonstrate a holistic view as to how Bermuda protects its jurisdiction and financial centre from suspect wealth. Further, its regional engagement with CFATF, and its conducting several recent and comprehensive NRAs, demonstrate compliance with the risk-based nature of the international AML/CFT movement.

In terms of the questions this book seeks to explore, this chapter has demonstrated that international standards regarding suspect wealth are highly visible and prevalent in Bermuda. It is clear from the reviews considered in this chapter that Bermuda has developed an upward trajectory of engagement and compliance with international standards. In terms of safeguarding its financial sector from receiving suspect wealth, the legal and regulatory reforms which have been long underway in Bermuda stand the territory in good stead. However, as has been identified, certain areas such as real estate and DNFBPs need further attention, something domestic awareness-raising and high-level training functions ought to focus on moving forwards. It will be interesting to monitor Bermuda's creation of a public register and the extent to which this will have an effect on Bermuda's regulated environment and ability to disrupt financial crime. It is imperative to monitor Bermuda's application and effectiveness of recently reformed or enacted legislation. Bermuda's response to economic crime demonstrates a robust approach to regulating its domestic environment and cooperating with international standards as they develop.

References

America's Cup Bermuda Ltd (2017) 'America's Cup Bermuda Legacy Impact'. Available: https://11thhourracing.org/wp-content/uploads/2017/12/35thamericascupbermudalegacyimpact.pdf

Atkinson, A. B. (1977) 'Optimal Taxation and the Direct versus Indirect Tax Controversy', *Canadian Journal of Economics*, 19: 590–606.

BBC Panorama (6.11.2017) 'The Billion Pound VAT Scam'. Available: www.bbc.co.uk/programmes/b09hm8q4

Beccaria, C. (1764/1986) *On Crimes and Punishments*, H. Paolucci (Trans.), New York: Macmillan.

Bermuda Business Development Agency (2016) 'Bermuda is Different'. Available: https://www.globenewswire.com/news-release/2016/04/05/826101/0/en/Bermuda-is-different-BDA-responds-to-Panama-Papers.html

Bermuda Government (2016) 'Visitor Arrivals Report Full Year'. Available: https://www.gotobermuda.com/sites/default/master/files/2016_visitor_arrivals_report0320.pdf

Bermuda Government (20.5.2016) Hon. Trevor Moniz 'Ministerial Statement: Modernizing Bermuda's Law on Bribery & Corruption'. Available: https://www.gov.bm/articles/minister-trevor-moniz-ministerial-statement-modernizing-bermuda%E2%80%99s-law-bribery-corruption-0

Bermuda Government (2017a) 'Department of Statistics, Digest of Statistics 2017, Table 6.1'. Available: https://www.gov.bm/sites/default/files/2017-Digest-of-Statistics.pdf

Bermuda Government (2017b) 'Department of Statistics: Bermuda Job Market Employment Briefs'. Available: https://www.gov.bm/sites/default/files/7530_EB_May_2017_REVISED_JULY_0.PDF

Bermuda Government (2017c) 'Report: Assessment of Bermuda's National Money Laundering and Terrorist Financing Risk (Bermuda NRA)'. Available: https://www.gov.bm/sites/default/files/9171_Public%20NRA%20Report_Final_3.pdf

Bermuda Government (14.3.2017) 'Ministerial Statement, Minister of Economic Development'. Available: https://www.gov.bm/articles/registrar-companies-compliance-measures-act-2017

Bermuda Government (17.11.2017) Ministerial Statement, Minister of National Security, 'Reducing Gang Violence'. Available: https://www.gov.bm/articles/reducing-gang-violence-bermuda

Bermuda Government. Cabinet Office (22.5.2017) 'Enhancements to Bermuda's Beneficial Ownership Regime Proposed'. Press Release. Available: https://www.gov.bm/articles/enhancements-bermuda%E2%80%99s-beneficial-ownership-regime-proposed

Bermuda Government. Employment Survey 2020.

Bermuda Government. Finance Ministry, 'Financial Statements of the Consolidated Fund' 2019.

Bermuda Government. Finance Ministry, 'National Economic Report of Bermuda 2015'. Available: https://www.gov.bm/sites/default/files/2015-National-Economic-Report.pdf

Bermuda Government. Ministry of Legal Affairs (2016) 'Bribery Act Guidance Note'. Available: https://www.gov.bm/sites/default/files/BRIBERY-ACT-2016-Guidance-FINAL2.pdf

Bermuda Government. Police Service (2012) 'Making Bermuda Safer: Strategic Plan 2012–2015'. Available: http://www.bermudapoliceservice.bm/upload/PDFs/2012-2015%20Bermuda%20Police%20Service%20Strategic%20Plan.PDF

'Bermuda Tax Reform Commission 2018 Report'. Available: https://www.gov.bm/sites/default/files/Tax-Reform-Commission-Report-Final-2018-11-19.pdf

Bernhard, V. (1985) 'Bermuda and Virginia in the Seventeenth Century: A Comparative View', *Journal of Social History*, 19(1): 57–70.

Brauner, Y. (2014) 'What the BEPS?', *Florida Tax Review*, 16(2): 55–115.

Carey Olsen (6.4.2020) 'Application of Bermuda's Bribery Act Considered by Supreme Court'.

Cayman Compass (11.1.2021) 'Bermuda to Reform "Unfair" Tax System'. Available: www.caymancompass.com/2021/01/11/bermuda-to-reform-unfair-tax-system/

CFATF (2014) '5th Follow-Up Report'. Available: https://www.cfatf-gafic.org/cfatf-documents/follow-up-reports-2/bermuda/3556-bermuda-5th-follow-up-report-1/file

CFATF (2020) '4th Round MER'. Available: https://www.cfatf-gafic.org/home-test/english-documents/4th-round-meval-reports/13596-bermuda-4th-round-mer/file

Commission of Inquiry into the Report of the Auditor General on the Consolidated Fund of the Government of Bermuda for the Financial Years March 31 2010, March 31 2011 and March 21 2012, Report of Commission, February 2017.

D'Angheria, P. M. (1511) 'Legatio Babylonica', cited in Jones, R. (2004) *Bermuda Five Centuries*, Hamilton: Panatel VDS.
Department for Business, Energy and Industrial Strategy (3.2018) 'A Register of Beneficial Owners for Overseas Companies and Other Legal Entities: The Government's Response to the Call for Evidence'. Available: https://assets.publishing.service.gov.uk/government/uploads/system/uploads/attachment_data/file/681844/ROEBO_Gov_Response_to_Call_for_Evidence.pdf
DeShields, S., and Riley, C. (2015) 'The Economic and Social Impacts of Bermuda Hosting the 2017 America's Cup Races'. Available: https://www.researchgate.net/project/The-Economic-and-Social-Impacts-of-Bermuda-Hosting-the-2017-Americas-Cup-Races
Docquier, F., Lohest, O., and Marfouk, A. (2007) 'Brain Drain in Developing Countries', *The World Bank Economic Review*, 21(2): 193–218.
EU Commission, Special Committee on Tx Crimes, Tax Evasion, and Tax Avoidance, Meeting 21 June 2018, Hearing on 'Lessons Learnt from the Paradise Papers', Panel II Alleged Aggressive Tax Planning Schemes Within the EU.
EU List of Non-Cooperative Jurisdictions for Tax Purposes, Council Conclusions (Adopted 5/12/17).
European Parliament (9.1.2019) 'Parliamentary Questions, E-000064-19'. Available: https://www.europarl.europa.eu/doceo/document/E-8-2019-000064_EN.html
Farles, T. (21.11.2012) 'Guide to Anti–Money Laundering and Anti-Terrorist Financing in Bermuda'. Available: https://www.mondaq.com/money-laundering/207538/guide-to-anti-money-laundering-and-anti-terrorist-financing-in-bermuda
Faulhaber, L. V. (2010) 'Sovereignty, Integration and Tax Avoidance in the European Union: Striking the Proper Balance', *Columbia Journal of Transnational Law*, 48: 177–241.
Findley, M. G., Nielson, D. L., and Sharman, J. C. (2014) *Global Shell Games: Experiments in Transnational Relations, Crime, and Terrorism*, Cambridge: Cambridge University Press.
G20 (2012) 'Leaders Declaration', Mexico. Available: https://www.oecd.org/g20/summits/los-cabos/2012-0619-loscabos.pdf
Glover, L., and Smith, D. B. (2008) *The Shipwreck that Saved Jamestown: The Sea Venture Castaways and the Fate of America*, New York: Henry Holt.
Hawley, S. (8.12.2014) 'How Effective is the UK Bribery Act?', *Corruption Watch*.
Home Office (2017) 'Criminal Finances Act 2017 Overarching Impact Assessment; and Criminal Finances Act 2017 Unexplained Wealth Orders Impact Assessment'. Available: https://assets.publishing.service.gov.uk/government/uploads/system/uploads/attachment_data/file/621192/Impact_Assessment_-_CF_Act_Overarching.pdf
Horder, J. (2013) Deterring Bribery: Law, Regulation and the Export Trade, 196–215', in J. Horder and P. Alldridge (eds.), *Modern Bribery Law: Comparative Perspectives*, Cambridge: Cambridge University Press.
House of Commons, Foreign Affairs Committee (2019) 'Inquiry: Global Britain and the British Overseas Territories: Resetting the Relationship', Fifteenth Report of Session 2017–2019. Available: https://publications.parliament.uk/pa/cm201719/cmselect/cmfaff/1464/1464.pdf
ICIJ (10.1.2019) 'Nike Could Owe Billions in Back Tax if New EU Probe Finds Against It'. Available: www.icij.org/investigations/paradise-papers/nike-could-owe-billions-in-back-tax-if-new-eu-probe-finds-against-it/#:~:text=Nike%20Could%20Owe%20Billions%20In%20Back%20Tax,EU%20Probe%20Finds%20Against%20It&

text=However%2C%20it%20would%20still%20be,in%20ICIJ's%20Paradise%20 Papers%20reporting

IMF (2008) 'Bermuda: Final Detailed Assessment Report Anti–Money Laundering and Combatting the Financing of Terrorism'. Available: https://www.imf.org/external/pubs/ft/scr/2008/cr08105.pdf

Irish Times (5.1.2019) 'Google Ramps up the "Double Irish" before Closing Time'. Available: www.irishtimes.com/business/technology/google-ramps-up-the-double-irish-before-closing-time-1.3747997

Jenkins, A. (2009) 'The Bermuda Islands Blow 'Sweet & Sour' on Employers' Liability for Internet Libel', *Computer Law and Security Review*, 25: 280–284.

Judiciary of England and Wales (2015) 'The Professions: Power, Privilege and Legal Liability', Peter Taylor Memorial Lecture, Lord Justice Jackson.

Kemme, D. M., Parikh, B., and Steigner, T. (2017) 'Tax Havens, Tax Evasion and Tax Information Exchange Agreements in the OECD', *European Financial Management*, 23(3): 519–542,

KPMG (2017) '(Re)insurance in Bermuda: View from the Bridge'. Available: https://home.kpmg/content/dam/kpmg/bm/pdf/2017/03/Charles-Thresh-Mike-Morrison.pdf

Nagin, D. S. (2013) 'Deterrence in the Twenty-First Century', *Crime and Justice*, 42(1): 199–263.

Neslund, K. (2009) 'Why Tax Information Exchange Agreements are Toothless', *Tax Insider*.

OECD (1998) 'Harmful Tax Competition – An Emerging Global Issue'. Available: https://www.oecd-ilibrary.org/taxation/harmful-tax-competition_9789264162945-en

OECD (2000) 'Towards Global Tax Co-operation. Progress in Identifying and Eliminating Harmful Tax Practices'. Available: https://www.oecd.org/tax/harmful/2090192.pdf

OECD (2017) 'Global Forum on Transparency and Exchange of Information for Tax Purposes, 'Tax Transparency 2017' Progress Report'. Available: http://www.oecd.org/tax/transparency/documents/global-forum-annual-report-2017.pdf

OECD (2020) 'Automatic Exchange Portal'. Available: https://www.oecd.org/tax/automatic-exchange/

Ogletree Deakins (14.5.2019) 'Bermuda: First Investigations Under New Anti-Bribery Legislation'. Available: https://ogletree.com/international-employment-update/articles/june-2019/bermuda/2019-05-14/bermuda-first-investigations-under-new-anti-bribery-legislation/

Oxfam (12.1.2016a) 'Bermuda Named World's Worst Tax Haven'. Available: www.oxfam.org.uk/media-centre/press-releases/2016/12/bermuda-named-worldsworst-tax-haven

Oxfam (2016b) 'Tax Havens Serve No Useful Economic Purpose: 300 Economists Tell World Leaders'. Available: https://www.oxfam.org/en/press-releases/tax-havens-serve-no-useful-economic-purpose-300-economists-tell-world-leaders

PWC (2016) 'Tax Information Exchange – What Will Change and How Taxpayers Should Respond'. Available: https://www.pwc.com/ng/en/assets/pdf/tax-information-exchange-to.pdf

PWC (2017) 'Economic, Environmental and Social Impact of the 35th America's Cup on Bermuda'. Available: http://parliament.bm/admin/uploads/report/96b48b507bc2a99e9fb84c37559da759.pdf

PWC (2018) 'The Global Economic Crime and Fraud Survey'. Available: https://www.pwc.co.uk/services/forensic-services/insights/global-economic-crime-survey-2018---uk-findings.html

Reuters (21.10.2016) 'Credit Suisse Reaches 109.5m Euro Settlement in Italy'. Available: www.reuters.com/article/uk-italy-creditsuisse-tax/credit-suisse-reaches-109-5-million-euro-settlement-in-italy-idUKKCN12L1TC?edition-redirect=uk

Reuters (3.1.2019) 'Google Shifted $23billion to Tax Haven Bermuda in 2017: Filing'. Available: www.reuters.com/article/us-google-taxes-netherlands/google-shifted-23-billion-to-tax-haven-bermuda-in-2017-filing-idUSKCN1OX1G9?utm_source=reddit.com#:~:text=AMSTERDAM%20(Reuters)%20%2D%20Google%20moved,the%20Dutch%20Chamber%20of%20Commerce

Richards, E. T. B. (2017) *Bermuda: Back From the Brink*, Hamilton: Self-Published.

Royal Gazette (24.4.2017) 'Minimum Wage Would Mean More Jobs for Bermudians', Sheelagh Cooper. Available: www.royalgazette.com/other/article/20170424/minimum-wage-would-mean-more-jobs-for-bermudians/

Royal Gazette (10.1.2019) 'Economic Substance Incentives Unveiled'. Available: www.royalgazette.com/other/news/article/20190110/economic-substance-incentives-unveiled/

Ryder, N. (2015) 'The Legal Mechanisms to Control Bribery and Corruption', 381–393, in B. A. K. Rider (ed.), *Research Handbook on International Financial Crime*, Cheltenham: Elgar.

San Antonio Express (5.8.2016) 'U.S. Takes $2.8 Million Allegedly Embezzled from Mexican Border City Matamoros'. Available: www.expressnews.com/news/local/article/U-S-takes-2-8-million-allegedly-embezzled-from-9125779.php

Sharman, J. C. (2006) *Havens in a Storm*, Ithaca, NY: Cornell University Press.

Stanton, J. (2016) 'The Currency Board Monetary System Over 100 Years in Bermuda (1815–2015)', *Studies in Applied Economics*, No. 50.

Stubbs, R. J. (2016) 'Bermuda in 2016: An Economic Analysis and Political Critique of Where We Are, How We Got Here and The Way Out'. Available: https://issuu.com/robertstubbs0/docs/bermudain2016

Sutherland, E. H. (1949/1985) *White Collar Crime*, New Haven: Yale University Press.

Tax Journal (8.1.2020) 'Google to End "Double Irish" Tax Structure'. Available: www.taxjournal.com/articles/google-to-end-double-irish-tax-structure#:~:text=8%20January%202020-,Google's%20parent%20company%2C%20Alphabet%2C%20has%20announced%20a%20restructure%20which%20will,large%20extent%20from%20the%20EU

Thomas-James, D. (2017) 'Unexplained Wealth Orders in the Criminal Finances Bill: A Suitable Measure to Tackle Unaccountable Wealth in the UK?', *Journal of Financial Crime*, 24(2): 178–180.

TJN (2012) 'The Price of Offshore Revisited'. Available: https://www.taxjustice.net/cms/upload/pdf/Price_of_Offshore_Revisited_120722.pdf

Transparency International (2017) '3 Things We've Learned Since the Anti-Corruption Summit in London 2016'. Available: https://www.transparency.org/en/news/3-things-weve-learned-since-the-anti-corruption-summit-in-london-2016

Transparency International (2018) 'The Cost of Secrecy'. Available: https://www.transparency.org.uk/sites/default/files/pdf/publications/TIUK-CostofSecrecy-WEB-v2.pdf

Transparency International (2018) 'G20 Leaders or Laggards? Reviewing G20 Promises on Ending Anonymous Companies'. Available: https://images.transparencycdn.org/images/2018_G20_Leaders_or_Laggards_EN.pdf

Trautman, L. J. (2017) 'Following the Money: Lessons from the Panama Papers, Part 1: Tip of the Iceberg', *Penn State Law Review*, 121(3): 807–873.

UK Committee on Public Accounts (2016) 'HMRC's Performance in 2016–2017, HC456'. Available: https://publications.parliament.uk/pa/cm201719/cmselect/cmpubacc/456/456.pdf

UNODC Statistics Online, Murder Rate by Country.

US Department of Justice (16.10.2017) 'Wife of Former Mexican Official Convicted in Bank Fraud Conspiracy', Press Release. Available: https://www.justice.gov/usao-sdtx/pr/wife-former-mexican-official-convicted-bank-fraud-conspiracy

Wood, P. R. (2008) *Maps of World Financial Law*, London: Sweet and Maxwell.

World Bank Development Indicators Database: Bermuda. Available: https://data.worldbank.org/country/bermuda?view=chart

5 The Turks and Caicos Islands

5.1 TCI: an overview

In his final speech as Governor, having served in the islands between 2005 and 2008, Richard Tauwhare said: "These islands have huge, huge potential. . . . The future of TCI holds great promise [as] we have a huge amount going for us" (*TCI Weekly News* 2008). Tauwhare was confident in 2008 that TCI had reached a turning point in its history. Yet, the context of this faith came at a time the islands were about to face yet another constitutional crisis which would dramatically impact its social, governmental and economic development. Direct rule lasted between 2009 and 2012 following the UK's partial suspension of TCI's Constitution. This followed the findings of systemic corruption by the Commission of Inquiry 2008–9, which examined possible corruption or other serious dishonesty in relation to elected members of the Legislature in recent years, led by the Rt. Hon. Sir Robin Auld (the Auld Commission). Despite Tauwhare instigating the Inquiry, his confidence perhaps resided in a belief emanating from his experience of the resilience of the TCI people.

The islands are no stranger to intervention from the UK, nor alien to problems relating to economic crime and unaccountability. Since 1976, there have been instances of corruption and other misconduct levelled against three Premiers or Chief Ministers. In 1985, Chief Minister Norman Sanders was sentenced to 8 years in US prison for offences relating to conspiracy to traffic narcotics into the US. In 1986, a Commission of Inquiry led by Mr Louis Blom-Cooper QC (Blom-Cooper Inquiry) found Chief Minister Nathaniel Francis to be guilty of unconstitutional behaviour and ministerial malpractices (Blom-Cooper Report, 109). Finally, in 2008–9, a further Commission of Inquiry led by Sir Robin Auld (Auld Commission) recommended a criminal investigation into Premier Michael Misick who was, following his resignation and period of direct rule ensuing in TCI, arrested in Brazil and returned to TCI to be charged with offences relating to money laundering and bribery. His trial is ongoing.

These circumstances demonstrate that key constituent elements of developed society such as the rule of law, integrity in public life, due process and accountability have been lacking in TCI at the highest levels. Two periods of direct rule in a relatively short time span of 30 years, whereby TCI effectively 'lost' its sovereignty, have impacted upon TCI's development and its relationship with the UK. In this chapter, TCI's levels of compliance with international standards to combat economic crime and suspect wealth will be examined, set against this important contextual backdrop. Reforms of the past decade are of particular relevance in assessing TCI's progress.

While TCI is relatively young in developmental terms, it has a rich history in its pre-colonial context and in its modern status of recent years as a fast-growing Caribbean tourism destination (Caribbean Tourism Organisation 2016). Its original inhabitants were Taino (later known as Lucayan Indians) who resided there for nearly 700 years. Their legacy remains through industries like seafaring, fishing and farming. In the early 16th century, Bermudians arrived and engaged in salt-raking to take salt back to Bermuda. Britain lay claim to TCI in 1764 and it was placed under the jurisdiction of the Bahamas by the UK. In 1848, the islands were separated and TCI was self-governing for a quarter of a century in a period known as the 'Presidency era'. TCI was later annexed to Jamaica due, in part, to its unviability and unsustainability vis-à-vis taxation to offset debt. It was annexed until 1962 when Jamaica obtained independence from British colonial jurisdiction. TCI returned to Bahamian jurisdiction until the Bahamas became independent in 1973. Consequently, TCI installed its first Governor. Its constitution was enacted in 1976 along with an election, following which the first ministerial-style government was elected in the islands.

TCI has had two periods of direct rule imposed by the UK. On 24 July 1986, the UK government, led by Prime Minister Margaret Thatcher, dissolved TCI's government and imposed direct rule following the 1986 Blom-Cooper Commission of Inquiry, which lasted until 8 March 1988. The second period followed the 2008–9 Auld Commission of Inquiry and lasted from 16 August 2009 until 13 November 2012, when it was brought to an end following a General Election and enactment of a revised constitution.

TCI is a self-governing Overseas Territory and parliamentary dependency under constitutional monarchy. Its population is 34,900. The Governor, presently H.E. Nigel Dakin, appoints a Deputy Governor responsible for the Public Service, and a Premier capable of commanding a Parliamentary majority. TCI's Assembly consists of 19 members, 15 of whom are elected, 2 are nominated by both political parties, and 2 are appointed by the Governor. The two parties are the People's Democratic Movement (PDM) and the Progressive National Party (PNP). The PNP are in government and Hon. Washington Misick is TCI's Premier. The legislature is tasked with making laws for the peace, order and good governance of the island. TCI's political framework largely mirrors Westminster's. Its community is well engaged in participatory democracy and, despite a small electorate as only 'Belongers' aged over 18 can vote, there was a turnout of 80.41% in the 2016 election (TCI Election Centre 2016). Belonger status in TCI is conferred as of right (e.g. birth) or by way of grant (e.g. long residence or special service).

TCI's legal system is based on common law. Intervention by the UK via Orders in Council is provided for in legislation, which is a highly controversial and complex area of law and international relations. This function was also emphasised in the 2012 White Paper on the Overseas Territories. This power is particularly acute in the context of TCI. While an interventionist tool might conjure up imagery of colonialism, successful attempts to legislate on behalf of the Overseas Territories were seen in 2017–18 in compelling them to create public beneficial ownership registers under section 51, SAMLA. Some scholars, such as Sharman (2006, 18), have argued that for fiscal issues this power would not be used by the UK. While the UK Parliament had previously opposed this, due to the constitutional and political tensions which would arise, it manifested in the form of a legislative ultimatum which undermines convention. The most impactful UK intervention in TCI was direct rule between 2009 and 2012 (House of Commons Library 2012, 6). The Auld Commission concluded that TCI was in "dire constitutional, political and economic straits". After a period which some defined as a foreign invasion (Caribbean Insight 2009), both will and high-level commitments on the part of the islanders were necessary to implement progressive controls.

5.2 Economy and development as a financial centre

TCI is geographically well-situated, being 48 km south of the Bahamas and 925 km east-southeast of Miami. This has enabled TCI to develop a major tourism industry. With a GDP per capita of $27,877, TCI is considered 'developed'. TCI's economy has seen periods of substantial economic growth, such as real GDP growth of 11.4% in 2005, 17.9% in 2006 and 8.3% in 2008 (TCI Statistics Department 2018). It suffered a significant crash in 2009 where GDP decreased by 19.6%, partly due to the global financial crisis but doubtless exacerbated by the constitutional crisis following the Auld Report. Its tourism industry has sustained increasing momentum since the 1980s, partly attributed to the islands' strategy of focusing on wealth tourism. It received 1.3 million visitors in 2016, and a cruise liner port opened in 2007 (TCI Tourist Board 2016). TCI has among the highest visitor-spending per capita in the region. Other areas include fishing and agriculture, employing 20% of its labour force.

Given its natural beauty and corresponding luxury tourism sector, TCI has developed a significant property industry. However, through this sector it remains vulnerable to economic crime, and it was identified as a money laundering risk in FATF's 2008 report and subsequent NRA (CFATF 2008, 150). Within this, the construction industry presents risk to the islands' natural beauty, biodiversity and heritage given that construction and development decisions often impact coastal land. This area presents challenges as to the receiving of suspect wealth, on the basis that lack of controls can facilitate both domestic and overseas bribery (e.g. from a non-Belonger) as well as facilitating an investment vehicle into the jurisdiction to dispose of foreign suspect wealth.

Like many other small island jurisdictions, TCI has an indirect taxation model. While non-collection of traditional taxes classifies TCI as a tax-neutral jurisdiction, it collects public revenue through various sources including customs excise duty on imported goods and stamp duties in respect of real estate sales. TCI collects stamp duty on consideration passing on the transfer of shares of companies holding local land, and there is a nominal duty on the transfer of a domestic company's shares.

In 1981, TCI entered the offshore financial services market. This represented a growing trend in the Caribbean, for example Antigua and Barbuda did the same in 1982 and BVI in 1984. TCI's financial services sector contributed to circa 17% of GDP in 2019. This sector has traditionally focused on international investment through property and construction. TCI provides many typical offshore financial services. Its regulated financial activities are overseen by the FSC under the FSC Ordinance 2001. Regulated activities in the jurisdiction include company incorporation, banking, partnerships, insurance, money transmitters, trust companies, investments and management. There are many reasons why TCI has remained competitive amongst its fellow offshore centres in the Caribbean, including time zone, legal system, and connectivity to the US. As Moore (1997) observes, TCI's legal system is far more favourable than the civil law deriving from Napoleonic times, as is the case in Aruba or the Netherlands Antilles. While its offerings are typical of offshore centres, TCI's are not as sophisticated or innovative as some of its competitors. This lends support to the argument made in this work for viewing these jurisdictions as distinct islands, rather than as a collective. For example, while trust services are available, special and complex trusts are more commonly seen in jurisdictions like BVI.

The make-up of TCI's licensed and regulated financial sector can be summarised as 7 banks, 36 CSPs, 3 money service businesses, 69 captive insurance companies, 7,504 producer-owned reinsurance companies, 7 investment companies, 11 mutual fund administrators and 9 trust companies. TCI's business sector is supported by 43 law firms and 23 accountancies. Its companies and incorporation sector is significant, with 16,875 companies and 74 partnerships (CFATF 2020, 27; 133).

5.3 Domestic corruption and impact on development

TCI's response to economic crime and suspect wealth, and in particular bribery, has to be set against a history whereby corruption has significantly impacted its development. While not implicated in the most recent ICIJ offshore data leak, corruption scandals implicating TCI have made international headlines, led to Commissions of Inquiry, and twice caused suspension of TCI's Constitution. Other than the general stigma attached to tax havens, which is something TCI also contends with, these instances have caused harm in different ways.

The findings of the Auld Commission indicate the ease with which domestic corruption undermined institutional processes, and how the local construction market facilitated substantial investment from overseas. When controls are lacking in a jurisdiction, this type of environment makes it particularly attractive to foreign individuals and entities with nefarious intent. Evidence from the Auld Commission indicated that in TCI this facilitated an ability to corruptly profit from large Crown land deals. The mere presence of suspicion or the perception that the jurisdiction is non-compliant with international standards renders negative impact.

On 13 March 1985, the *New York Times* reported 'In Old Pirate Haunt, Daunting News of Drug Trade'. This was in reference to accusations made against TCI's Chief Minister, Norman Saunders, and other officials of conspiracy and bribery relating to narcotics trafficking. Saunders allegedly received bribes to permit smugglers to refuel aircrafts at his airport station (Griffith 1993, 33). He was arrested in Miami with Development Minister Stafford Missick and a Canadian businessman. The US charged them with conspiracy offences including conspiring to violate the US Travel Act 1961 and import narcotics. Video evidence emerged showing Saunders allegedly accepting $20,000 from an undercover agent to protect drug shipments passing through TCI to the US. All 3 were convicted of conspiracy offences. This history is important, as it illustrates problems at earlier stages of TCI's development set against developing increased autonomy.

In 1986, Governor Christopher Turner appointed British barrister Louis-Blom Cooper QC as Commissioner of Inquiry into allegations of arson of a public building, corruption and other matters. The Commission found the Chief Minister, Health and Education Minister and Minister of Works guilty of unconstitutional behaviour, ministerial malpractice and "unfitted to carry out ministerial responsibilities" (Blom-Cooper Report, 107). It recommended suspending the 1976 Constitution and implementing direct rule, which lasted between 1986 and 1988, where governance rested with the Governor and an Advisory Executive Council.

Blom-Cooper's findings are historically relevant, given their severity and the striking similarities to the Auld Commission's findings in 2009. The 1986 Report, proximate to the aforementioned conviction of Saunders, warned: "The time has come to disperse the cloud that hangs like a brooding omnipresence in a Grand Turkan sky". Blom-Cooper noted that the November 1985 by-election saw three new members elected who were "closely associated with the previous Chief Minister . . . and his two colleagues found guilty of serious drug offences". He suggested that this rendered a sense of hopelessness for change with elections. He averred that significant instances of corruption are prefaced by a failed state of public affairs, administration and controls. He called it a "disease in the body politic" which seemed endemic and ineradicable in TCI, at least for that generation. As well as the Chief Minister's conviction, Blom-Cooper's Report paints a bleak picture of governance in the mid 1980s. Of particular note, the Report suggested:

> making allowance for the general lack – (a) of educational attainment of many Islanders; (b) of specialist training in public administration resulting in a low general standard of local civil servants; and (c) of political sophistication among Ministers . . . the time has come to disperse [of] persistent unconstitutional behaviour [and] maladministration . . . at every level of government.

During the 1990s, Governor Martin Bourke stated that the islands were at a peak of narcotics trafficking, its police force was corrupt and crime was increasing

(*Independent* 14.4.1996). A well-known figure in TCI, Alden 'Smokey' Smith, who had been imprisoned in the US for his involvement in the 1985 Saunders affair, was acquitted in the 1990s on drug trafficking charges, to cheering crowds. Many islanders compared this to the acquittal of O. J. Simpson.

The Caribbean became synonymous in the field of transnational organised crime with drugs and its proceeds in the 1970s and 1980s (Sharman 2006). There has been considerable scholarly work on the impact of narcotics trafficking on the Caribbean. A similar example to Chief Minister Saunders' conviction were the accusations levelled at Bahamian Prime Minister Lynden Pindling in the late 1980s for allegedly accepting protection money to facilitate narcotics trafficking through the Bahamas (*New York Times* 14.1.1988; 29.4.1988).

In TCI, Blom-Cooper (1986, 22) observed that up to 1985, drug trafficking was an alternative source of income: "Several good quality airports and their position midway between Florida and the drug producing countries of South America, earned a substantial income as an entrepot and made, albeit illegally, a significant contribution to the economy". Indeed, it was the attack against narcotics trafficking in the War on Drugs which provided the architecture for modern AML policies.

There is consensus that drug trafficking and associated forms of crime like corruption have ravaging effects on a country's economic, social and institutional development, not least given that it is commonly understood that drug use among local populations increases with the presence of a trafficking industry. Secondary problems include prostitution, gangs and violent crime. However, similar to the 'corruption can facilitate development' argument, the fact remains that the drugs industry earned sizeable income for TCI. This was not simply for the elites, as Blom-Cooper noted that evidence suggests that profits filtered down amongst the people. He posited that this might account for the equivocal response of Belongers to Saunders' conviction. After his release, he returned to politics serving in the Legislative Council. By one account, he was as popular as ever (*Independent* 14.4.1996).

Direct rule was imposed again on TCI in 2009. The former Premier, Michael Misick, is presently on trial for corruption and money laundering offences, along with other former Ministers. Misick was very much the focus of the Commission which found that he had failed repeatedly throughout to make full and accurate declarations of his interests as required under the Registration of Interests Ordinance 1993 (Auld Report, 244). There was evidence that he abused his position by personally using PNP funds, hence the Commission's recommended criminal investigation. Allegations related to disproportionate political donations and finder's fees in respect of selling Crown land for development, and contracts for his then wife, who is a famous actress, to promote TCI. What is particularly interesting about Misick's case is his popularity in TCI – perhaps comparable to that of Saunders in the 1980s. Many perceive that he largely increased TCI's development (*TCI The Sun* 15.1.2014). Despite indictments, and his assets being subject to restraint under the Proceeds of Crime Ordinance, Misick remains an extremely popular figure, evidenced by thousands of guests and celebrities attending his birthday. As such, in *Misick and Others (Appellants) v The Queen (Respondent) (TCI)* [2015], at 55–56, it was argued that he could not have a fair trial. In earlier submissions to the Auld Commission, Misick's barrister had argued that the adverse media and contamination of any potential jurors by rumour, or public disclosure of inadmissible evidence meant that there was no prospect Misick could receive a fair trial. This was clearly convincing as the Commissioner, Sir Robin, recommended a judge-alone trial. Interestingly, this concern also featured in the Blom-Cooper Report (1986, 97): "With such a manifest commitment to party politics [in TCI] it would be impossible to achieve impartiality in a jury". As perhaps with any small community, there is a familiar nature in TCI. An example being the Premier, Washington Misick MP, who is Michael Misick's brother. Small parishes in the islands consist of a few hundred people who constantly interact. Misick's continued integration is evidenced by his 2016 return to politics standing as an independent candidate in the election (as did another defendant).

Under Misick's premiership, *prima facie* TCI's economy grew significantly through property development, tourism and land sales. This had an impactful effect on tourism and investment as well as other areas of the islands' development, such as education, land ownership and healthcare. However, the reality is that this growth was underpinned by alleged misconduct and mounting debt. While denying corruption, Misick admitted that there were times he had been at fault, such as not disclosing interests to the Registrar, and he argued that this was part of a practice of neglect and carelessness which resided in TCI for years, while asserting the value of having good relations with property developers (House of Commons Library 2012, 5).

The question arises: Are certain types of behaviour normative in TCI? The Auld Commission identified that bribing of voters was a major concern, and despite a tiny electorate (7,000 people at the time, due to the franchise being limited to Belongers) there was a disproportionate level of funding in the party system. Some $4 million went in and out of the PNP's bank account in the 6 months preceding the 2007 election (Auld Report, 66). Some further selected findings from the Auld Commission include that there was a possibility of corruption regarding the chain of events leading to the disposal of an area of Crown land at Joe Grant Cay, sold to a consortium at a price significantly below market value. The Commission further averred that a payment of $150,000 made by a developer of a local resort to a Minister the day before the election resulted in said Minister paying it into the business account of his company, rather than used as a campaign donation. The Commission held that a Minister had ignored or created conflicts of interest by dishonestly transacting to offering grants of Crown land to himself or companies he substantially owned or controlled (Auld Report, 247–257).

Worryingly, there are parallels between the Blom-Cooper and Auld reports, despite over two decades separating them. As is evidenced by the various findings, some of which are alluded to above, there has been a trend with the types of misconduct found by both Commissions. Sir Robin Auld noted at 22:

"[Blom-Cooper's] general conclusion on those matters suggest that little has changed over the last 20 or so years leading to this Inquiry, except as to the possible range and scale of venality in public life". At least, for a micro-population jurisdiction with a relatively high GDP, it is quite understandable that the presence of new luxury resorts creating jobs and attracting international visitors would be perceived positively. This appears to be the case in the fallout from Misick's premiership, where there was a continuous GDP growth. However, if corruption is normative in a society, then long-term damage is caused to social, legal and political institutions. This is essentially the cost. The Commission's findings pointed to instances of corruption in office, conflicts of interest going unchecked, non-transparent processes such as selling Crown land, vested interests influencing decisions, inadequate rules governing donations, donations resembling bribes, inadequate disclosure of interests or payments, use of outdated land valuations and land-flipping. Notwithstanding the difficulties in measuring the social harm or tangible costs of all this, the reality is that the growth was built on a credit bubble which could not sustain wider financial pressures in the late 2000s. While growth at the expense of standards in public life may provide an interim economic boost, it can significantly damage the prospects of institutional development. The loss of sovereignty and reduced autonomy clearly evidences this. For example, if Crown land is sold based on outdated valuations, then despite the new luxury resort being built and all the benefits which come with that, the country has lost revenue from open bidding at market value. Or, if Belongerships are given to developers, this could erode land-price protection for native islanders. If donations can buy influence or subvert competition and procedures, this impacts institutional process and also facilitates the transiting of suspect wealth if the funds are of dubious origin. In *R v Misick and Others*, evidence was adduced that under Misick's premiership, TCI lost $42 million in 1 year due to exemptions and concessions made under development orders (*TCI Weekly News* 25.1.2016). Set against a context of land-flipping and allegations of bribery in development projects, this shows how public money can be lost due to unaccountability in decision-making.

Further, granting Belongerships to individuals under discretionary powers was one of the areas of risk and abuse found by the Auld Commission. Belonger empowerment means that they can purchase land at heavily discounted rates, compared to non-Belonger foreign purchasers. Attaching these premiums is a significant means of revenue-building. This, together with allocation of contracts to those with recently granted Belonger status meant that in TCI's case, foreign investors were able to capitalise on this discretionary system and domestic unaccountability to facilitate lucrative development in TCI.

5.3.1 Trial of former ministers

The ongoing trial of former Premier Misick and other former politicians raises important questions. So far, this book has pointed out that a jurisdiction's ability to protect itself from receiving suspect and illicit wealth depends greatly on the ability of domestic laws, effectiveness of controls, and the will for enforcement. The trial is a significant, ongoing example of criminal prosecutions relating to corruption and money laundering arising from the Auld Commission. A total of 13 people were charged with 11 individuals facing trial, including four former Cabinet members. Five of the 11 defendants are PEPs (CFATF 2020, 75).

The trial involves offences relating to infractions of domestic TCI criminal laws. The catalogue of offences includes conspiracy to receive bribes, conspiracy to defraud, conspiracy to disguise criminal proceeds and to conceal or transfer the proceeds of crime, and entering into or becoming concerned with a money laundering arrangement, conspiracy to pervert the course of justice, and other related money laundering offences. The Auld Commission pointed out that if domestic standards are non-existent, then this serves as a target for abuse to facilitate international financial crime.

There is no scholarly literature considering the critical procedural issues raised by this trial, with the only information available being media reports and government updates, as well as those reported documents emanating from related proceedings. As Hughes LJ, at 19, commented in *Misick and Others v The Queen* [2015]: "[These are] very exceptional trials for the very small courts system of TCI. . . . A special courthouse has had to be constructed on one of the principal islands to hear them. Almost all the leading advocates appear to have been recruited from outside the Islands".

There are steadfast reservations about the trial (*TCI The Sun* 1.6.2018a). There also exists a perception that Misick's conduct did not amount to corruption because laws were vague and did not specify methods by which politicians could receive donations. At the procedural level, Misick and others have made applications about not receiving a fair trial and have averred that diplomatic solutions should be sought after the lengthy timeframe and disproportionate expense. The right to a fair trial is enshrined in numerous sources of domestic and international law, including Article 10 Universal Declaration of Human Rights and Article 6(1) European Convention on Human Rights (ECHR). Section 6(1) TCI Constitution mirrors the ECHR and states that defendants must be "afforded a fair hearing within a reasonable time by an independent and impartial court". During direct rule, the 2006 Constitution was suspended and, as such, the unqualified right to jury trial in TCI was suspended. Today, while trial by jury is conventional, if the interests of justice require, then a judge-alone trial may be ordered. In the 2015 UKPC appeal, the defendants argued that the trial undermined their constitutional right to a fair trial on the basis that the judge had insufficient security of tenure to maintain independence, and that in deciding to have a judge-alone trial he had failed to ascertain whether there was no reasonable doubt that the interests of justice required a trial without a jury.

The 2015 UKPC appeal emphasised that the trial issues were complex and that a jury would have had to have been selected form the 6,000 Belongers. Hughes LJ, at 55, noted that in modern times the cardinal virtue and safeguard of trial by jury is the ability to "produce fact finders who are entirely unconnected with the events under examination, and wholly disinterested". A jury in this case would have been quite the opposite as they would invariably have had some connection to events or defendants. With the change in law to give the judge power to determine trial by jury or judge, it appeared inappropriate to proceed on the basis of a jury trial given these procedural concerns. It could have resulted in a jury composed of stoic critics or ardent supporters of the defendants. Sections of the local population strongly resented direct rule, which is unsurprising given TCI's complex history.

After a 7-year investigation following the Commission, the trial commenced in 2015. The prosecution took 3 months to call its first witness and its case ended in late 2018. This was followed by unsuccessful no-case submissions from the defence. Several significant delays have occurred, and other concerns over poor management include the prosecution overburdening the case with defendants and counts that were not sufficiently narrowed. One defence barrister stated: "No case should last three to four years [and no one] could possibly be expected to remember the witnesses . . . the evidence given (and) whether it was immediately believable or whether there was a question mark over it" (*TCI Weekly News* 21.1.2019). They averred that none of the lawyers or judge would have accepted the brief had they thought it would last this long. As at 2021, the trial was still ongoing, yet was stopped following the trial judge, Mr Justice Harrison, passing away. At the time of writing, prosecutors have brought fresh charges for a new trial to commence.

While the trial exhibits a sense of accountability, or at the least in line with the jurisprudential doctrine that justice must also be seen to be done, the trial demonstrates concerns about TCI's ability to administer justice in respect of these past instances of corruption and money laundering. Notwithstanding disruption and suffering from the 2017 hurricanes and Covid-19, the trial was in its fifth year. It could be argued that administering justice in respect of those high-profile individuals charged is a necessary element of TCI's broader approach in strengthening domestic law and financial crime enforcement. The act of prosecuting high-profile individuals is well-established as demonstrating equality before the law. Whether this is consistent with due process in respect of these defendants, however, is a matter of contention.

The legal principle that justice delayed is justice denied is certainly apt in this case. Had the case concluded in 2021, then its disposal would have taken 6 years. In the context of a potential new trial, there are very real concerns about this from a constitutional perspective, so it will be interesting to monitor this and whether any verdicts, if they arrive, will be appealed.

5.3.2 Civil recovery

The trial arguably evidences a renewed sense of accountability in TCI and demonstrates that domestic controls are being utilised. This contrasts with the former perception that the lack of controls enabled its systems to be abused. Crown land has been a politicised asset in TCI for years and its most precious sustainable development resource. Decisions pertaining to its disposal and development rest with Ministers, which has presented evident procedural risks. It is incumbent on those in office to raise awareness about the rarity of Crown land which, in Providenciales, accounts for a quarter of all land including land occupied by government offices, parks, housing and hotels. The Auld Commission highlighted that Crown land was viewed as dispensable and incorrectly valued. It found a culture which empowered the engagement in 'land-flipping' (land purchased at under-market value and immediately sold for substantial profits) and returning to Ministers to purchase more.

The Auld Commission recommended establishing a recovery unit. While controversial, this has represented the most successful legal proceedings brought to date. In 2013, the UK government reported that 2,500 acres of Crown land had been recovered (Governor's Office 23.5.2013), later rising to $23.3 million and 3,100 acres. There have been more than 70 cases involving recovery of land, cash and damages, and it has been considered one of the world's largest asset recovery programmes. The recovery team, overseen by the Attorney General's Chambers and lawyers from London, emphasised that while cash represents a more pressing concern due to current domestic economic hardship, the recovery of improperly sold land represents the future prosperity of the islands. Examples of successful cases under this include a judgment for $1.35 million in damages against an individual who had acquired Crown land for $50,000 and sold it immediately for $1.35 million. It was found that a former Minister breached fiduciary duties by directing use of an outdated valuation.

In the context of the civil recovery efforts, money is returned to TCI's government. Civil mechanisms can be utilised either in conjunction with criminal procedures, or when they are unlikely to yield results (Does de Willebois and Brun 2013, 615). Indeed, the UK itself has strengthened its civil recovery toolkit with the adoption of various mechanisms under the Criminal Finances Act 2017, such as unexplained wealth orders.

As per the French maxim "*Là où il y a de la terre, il y a la guerre*" (where there's land, there's war), the civil recovery proceedings are costly particularly when recovering sizeable land. Defendants in civil and criminal proceedings have made full use of TCI's highest appeals court, the UKPC. Government expenditure in 2013–14 for the SIPT was $4.66 million and $6 million for civil recovery. In evidence to the FAC Inquiry 2018, Premier Robinson averred that the criminal trial cost was approaching $100 million (FAC 2018b, Q165). While the criminal prosecution is ongoing, and notwithstanding its cost, the civil recovery team has achieved successes. When examining tangible outcomes of the Auld Commission, civil recovery is fulfilling various objectives in the context of recovering important development resources.

5.4 Implication in international economic crime cases

Having discussed the ongoing impact that domestic allegations and findings of economic misconduct have had on TCI's development, and prior to examining its contemporary legal and regulatory response to the same, this section briefly considers the extent to which TCI's own offshore financial sector has been implicated internationally in financial crime and other misconduct. As the above examples demonstrate, controls have been lacking in TCI in its history, which presents significant risk of abuse.

A good starting point is to consider the impact of the Panama and Paradise papers. Revelations from these publications paint a negative picture of the specifically named offshore jurisdictions. However, TCI was not mentioned in the Panama papers as being a jurisdiction in which any legal entities named were registered, although it was implicated in the Paradise papers with 26 legal entities named as being registered in TCI. Of those 26, only 2 were active, with the other entities listed as closed at the time of publication (*ICIJ* Offshore Leaks database, Paradise papers). In some cases, entities mentioned had closed back in the 1990s. In both publications, TCI is mentioned in other contexts including as registered addresses for intermediaries. Therefore, in circumstances whereby information was published relating to some 500,000 legal entities, only 2 active TCI-registered entities were named. Despite the almost exclusively adverse tone of media and government coverage of the publications, the data specific to TCI does not tell us anything other than demonstrating a few entities were incorporated there or have existed there, and that several dozen intermediaries are present. In real terms, the evidence shows that TCI provides offshore financial services, which is not in dispute. There is certainly a *prime facie* case that TCI is not mentioned to any statistically significant degree, relative to the 500,000 named entities. Given that the data omits any contextual information on the entities' commercial activities or purpose, information relating to TCI is somewhat *de minimis*. Further, TCI has not been implicated in any civil or criminal enforcement actions stemming directly from information disclosed in the data breaches at the time of writing.

The information from these publications does not exculpate TCI, nor does it demonstrate anything sinister – if it is accepted that offshore entities are, in and of themselves, not sinister. As the recent English judgment in *NCA v Baker and ors* [*2020*], the High Court re-emphasised that offshore structures in and of themselves are not enough to give rise to suspicion of wrongdoing. Of course, it is not to say TCI offshore entities are not susceptible to abuse. The publications, which targeted major offshore law firms – which are engaged in activities relating to corporate services on behalf of clients – effectively exposed only 2 active companies registered in TCI and 6 intermediaries linked to TCI. While the ICIJ stresses that its aim is not to imply criminality of those entities or persons named in its databases, the question of proportionality is raised in the context of the UK's decision to impose open registers on all Overseas Territories, due to a perceived problem exposed by the publications.

Looking beyond the data breaches, TCI's offshore financial sector has been implicated in various cases internationally as facilitating financial crime and being used to conceal its proceeds. Evidence from case law, particularly from the US, demonstrates this. In *United States v Bognaes* (2016),[1] a lawyer was convicted for

1 See also US Department of Justice, Press Release (12 April 2016) 'Fugitive Convicted of Federal Tax Crimes Arrested by the US Marshals Service in Arizona After More Than 14 Years on the Run'.

offences relating to tax evasion and fraud for setting up business organisations for his clients to evade tax. He was said to have instructed them on how to conduct transactions via nominees and on wiring funds offshore to TCI. Similarly, in *United States v Meyer* (2016),[2] a financial services executive pleaded guilty to obstruction of justice by concealing assets subject to a freezing order and seizure warrant. On learning of an SEC investigation, he was said to have concealed $4.8 million in assets via a series of offshore accounts and a shell company. Assets included a luxury property in TCI as well as home renovations, deemed to be criminal proceeds and thus forfeited.

In *United States v Hall* (2013),[3] an insurance salesman pleaded guilty to operating a sham investment scheme including money laundering and wire fraud. The scheme lasted a decade in which 50 investors were defrauded of $4 million. It was facilitated by a shell company in TCI, with its only activity being a postbox, of which he was listed as a director. In *United States v Lopez* (2013),[4] a company executive was charged with securities fraud relating to operating TCI-registered shell companies for the purpose of issuing stock to settle debts and creating purposefully defaulted loan agreements with the shell companies to then instigate sham lawsuits. In *United States v Chapman* (2013),[5] which involved a $270 million fraudulent investment scheme, court documents show that the perpetrator failed to repay clients' money and spent it on a lavish lifestyle, including purchasing TCI properties. The case of *United States v Mebiame* (2016) involved a joint venture between a wholly owned subsidiary of a US hedge fund and a TCI subsidiary company concerned in acquiring African mining rights and uranium concessions in Chad, Niger and Guinea. The defendant was a consultant acting for the joint venture and was alleged to have bribed African officials to obtain the rights. In violation of the FCPA, Mebiame was said to have conspired in the US to bribe, and following a guilty plea was sentenced to 24 months' imprisonment. The TCI entity and owner were known to US authorities,[6] and named as a co-conspirator in the indictment. At all material times, Mebiame was acting as a consultant to the entities, and the conduct he was charged with related to conspiracy while in the US. In respect of TCI, some important points include the fact that Mebiame was not a director, controller or owner of the TCI entity. As such, and like any other company, there would be no requirement to register him in terms of company information. In other words, the TCI company's register

2 See also US Department of Justice, Press Release (24 March 2016) 'Financial Services Company Executive Pleads Guilty to Obstruction of Justice'.

3 See also US Department of Justice, Press Release (27 December 2013) 'Jacksonville Man Pleads Guilty to Operating a Fraudulent Investment Scheme'.

4 See also US Department of Justice, Press Release (22 January 2013) 'Former CEO-President of San Diego–Based Company Charged in $28 Million Stock Fraud Mark Lopez Also Accused of Obstructing SEC Investigation by Hiding Emails in Manila Folders Marked "Files Deleted" and "Not Released to SEC Subpoena (Delete)"'.

5 See also US Department of Justice, Press Release (6 December 2013) 'Sterling Man Sentenced for Conducting $270 Million Investment Fraud Scheme'.

6 Charges, [1].

would not be aware of his involvement with the company. However, had he been the company's director, his personal circumstances would have likely been red-flagged given his status as a PEP, being the son of the former Gabon Prime Minister. Many of these case examples show that criminality abroad has not only been facilitated by use of TCI companies and services to conceal wrongdoing or provide enrichment, but also that TCI's property market represents a risk of being used to launder the proceeds of crime.

In Transparency International's (2018) report *The Cost of Secrecy*, the Mebiame case was used as evidence to suggest that if TCI's beneficial ownership register was 'open', then such matters would be easily detectable. They aver that TCI companies are highly secretive with no information published about their owners or directors. They state that TCI's "aggressive secrecy may indicate why more corruption schemes involving [TCI] companies have not come to light" (Transparency International 2018, 3). However, as mentioned, even if the register is public, this information may have been lacking as he was only, as the Justice Department put it, a "fixer" for the US-based and TCI-based entities (US Department of Justice 31.5.2017). While the Mebiame case clearly relates more to the conduct of a Gabonese-French dual citizen furthering his scheme on US soil, another important point relates to the co-conspirator named in the court documents as the controller of the TCI entity for whom Mebiame worked in acquiring the rights via bribes. While there is limited information about the co-conspirator, it is concerning that the controller of a TCI company was named with respect to bribes paid to African officials. It raises questions as to whether this fell within the purview of TCI's Bribery Ordinance.

5.5 Analysis of TCI's legal and regulatory response to economic crime and suspect wealth

5.5.1 Anti-bribery

So far, this chapter has demonstrated that corruption and unaccountability has been a significant problem in TCI's history. Due to the Overseas Territories not being signatories to international treaties, UNCAC has not been extended, but many including TCI are actively seeking extension. TCI's Bribery Bill 2017 sought to reform TCI's anti-corruption legislation and provide a new scope of bribery offences to reflect corruption's global character. Section 4, Bribery Ordinance 2017 deals with the offence of bribing others, while section 5 deals with the offence of being bribed. It also makes it an offence to bribe foreign officials with extraterritoriality provisions, as well as creating the now-familiar failure to prevent bribery offence on the part of corporates as per section 10. The legislation gives guidance on this. It is fair to say that many of its aspects are based on the UK's Bribery Act and was implemented to better address the requirements of the OECD Anti-Bribery Convention. The reformed legislation in TCI brings the jurisdiction in line with international anti-corruption standards from a legislative standpoint. TCI's anti-corruption laws closely mirror key provisions of UNCAC;

for example, section 9 TCI Bribery Ordinance clearly complies with Article 16 of the Convention, which deals with bribing foreign officials. It shows that TCI recognises the importance of updated legislation, something still lacking in many offshore jurisdictions. Modern bribery laws are as much about common-sense standards for domestic businesses as for large multinational entities. It is therefore suitable for TCI, particularly in instilling a common-sense approach about the different risks that bribery can pose domestically and from abroad. With TCI's growing property and construction sectors, set against a backdrop of past corruption involving this market, properly defining bribery and making international investors aware that all-encompassing legislation exists relating to individuals and entities in TCI is useful.

Since 2012, there has been visible commitment from the political directory to ensure the strengthening of institutions and frameworks by reforming anti-corruption laws and instigating various related initiatives. Law reform takes up valuable space on legislative agendas, not to mention technical and financial resources. One example has been to strengthen the Integrity Commission's legislation established by the Integrity Commission Ordinance 2008 and enshrined in the constitution at section 102. Other statutory bodies and institutions protecting governance in TCI include the Director of Public Prosecutions, Human Rights Commission and Complaints Commissioner. Institutions like the Integrity Commission, Registrar of Interests and Supervisor of Electors are particularly important in the context of the Auld Commission's findings of electoral impropriety in terms of bribery, donations and non-declarations of interests.

The statutory responsibility of the Integrity Commission is to promote integrity, honesty and good faith in public life. It educates the public about integrity and maintains a Code of Conduct for Persons in Public Life (section 102(4) TCI Constitution). This was the first of its kind in the Caribbean and Overseas Territories. This recognises the important role that domestic institutions can play in tackling corruption, often seen in OECD countries with ethics checklists and associated initiatives (Mills 1998). The ethos of establishing a framework of good governance upon which integrity can be fostered in TCI is accompanied by the number of individuals in public life having to make declarations under the 2008 Ordinance increasing by 100% since 2010. The Code of Conduct was timely in the immediate aftermath of the 2012 election and reinstatement of self-rule. Complementing this, the Commission adopted the Seven Principles of Public Life developed in 1995 by the UK Committee on Standards in Public Life and included in the 2012 White Paper. These reinforce the principles of integrity, objectivity, selflessness, accountability, openness, honesty and leadership. Drawing upon experiences from Caribbean neighbours such as Trinidad and Tobago, the Commission also published a 'Guide to Identifying, Avoiding and Managing Conflict of Interest'. Following elections, the Commission reported robust implementation of the Political Activities (Amendment) Ordinance 2016. Further developments include establishing whistle-blower protection – a standard espoused by various international bodies (OECD 2016, 3). The Commission's Deputy Director noted that trust in small, close-knit communities is difficult to harness and that it is challenging to get individuals to understand that protection exists (Been 16.11.2016). Despite this, the regime is said to have increased the number of individuals bringing complaints about public corruption. Given that the Commission not only has regulatory and oversight responsibilities but also an investigative function, their employees swear an oath of secrecy due to the sensitive information they encounter. The doctrine of confidentiality is taken seriously in TCI. In 8 years of establishment, the Integrity Commission has had no leaks of confidential reported information, which helps engender respect for, and confidence in, this system.

The Auld Report further found deficiencies with the political process with donations being a significant concern. It alleged that developers, often international, were able to make disproportionate political donations which coincided with their bids for developments, sales of Crown land or planning applications being approved by the Cabinet. These findings were actioned by the Integrity Commission. In its 2016 post-election report, they found that the election saw no formal breaches of the Ordinance, and there was evidence to show remarkable improvement in the quality and regularity of statutory returns under the Political Activities Ordinance, particularly from the main parties.

The Integrity Commission's awareness-raising activities fulfil an important statutory function as part of TCI's anti-bribery framework. In the context of past events, it is crucial for TCI's long-term development that history does not repeat itself, nor that TCI identifies itself by its past in this respect, as labelling theory would suggest. A label is a creation of social reaction (Berk 2015, 150–154) and is a formation embedded in the concept of stigma. This is clearly seen with the 'tax haven' label fast displacing any positive perception about tax competition or offshore financial services.

Promoting integrity at the societal level is a purposeful strategy in protecting small jurisdictions from domestic and international corruption abuse. Recognising the importance of youth education, in fulfilment of its statutory education function, the Integrity Commission organises an annual integrity competition designed to engage students and educators in activities such as creative arts and debate on the subject of integrity. Promoting integrity at early educational stages demonstrates a recognition that corruption can be tackled through shifting mindsets. It also demonstrates multi-stakeholder appetite in the jurisdiction to foster principles that will augur well for future generations of leaders. At the Third High-School Debate in 2017, TCI's Youth Director emphasised the fact that people watch whether what we claim to believe on Sunday is put into practice on Monday.

In the science of education scholarship, there is consensus that in the early part of the 20th century, world events presented the opportunity to enhance basic values through education. As Brehony (2004, 740) notes, following World War II "the future of education was to foster international understanding, to develop a world consciousness and to give an introduction to the duties of world citizenship". This period saw Stalinism and Nazism, which made research into education from the 1940s onwards critical to eradicate such evils by strengthening values. In the context of promoting integrity to protect against economic crime, theories of public education which engage morality, spirituality and a basic values approach are purposive. Scholars like Jung (1957) have emphasised the utility of this, particularly following oppressive political and social instances of the past century.

Given the scourges of corruption that TCI has experienced, there is a moral imperative for prioritising this alongside high-end international commitments and implementing sophisticated bribery laws. Critics might argue that this type of activity is window dressing to present a *prima facie* bribery response. However, TCI's progress in this context, measured against its recent past, is significant and involves key legislative reform, domestic initiatives, a strengthened Integrity Commission and its activities, and a redressing of key social principles. While this has not yet translated to prosecutions and convictions, as experience from other jurisdictions suggests this takes time, certain things paint a positive picture such as the creation of a whistle-blower programme, or no leaks of confidential information from the Commission's work, and adoption of registers of interests.

5.5.2 *Anti–money laundering and counter-terrorism financing, including FATF compliance and national risk assessments*

TCI has been proactive in enhancing its AML framework. Its recent NRA acknowledged its vulnerability to money laundering, which has also been identified by various international assessors. Given its history, and evidenced by the current SIPT trial involving money laundering charges, it is not unreasonable to suggest that there was formerly an absence of recognition of this vulnerability. This is all the more serious when considering foreign criminal cases in which TCI entities have been implicated.

Prior to the CFATF 2008 MER, the Auld Report identified a serious crisis of ethics in public life. Given the allegations of officials' misconduct at the time of the MER, it is unsurprising that political will was lacking in acknowledging money laundering to be a problem, or that its financial system had, or could facilitate the transiting of suspect wealth at home or from overseas. This was set against a context of Crown land being sold to developers at an alarming rate, depriving the government of revenue and enriching those brokering the deals. For example, it was reported that a Slovakian developer, accused of engaging in corrupt dealings with the former Premier, had allegedly entered into a 99-year lease for 222 acres of land for $1 (*TCI Weekly News* 21.7.2012).

The suggestion that both controls and political will were weak is, in part, supported by CFATFs (2008) assessment that TCI's AML framework had significant problems. The MER identified serious AML deficiencies including being Non-Compliant with 15 recommendations such as Recommendation 5 (customer due diligence), Recommendation 6 (PEPs), and Recommendation 12 (DNFBPs); and Partially Compliant with 24 recommendations such as Recommendation 1 (offence of money laundering) and Recommendation 13 (suspicious transaction reporting). In consequence, TCI was placed under 'expedited follow-up' requiring regular reports to CFATF Plenaries. This status remained in 2010, with CFATF concluding that limited progress had been made and that most of the Core and Key Recommendations were outstanding. At the May 2011 4th Follow-Up, TCI was told that it had to report back by November 2011 for the 5th Follow-Up, given that 7 Core and Key Recommendations were either not met or only partially met.

In 2012, TCI graduated the expedited process based on progress made with implementing findings and addressing deficiencies. The 2012 Report recommended that TCI be allowed to exit the 3rd Round Follow-Up process. CFATF stated that it

> acknowledged the significant progress made by [TCI] in improving its AML/CFT regime and notes that [TCI] has established the legal and regulatory framework to meet its commitments in its agreed Action Plan regarding the strategic deficiencies that CFATF had identified.

It stated that TCI was therefore no longer subject to CFATF's International Cooperation Review Group's monitoring process. This demonstrates that since 2008 – where engagement with these initiatives was weak – TCI has worked under the supervision of the regional monitoring body which has enabled cooperation in identifying risks and vulnerabilities, bringing many aspects of its regime into compliance.

The 2016 13th Follow-Up report showed progress. Findings of note include increased focus on enacting, amending and implementing legislation to strengthen its AML framework, as well as the extent to which implementation of these have been successful.[7] The report noted that between 2009 and 2015, TCI commenced 25 money laundering investigations, with 11 resulting in prosecutions. At the time of that report, 2 had been completed, resulting in 1 conviction. Of the 25 instances of reported money laundering, 4 resulted in restraint orders for which civil recovery followed in 3 cases, 1 of which was a confiscation of $10 million. Despite the low conviction rate at the time, it represents quite a high number of prosecutions resulting from investigations.

The 4th Round MER process measures implementation of FATF standards, with emphasis on technical assistance and effectiveness. Virtually all jurisdictions engaged in the 4th Round face challenges with regards to the effectiveness component. TCI conducted and published its first NRA for money laundering and terrorism financing in preparation, thereby demonstrating a preparedness to engage in the process. TCI's AML Committee was established under section 115 Proceeds of Crime Ordinance 2007 and is chaired by the Attorney General. Its members include the Collector of Customs, FSC Managing Director, Commissioner of Police, FIA Director and DPP. Its functions include the development of a national action plan to assist in coordination between authorities and advising

7 See: CFATF (2016), [8] for a full list of legislation enacted in TCI since the 2008 MER.

on policy development and TCI's participation in international initiatives. It played a foundational role in TCI's NRA.

TCI has demonstrated regional leadership and advocacy with regards to AML compliance. Its wider involvement and engagement with CFATF buttresses this point. In 2015, TCI was unanimously elected CFATF Deputy Chair, and Chair for the 2016–17 term. Taken with the work of the National AML Committee and resulting NRA, this evidence demonstrates investment of time and resources in these issues and seeking to strengthen underlying awareness of them.

The FSC is tasked with oversight of the financial sector, offshore activity and AML/CFT. Its statutory function is enshrined under the Financial Services Commission Ordinance 2007 and includes supervising conduct of financial service business, administering the Ordinance and monitoring its effectiveness in providing for regulation to meet internationally accepted standards. It works to promulgate codes of conduct in financial services and promotes continuing development of professional standards. Further, it is the supervisory authority of DNFBPs and the non-profit sector, per section 3, Non-Profit Regulations 2014. The FSC was also instrumental in the production and administration of TCI's NRA. In its 2016–17 report, the FSC's training and supervision initiatives were outlined and include co-sponsoring a seminar on risk-based supervision with the Caribbean Group of Banking Supervisors from 11 jurisdictions, establishing partnerships with the international insurance sector, improving the Commission's strategy for regulating Producer Owned Reinsurance Companies and providing technical assistance on beneficial ownership registry by hosting and staffing it (TCI FSC 2016–2017, 10).

The NRA covered the period 2014–17. It was the first of its kind in TCI and analysed its regulatory and supervisory frameworks. The purpose was to identify money laundering and terrorism financing vulnerabilities and risks requiring greater resource allocation. It concluded that the risk of money laundering is 'Medium High' and terrorism financing 'Low'. The NRA noted important features of TCI, including its archipelagic structure making it susceptible to drug and cash smuggling via watercraft. This feature, which is of course shared by many similar island jurisdictions, has been identified by other overseas monitoring bodies such as the US Department of State, whose 2018 Narcotics Control Report and Assessment both point to successful counternarcotics initiatives TCI has engaged with, including counternarcotics cooperation efforts as part of Operation Bahamas-TCI – the joint narcotics interdiction operation. This puts context to the conclusion in the NRA that narcotics and cash smuggling from overseas is not prevalent today, despite formerly being so.

With regards to money laundering, the NRA indicates that financial flows in and out of TCI present money laundering opportunities. This is partly due to TCI's financial sector and offshore services market as well as luxury property – a common laundering vehicle (Rameur 2019). According to FIA data submitted for the NRA, TCI is particularly prone to capital emanating from North America and that predicates crimes include smuggling, tax evasion, drug trafficking and fraud. This point is further supported by aforementioned cases such as *United*

States v Hall (2013) and *United States v Chapman* (2013). Domestically, TCI's implementation of legislation and enforcement against money laundering is shown to be productive. For example, the SIPT was initiated to try 9 individuals including former government Ministers, for some 24 offences of money laundering (among other things).

The NRA considered the level of SARs to be low for TCI's risk profile, given its status as an offshore financial centre and its proximity to North America. If there is a perception that SARs are low or inconsistent with the known risks, then this could expose TCI to potential abuse through financial transactions. Data from the AML Committee showed that there were 177 SARs submitted between 2014 and 2017, with the vast majority from the financial sector. Of the total SARs received, 36% came from commercial banks.

TCI's real estate market continues to be an identified money laundering risk, doubtless exacerbated by its increasing luxury tourism market. Its real estate sector recovered strongly following the global recession. TCI has seen increasing international arrivals and stopovers, with 435,000 in 2016 (TCI Tourist Board 2016) and an increase in visitors from the UK (around 80% of total), Canada, Europe and the wider Caribbean. Property is expensive, with the average villa costing $1.37 million. One villa sold for $27.5 million in 2016. The NRA also found that risks in this sector include the self-employed nature of many agents and relative ease of obtaining an agent's licence. They assert that the difficulty of achieving AML/CFT compliance there is supported by low levels of SARs to the FIA, with only two disclosures across 2016–17. It also flagged inexperience of real estate practitioners and other DNFBPs in terms of AML/CFT regulation and an imperative to provide training through the regulated framework. The report recommends that entry requirements to operate as agents should be raised and concludes that this area of the sector be classified as a 'Medium High' risk.

Contextually, it is important to note that TCI's development has been enhanced by construction of luxury hotels and villages in Providenciales and Grace Bay. Consequently, there is significant capital flowing as a result of such activity. During and since the NRA, the FSC and FIA have conducted a series of awareness-raising and training activities involving public and private sector stakeholders such as the Bar Council, Real-Estate Association and DNFBPs. The FSC held 12 training events between 2011 and 2015 collaborating with professional associations, audit companies and in many instances receiving hundreds of participants (CFATF 2016, 9). It is clear that sensitization initiatives play a significant role and demonstrate proactivity on the part of these associations.

In terms of legislation, 15 pieces of relevant legislation have been enacted in recent years including the Bribery Ordinance, Trafficking in Persons Ordinance, Prevention of Terrorism Ordinance and the AML/PFT (Prevention of Terrorist Financing) Regulations and Code in 2011. Moreover, various initiatives and institutions have been established tasked with oversight compliance and education, and ensuring that legislation acts as a deterrent through enforcement. While it is evident that progress is being made, certain risk areas are concerning, not particularly with terrorism financing but with money laundering such as the numbers of SARs (TCI Government 2017).

In 2018, TCI projected growth in its construction sector on an unprecedented scale (*TCI The Sun* 1.6.2018b). Therefore, regulatory controls need to advance to ensure repetition of past impropriety in this sector. Importantly for TCI's development, it is about incentivising individuals and organisations to join the government in these undertakings. Of course, initiatives might be met with resistance particularly when it is visible that international standards are not always consistently applied in larger, developed countries. However, TCI has moved from a system of imposing rules on organisations to realising the benefit in working with DNFBPs and engaging in broader discussions with them, realising that they know their business best.

In 2020, CFATF published the latest MER for TCI. As well as technical compliance, this review also assessed effectiveness of TCI's AML/CFT framework and progress since the last review. Acknowledging its recent NRA, it concluded that TCI has a 'fair' understanding of money laundering risks. While praising the participatory collaboration between public and private sectors, the report also draws attention to TCI not fully addressing laundering risks relating to legal persons, DNFBPs and FIs. It also notes that TCI does not fully understand the terrorism financing risk. It also referenced the limited number of SARs being incommensurate with TCI's risk level and that some FIs seem unaware with the reporting obligations under the STR regime. It highlighted, however, TCI's willingness to implement risk-based measures and the fact that its competent authorities have engaged in significant restructuring to better tackle risks. It refers to significant changes made to the islands' AML/CFT framework and legislative reform for AML/CFT and other offences. While acknowledging proactivity of the FSC, the report highlights the infancy of its supervisory regime. It also highlights that registration requirements regarding DNFBPs present an ongoing risk, and that this sector having limited to no understanding of the risks, including customer DD, beneficial ownership and PEPs. The report also concludes that CSPs underestimate the risks to their sector. They note that the NRA completed by TCI provided a 'fair understanding' of risks, but that there were gaps in data so as to provide an incomplete picture of the islands' risks. For example, impact of international predicate crimes on the jurisdiction were not assessed, despite posing the greatest risk. They also raised concerns that the low terrorism financing rating was not based on consideration of all relevant data and also the vulnerability of other sectors to this risk. However, the report also acknowledges development of a National Strategy, which indicates commitment in addressing these risk areas and broad participation across industries.

TCI was assessed as 'low risk' in terms of terrorism financing, although of particular note was the report's finding that TCI's Customs were not gathering data on outgoing cash and not referring declarations to the intelligence agency. As such, undetected cash leaving the jurisdiction was flagged as a concern, as was the weak system for allowing proper identification and investigation of terrorism financing. CFATF suggested lack of training, awareness and guidance were challenges in this regard.

The review notes that prosecutions and convictions for laundering offences have occurred in the jurisdiction. Some shortcomings in the beneficial ownership regime are highlighted, such as updating information in a timely manner, although the report does highlight that enforcement authorities have access to basic information and that generally it is available in a timely manner, and it references the legislative requirements now existing in TCI. In terms of mutual legal assistance and international cooperation, the review demonstrates that TCI provides assistance on international matters in a timely process.

As to TCI's technical compliance, the 2020 MER noted that TCI has "progressively advanced the legislative framework to address gaps in the country's AML framework". They concluded that this level of legislative implementation has significantly enhanced TCI's technical compliance. The 2020 review assessed TCI as being Compliant with 15 Recommendations, Largely Compliant on 9, and Partially Compliant on 16. On effectiveness, TCI was assessed as having achieved a moderate level of effectiveness for FATF's Immediate Outcomes (IOs) 1, 2, 5, 6, 10 and 11. It concluded a low level of effectiveness for IOs 3, 4, 7, 8 and 9.

While TCI's AML framework has certainly been enhanced in terms of legislation and membership and engagement with regional monitoring groups, measuring the effectiveness of this internationally advocated framework is difficult. Many pieces of legislation have only been recently updated. There has been quite a high level of investigations (28) and prosecutions (11), including the ongoing SIPT trial, which is the most complex. Data presented in the 2020 MER shows that the majority of charges in respect of money laundering related to acquiring criminal property (CFATF 2020, 74). It is notable that prosecutions have only arisen against natural persons, rather than legal persons. There has only been 1 conviction of a money laundering offence in TCI which involved foreign predicate criminality. The 2020 MER demonstrated that the sanctions imposed by TCI courts for money laundering have ranged from a fine or a prison sentence not exceeding 1 year, despite money laundering carrying up to 14 years' imprisonment on the statute books. However, in the review period, there was 1 conviction which resulted in a sentence of between 5 and 7 years. The lack of more convictions may be explained by other factors such as the complexity of trials, evidential difficulties or jury selection challenges, or the fact that there are many prosecutions which are still outstanding. However, addressing deficient legislation which services many purposes such as the deterrent function of law, as well as the frameworks in place to investigate and bring prosecutions, represents progress.

In the 2016 MER, CFATF deemed that the deficiencies in TCI's AML framework were addressed adequately. In 2020, CFATF averred that "TCI has progressively advanced the legislative framework to address gaps in the country's AML/CFT framework" and that these have "significantly enhanced its technical compliance framework" (CFATF 2020, 9). In its review of effectiveness of the 11 IOs, CFATF concluded that TCI has achieved a "moderate level of effectiveness" for IOs 1, 2, 5, 6, 10 and 11 and a "low level of effectiveness" for IOs 3, 4, 7, 8 and 9. The report concluded that TCI's understanding of money laundering risks is fair although not fully understood in the context of terrorism financing.

It did find that TCI demonstrates a willingness to implement risk measures in accordance with those identified in the NRA, although prioritisation appears unaligned with the most significant threats identified. It was critical of financial sector–wide understanding of risks and that DNFBPs have limited to no understanding of the risks.

Given the early stages of reformed AML and anti-bribery legislation in TCI, it is impossible to truly measure the utility of those rules based on current statistics. However, the fact that prosecutions are relatively high compared to investigations, delivers at least the perception that law enforcement's response thereunder is positive rather than *de minimis*. In other words, for would-be perpetrators of financial crimes in the jurisdiction, there are suitable laws in place, enforcement frameworks being utilised, and prosecutorial willingness and appetite to bring charges. Indeed, CFATF acknowledged the positive role played by the DPP in ensuring parallel financial investigations are conducted to identify possible money laundering. However, it appears that for investigations and prosecutions involving overseas predicate conduct, progress is needed.

5.5.3 *Company law, beneficial ownership, economic substance and tax transparency*

TCI's government has engaged in considerable statutory reforms in the area of company law and beneficial ownership information, seen in the Companies Ordinance 2017. With increasing attention on corporate ownership internationally, and the perceivably harmful role played by offshore centres, Section 145 Companies Ordinance 2017 created a register of beneficial ownership of companies. Prior to this reform, the framework was weaker and more susceptible to abuse, with far less reporting requirements for companies. Beneficial owners are defined under this legislation, aligning with the definition at section 6, UK Money Laundering Regulations 2007. Section 9(3) of the Ordinance states that "a person applying to incorporate the company shall provide the Commission with the prescribed beneficial ownership information in relation to each person who will . . . be a registrable person in relation to the company". Under the Ordinance, only the person proposed as the company's registered agent can make an application for incorporation. The legislation at section 133(2) requires companies to maintain a register of beneficial ownership, directors, members, charges and notices which must be kept at the office of the company's registered agent. It is the agent's responsibility to submit documents to the Commission. The agent must be licenced and regulated as a company manager/agent (TCI Company Management [Licensing] Ordinance) and, among other things, is responsible for filing documents and maintaining information at their offices. There are 37 such registered entities. Under section 149(1), there is a "reasonable steps" requirement on the company to ascertain and identify beneficial owners. Section 149(2) provides that the company is entitled to rely on the written response of a person in relation to this without further inquiry, provided it was made in good faith. This arguably presents risks to enforceability, given it places reliance on good faith and accuracy of representations. The agent is also required to update the beneficial ownership register when the company becomes aware of any changes to beneficial owners and registrable persons. As such, there are corresponding responsibilities of the company to keep information up to date under section 154, but principally the responsibilities adhere to the company's registered agent.

All TCI companies were required to voluntarily register under the Ordinance by November 2018. Eighty-five per cent responded, with 15% (roughly 1,000 companies) failing to respond. The effect of this was that they were automatically registered and would have to comply with the filing of notices, failing which they would be struck off. Companies, via their agents, are required to deliver a notice to the FSC no more than 14 days following incorporation setting out the prescribed beneficial owners' particulars. Any change must be notified to the FSC no more than 14 days after such change. Disclosure of information on the register is prohibited, save for certain circumstances under section 159, such as police requests.

This updated framework noticeably and significantly departs from the old method of placing such information exclusively in the hands of companies. Its functional impact places greater competence with the regulator and also more stringent requirements on companies and their agents who are subject to FSC oversight. Contraventions, like failing to provide updated information, can result in a $50,000 fine. As an aside, this amount raises questions of proportionality. Despite the international standard on beneficial ownership being unsettled, the updated legislation meets the substance of FATF Recommendation 24, which advocates that such information should be centrally held and made available to competent authorities.

In 2016, TCI entered into an EOI Agreement with the UK with respect to sharing beneficial ownership information. This commitment was made in the context of fulfilling internationally accepted standards such as the EU's Fourth Money Laundering Directive, FATF Recommendation 24 and the G20 High Level Principles on Beneficial Ownership Transparency. It enables mutual cooperation between competent authorities investigating money laundering, terrorism financing, tax evasion, corruption and other economic crime. It provides law enforcement with automatic provision of beneficial ownership information. It furthers commitments made under the Multilateral Convention on Mutual Administrative Assistance in Tax Matters, signing at least the OECD-required number of TIEAs, creating legislation to implement US (and UK) Foreign Account Tax Compliance Act 2010. TCI has engaged with the CRS, making exchange automatic, and has signed such agreements with 67 countries. TCI's cooperation with the UK and international standards in this regard indicates commitment to transparency and international cooperation.

In the 2020 MER, CFATF highlights TCI's technical compliance with Recommendation 24 (Largely Compliant) and Recommendation 25 (Compliant) regarding beneficial ownership information. Paradoxically, the above established framework has been eschewed by the UK government through its legislative ultimatum under section 51 SAMLA, without testing its viability or effectiveness – not least given recent reforms. Despite international standards being unaligned on the extent to which beneficial ownership information should be completely transparent to the public, or limited to competent enforcement authorities, the UK government has called for complete transparency. TCI's efforts in good faith have clearly been disregarded. It is surprising in the context of the UK recently acknowledging in the FAC Inquiry report that despite powers given to law enforcement, the exchange mechanisms were rarely used (FAC 2019, 15). Despite all this, TCI made commitments to create a public register in line with UK demands by the end of 2023. Given TCI's central register is established, it appears that a transition may be achievable provided that the concerns raised in relation to the UK register are prioritised as part of TCI's upgrade to a public one.

Further company law reforms include those under the Companies and Limited Partnerships (Economic Substance) Ordinance 2018, which implement EU standards on economic substance requirements for entities. The legislation aims to ensure TCI's omission from the EU blacklist of harmful tax jurisdiction, in which it was originally greylisted and removed in March 2019. This legislation applies to all domestic companies and limited partnerships, as well as foreign companies registered in TCI – except for those that are tax resident in a jurisdiction which is not on the EU's list. The effects of adhering to economic substance requirements not only furthers tax cooperation and compliance but, in the case of businesses carrying on relevant activities in the jurisdiction, it erodes 'form over substance' and strengthens the domestic regulated environment. It is worth noting, however, that not all legal persons are captured by the economic substance requirements, for instance companies which own real estate in the jurisdiction yet have no other commercial activity.

5.6 Development concerns and relationship with the UK

Examining TCI's compliance with standards requires acknowledging its significant development concerns. TCI graduated DfID's aid programme in 2003. However, given TCI's financial and constitutional difficulties later that decade, DfID committed to a 5-year financial arrangement through commercial bank lending (DfID 2012, 3). However, in 2018, the UK International Development Secretary announced that a change in foreign aid rules had been agreed with the OECD and funding would be provided, particularly in the case of future natural disasters.

While TCI is relatively prosperous, it is susceptible to natural disasters and is under constant emergency risk. In 2017, Hurricanes Irma and Maria highlighted the fragility of TCI's infrastructure and strategic response. This represents a risk of seismic proportions to small islands that rely predominantly on tourism and finance for economic stability. The hurricanes caused widespread damage, disrupting public services and hospitals, and displacing and injuring people. The UK government committed £32 million in relief and later announced £70 million funds and £300 million loan guarantees (FAC 2018a). Relief included military personnel, vessels, food, shelter kits, solar lanterns and water. However, there was prominent criticism about the response which noted bad planning and that the sum was split between the territories. Most criticism was not about the type of assistance but that the response should have been contingent on the predictability of hurricanes.

In terms of characterising the UK's relationship with TCI, over time the UK has emphasised the general relationship as being one of partnership. It could be argued that the above instances demonstrate that this partnership only manifests retroactively. Following the 1986 crisis, Lennon suggested that Whitehall had followed a policy of benign neglect towards TCI's inhabitants (*FT* 1.11.1986). There is some support for independence in TCI as its goal. The UK Government's policy for the Overseas Territories could not be worded more intelligibly: "A unique constitutional relationship, built on a shared history, common values and a spirit of collaboration and partnership" (UK Government 2017, para 3). The direct rule periods were arguably retroactive investigations rather than preventive actions, which suggests this policy needs re-thinking. However, the UK had no other choice and, as one FCO Minister stated at the time, "these are some of the worst allegations that I have ever seen about sitting politicians".[8] Direct rule was perceived by many as an infringement on TCI's right of self-rule and an erosion of democracy and institutions. Elections were prohibited, and there was tension about taxation without representation. As Rev. Conard Howell (2011) observed, "the handling of TCI for the last two years . . . resoundingly makes the case for the eradication of colonialism". Similar resistance was seen in 1986, where the then Chief Minister stated that direct rule "shows the British imperialistic and colonialist attitude which one would have thought was abolished years ago" (*FT* 1.11.1986). In 2006, the then Premier called on islanders to fight against the "occupation of the foreign invaders" (Caribbean Insight 2009). In both cases, there has been the view that action was too late and generally resistance was rife towards interventionism.

This raises the issue as to whether the UK government has been a good governance partner. While intervention led to positive actions which have been identified in this chapter, such as law and regulatory reform, and restoration of self-rule after winning the UK's confidence, the fact remains that TCI has lived through direct rule twice in three decades – unprecedented for those Overseas Territories whose degrees of autonomy have been solemnly recognised by the UK through Acts of Parliament. It could be argued that the UK government has repudiated its own policy and allowed national emergencies to precipitate. When a pattern emerges over a relatively short time, the approach needs re-evaluating. As Clegg (2013) notes, successive governments since the 1980s have attempted meaningful improvements to the relationship, with reviews undertaken in 1978, 1992 and 1999 motivated by existing problems, such as the 1995 Soufrière Hills volcano eruption in Montserrat. DfID's evaluation of this emergency detailed that ad hoc arrangements were implemented reactively while the eruption progressed (DfID 1999, 1–2). While different to TCI's direct rule, this example points to the UK's

8 HC Deb (16 March 2009) 'Written Ministerial Statement – TCI: Governance', Col 39–40WS.

strategy in monitoring and assisting Overseas Territories, as similar criticisms followed the 2017 hurricanes.

Prior to the Auld Commission's call for immediate action, TCI's problems had not been immobilised. While crises such as hurricanes often occur immediately, economic or political ones rarely emanate spontaneously. For example, the 1930s Great Depression was not solely attributable to the market crash but to a changing economic landscape, including the Federal Reserve changing its credit policy in 1928 making it more difficult to borrow and with bank borrowing for speculation becoming more expensive (Crafts and Fearon 2010). Similarly, in the collapse of Lehman Brothers, the indicators were apparent, yet management were not proactive in ascribing earlier risk-management provisions (Mwauto 2014). Regulators and credit agencies were also culpable, giving top ratings to low-quality sub-prime securities, many of which later downgraded or defaulted (Hill 2010, 585). Causes of crisis are often incremental, thereby making crises avoidable if risks are intelligible.

By the 1999 White Paper, a new approach to the Overseas Territories appeared to be conceptualised. There were those in Parliament who asserted that the relationship was not working (House of Commons 1997 per Baroness Symons, 162). The Paper emphasised partnership based on mutual obligations and responsibilities. Clegg posits a key question: Has the spirit of the 1999 White Paper amounted to nothing? With the few examples discussed, it appears many aspects of the UK's approach have not been pre-emptive enough to meet the spirit of this policy. The Auld Commission noted that there were chronic ills amounting to national emergency. A 'chronic condition' is something of slow progression, and Sir Robin's assessment clearly conjects that TCI's problems were rather more enduring than an overnight calamity. TCI generally responded well to the imposed requirements. Therefore, identifying problems and implementing measures prior to a national emergency being declared might have proven effective.

The most recent exploration of the TCI-UK relationship came during the 2018–19 FAC Inquiry. While aid, funding, education and concerns about Brexit were raised in evidence of Premier Robinson, one major concern were the constitutional tensions arising from SAMLA. As has been suggested throughout this book, the non-consultative nature of this demonstrates a problem at the core of the partnership.

5.7 Conclusion

TCI has faced fundamental development concerns across many dimensions which have undermined its ability to implement certain international standards. Persistent corruption allegations have stinted the development of important aspects of the rule of law and undermined institutions to the point of crisis. The most visible impact of suspect wealth was TCI's loss of sovereignty on two occasions in 30 years. Systemic corruption findings not only affected its development, in that it lost millions in concessions, thousands of acres of Crown land, and experienced a loss of autonomy, but it also inhibited TCI's regulatory and compliance developments. Even to this day, capacity issues affect TCI demonstrated by the inarguably protracted nature of the SIPT trial. While TCI was not significantly implicated in recent offshore data breaches, it is concerning that TCI has been connected to serious overseas economic crime cases. Considering evidence from criminal cases in the US, the argument that TCI entities have been used to subvert onshore domestic laws, thereby receiving suspect wealth or letting it enter its financial sector through property purchases, indicates that progress is still needed to understand the risks in these sectors – something CFATF observed in the latest follow-up.

However, in the past 10 years TCI has engaged in material reforms across legislation, regulation and institutional development to strengthen its response to economic crime and suspect wealth. TCI must be credited as it has shown significant progress since 2012 and resuming self-rule. It has implemented various international economic crime standards such as EOI, TIEAs, CRS and a central register of beneficial ownership. While the central register model was arguably viable in the context of the internationally advocated FATF standards, TCI's commitments to implement an open register of beneficial ownership demonstrates cooperation. Further, it has reformed many key laws which the international community have deemed necessary to tackle suspect wealth, as well as those which speak to international tax cooperation such as economic substance requirements to avoid EU blacklisting attempts. This exhibits TCI's ability and willingness to implement sophisticated laws and comply with international standards. Important examples include the register of Members' interests and modern bribery legislation. It has enhanced and amended its AML regime legislatively in terms of POCA and reformed its company laws and information reporting requirements. Its legal reforms have further empowered statutory bodies, such as the AML Committee and the Integrity Commission, under which public integrity education is now a development strategy. TCI has demonstrated regional engagement with CFATF and the completion of its NRA demonstrates willingness to adhere to the internationally accepted risk-based approach to AML/CFT. While some of these risks need greater attention, particularly for other sectors, TCI has made considerable progress compared to affairs in the 1980s and 2000s.

References

Been, R. (16.11.2016) 'Tropical Vibes 105', Interview.

Berk, B. B. (2015) 'Labelling Theory, History Of', in *International Encyclopaedia of the Social and Behavioural Sciences* (2nd ed., Vol. 13), Amsterdam: Elsevier.

Brehony, K. J. (2004) 'A New Education for a New Era: The Contribution of the Conferences of the New Education Fellowship to the Disciplinary Field of Education 1921–1938', *Paedagogica Historica*, 40(5–6): 733–755.

Caribbean Insight (8.2009) 'CARICOM Condemns UK Stance towards TCI', London: Caribbean Council.

Caribbean Tourism Organisation, State of the Industry Report 2016.

CFATF (2008) '3rd Round MER'. Available: https://www.cfatf-gafic.org/cfatf-documents/mutual-evaluation-reports/turks-and-caicos-islands-1/130-t-c-3rd-round-mer/file

CFATF (2011) '4th Follow-Up Report to the 3rd Round MER'. Available: https://www.cfatf-gafic.org/cfatf-documents/follow-up-reports-2/turks-and-caicos-islands/132-t-ci-4th-follow-up-report/file

CFATF (2016) '13th Follow-Up Report to the 3rd Round MER'. Available: https://www.cfatf-gafic.org/cfatf-documents/follow-up-reports-2/turks-and-caicos-islands/6732-t-ci-13th-follow-up-report/file

CFATF (2020) '4th Round MER'. Available: https://www.fatf-gafi.org/media/fatf/documents/reports/mer-fsrb/CFATF-Mutual-Evaluation-Report-Turks-Caicos-Islands.pdf

CFATF. 'Jurisdiction that was under CFATF-ICRG Review and Has Made Significant Progress in Addressing Its AML/CFT Deficiencies: Turks and Caicos Islands'. Available: https://www.cfatf-gafic.org/member-countries/turks-caicos-islands/357-jurisdiction-that-was-under-cfatf-icrg-review-and-has-made-significant-progress-in-addressing-its-aml-cft-deficiencies-turks-and-caicos-islands#:~:text=The%20CFATF%20acknowledges%20the%20significant,deficiencies%20that%20the%20CFATF%20had

Clegg, P. (2013) 'Governance in the UK Overseas Territories: The Case of TCI'. Available: https://sta.uwi.edu/conferences/09/salises/documents/P%20Clegg.pdf

Crafts, N., and Fearon, P. (2010) 'Lessons from the 1930s Great Depression', *Oxford Review of Economic Policy*, 26(3): 258–317.

DfID (1999) 'An Evaluation of HMG's Response to the Montserrat Volcanic Emergency, Vol 1, Ev 635'. Available: https://assets.publishing.service.gov.uk/government/uploads/system/uploads/attachment_data/file/67966/ev635.pdf

DfID (2012) 'Operational Plan 2011–2015', DfID Overseas Territories Department.

FCO (2012) 'The Overseas Territories: Security, Success and Sustainability', White Paper. Available: https://assets.publishing.service.gov.uk/government/uploads/system/uploads/attachment_data/file/14929/ot-wp-0612.pdf

FT (1.11.1986) 'Corruption in TCI: A Little Local Difficulty'. FT archive.

G20 (2014) 'G20 High-Level Principles on Beneficial Ownership Transparency'. Available: http://www.g20.utoronto.ca/2014/g20_high-level_principles_beneficial_ownership_transparency.pdf

Governor's Office Waterloo Grand Turk (23.5.2013) 'Civil Recovery Retrieves $19.5m and 2500 Acres with More to Come', Press Release. Available: https://www.gov.uk/government/news/civil-recovery-retrieves-195m-and-2500-acres-with-more-to-come

Griffith, I. L. (1993) 'Some Security Implications of Commonwealth Caribbean Narcotics Operations', *Conflict Quarterly*, Spring 1993: 25–45.

Hill, C. A. (2010) 'Why Did Rating Agencies Do Such a Bad Job Rating Subprime Securities?', *University of Pittsburgh Law Review*, 71: 585–608.

House of Commons. International Development Committee, Montserrat, First Report, 18.11.1997.

House of Commons. Library (31.12.2012) 'The Turks and Caicos Islands', Research Briefing. Available: https://commonslibrary.parliament.uk/research-briefings/sn05038/

Howell, C. (2011) 'Statement TCI All-Party Commission of the Constitution and Electoral Reform', UN Third International Decade for the Eradication of Colonialism, Caribbean Regional Seminar, St Vincent and the Grenadines, 31 May–2 June 2011.

ICIJ Offshore Leaks database, Paradise Papers. Available: https://offshoreleaks.icij.org/

Independent (14.4.1996) 'Our Man in Hot Water: When the British Governor of TCI Claimed Drug Trafficking Was Rife, It Was the Last Straw for Locals'. Available: www.independent.co.uk/news/our-man-in-hot-water-1304963.html

Jung, C. (1957/2002) *The Undiscovered Self*, Abingdon: Routledge Classics.

Mills, A. (1998) 'Strengthening Domestic Institutions Against Corruption: A Public Ethics Checklist', in UN Development Programme (1998) 'Corruption and Integrity Improvement Initiatives in Developing Countries', ch.9.

Moore, G. C. J. (1997) 'Selecting An Offshore Jurisdiction: Why TCI?', *Mondaq*, 21 March 1997. Available: www.mondaq.com/x/2191/Trusts/Selecting+An+Offshore+Jurisdiction+Why+Turks+Caicos

Mwauto, J. K. M. (2014) 'The Failure of Lehman Brothers: Causes, Preventive Measures and Recommendations', *Research Journal of Finance and Accounting*, 5(4): 85–91.

New York Times (14.1.1988) 'Bahamas Leader Tied to Drug Bribe'. Available: www.nytimes.com/1988/01/14/us/bahamas-leader-tied-to-drug-bribe.html

New York Times (29.4.1998) 'Bahamian Leader Is Subject of U.S. Drug Inquiry'. Available: www.nytimes.com/1988/04/29/world/bahamian-leader-is-subject-of-us-druginquiry.html

OECD (2016) 'Committing to Effective Whistle-blower Protection'. Available: https://read.oecd-ilibrary.org/governance/committing-to-effective-whistleblower-protection_9789264252639-en#page1

Rameur, C. (2019) 'Understanding Money Laundering through Real Estate Sectors', European Parliament Research Briefing, European Parliamentary Research Service PE633.154.

Sharman, J. C. (2006) *Havens in a Storm*, New York: Cornell University Press.

TCI Commission of Inquiry (1986) 'Report of Mr Louis Blom-Cooper QC into Allegations of Arson of a Public Building, Corruption and Related Matters'. Available: https://turksandcaicosislands.org/CofI1986BlomCooperQC.pdf

TCI Commission of Inquiry (2008–2009) into Possible Corruption or other Serious Dishonesty in Relation to Past and Present Elected Members of the Legislature in Recent Years, Report of the Commissioner, the Right Honourable Sir Robin Auld, 2009.

TCI Election Centre (2016) 'General Election Results 15 December 2016'. Available: http://www.caribbeanelections.com/tc/elections/tc_results_2016.asp

TCI FSC Annual Report 2016–17. Available: https://tcifsc.tc/wp-content/uploads/2019/02/tcifsc-annual-report-2016-2017-1.pdf

TCI Government (2017) 'National Risk Assessment on Money Laundering and Terrorist Financing'. Available: https://www.customs.gov.tc/webuploads/currdoc/TCI%20National%20Risk%20Assessment%20on%20money%20laudering%20and%20terrorist%20financing.PDF

TCI Statistics Department (2018) 'National Economic Statistics'. Available: https://www.gov.tc/stats/

TCI The Sun (15.1.2014) 'Michael Misick Gets Hero's Welcome in TCI: Granted Bail with Conditions'. Available: https://suntci.com/suntv-news-p1173-122.htm

TCI The Sun (1.6.2018a) 'TCI MP Calls on Prosecutor to Quit'. Available: https://suntci.com/turks-and-caicos-islands-mp-calls-on-prosecutor-to-quit-p3209-129.htm

TCI The Sun (1.6.2018b) 'Huge Construction and Investment Boom'. Available: https://suntci.com/huge-construction-and-investment-boom-p3405-126.htm

TCI Tourist Board Department, Statistics 2016. Available: https://caribbeanhoteland tourism.com/wp-content/uploads/2017/03/Turks-Caicos-Final-2016-Tourism-Statistics.pdf

TCI Weekly News (2008) 'Governor Tauwhare Bids a Fond Farewell'. Available: http://tcweeklynews.com/governor-tauwhare-bids-a-fond-farewell-p770.htm

TCI Weekly News (21.7.2012) 'Hoffman Hands Back Salt Cay Land – Developer Agrees to Out of Court Settlement'. Available: http://tcweeklynews.com/hoffmann-hands-back-salt-cay-land-developer-agrees-to-out-of-court-settle-p2739-1.htm

TCI Weekly News (25.1.2016) 'Misick Government's Import Concessions Cost TCI $42m'. Available: https://tcweeklynews.com/misick-governments-import-concessions-cost-tci-m-p6796-127.htm

TCI Weekly News (21.1.2019) 'Defence Calls for End of Trial'. Available: www.ieyenews.com/tci-michael-misick-trial-defence-calls-for-end-of-trial/

Transparency International (2018) 'The Cost of Secrecy'. Available: https://www.transparency.org.uk/sites/default/files/pdf/publications/TIUK-CostofSecrecy-WEB-v2.pdf

UK FAC (2018a) 'The UK's Response to Hurricanes in its Overseas Territories', 27.2.2018. Available: https://publications.parliament.uk/pa/cm201719/cmselect/cmfaff/722/722.pdf

UK FAC (2018b) 'Evidence of Premier Cartwright Robinson, Q165'. Available: http://data.parliament.uk/writtenevidence/committeeevidence.svc/evidencedocument/foreign-affairs-committee/the-future-of-the-uk-overseas-territories/oral/93391.html

UK FAC (2019) 'Global Britain and the Overseas Territories: Resetting the Relationship', Fifteenth Report of Session 2017–2019.

UK Government (2017) 'Overseas Territories Joint Ministerial Council 2017 Communiqué'. Available: https://www.gov.uk/government/publications/overseas-territories-joint-ministerial-council-2017-communique

US Department of Justice (31.5.2017) 'Gabonese-French Dual Citizen Sentenced to 24 Months Imprisonment for Bribing African Officials', Press Release.

US Department of State, 2018 International Narcotics Control Strategy Report. Available: https://www.state.gov/2018-international-narcotics-control-strategy-report/

Van de Does de Willebois, E., and Brun, J-P. (2013) 'Using Civil Remedies in Corruption and Asset Recovery Cases', *Case Western Reserve Journal of International Law*, 45: 615–651.

6 Anguilla

6.1 Anguilla: an overview

Anguilla is a parliamentary dependency under constitutional monarchy located in the Eastern Caribbean Sea. With a population of 15,094, it is located 20 km north of Saint Martin and 96 km west of Saint Kitts. As a gateway to the Panama Canal, Anguilla sits in a shipping superhighway. Its main economic sources are tourism, financial and business services, agriculture and fishing (ECCB 2018, Anguilla). Other significant contributors include construction, real estate, transportation, storage and communications.

Anguilla has been a British territory for 370 years. In the 1830s, Anguilla unionised with Saint Kitts and Nevis, forming Saint Kitts–Nevis–Anguilla – largely for administrative purposes on Britain's recommendation. In the 1950s, Anguilla became part of the West Indies Federation and gained statehood after the Federation collapsed in the 1960s. While the 1960s and 1970s saw increasing independence across the Caribbean, such as Barbados in 1966, the Bahamas in 1973 and Saint Vincent in 1979, Anguilla resisted Saint Kitts and the UK Government to remain British. The Anguillian Revolution (1967–69) replaced the Saint Kitts–administered colony with direct British colonialism (Petty and Hodge 1987, 6). Anguilla became a separate dependent territory of the UK in 1980 and has since remained an Overseas Territory.

Anguilla is internally self-governing. Its Assembly has 7 elected members, 2 ex officio, and 2 appointed members. The main political parties are the Anguilla United Front and the Anguilla Progressive Movement. As with the other territories, the Queen appoints a Governor, who appoints a Premier.[1] The present Governor is H.E. Dileeni Daniel-Selvaratnam and the Premier is Hon. Ellis Webster. Anguilla's legal system is based on English common law and includes domestic statutes such as the Anguilla Constitution Order 1982 – widely regarded as an outdated instrument. Anguilla is part of the Eastern Caribbean Court. Its High Court hears criminal and civil matters including appeals, with the UKPC being Anguilla's final appellate court.

1 Until 2019 and the passage of the Anguilla Constitution (Amendment) Order 2019, the office was known as Chief Minister.

A former Chief Minister and 'Father of the Nation', Ronald Webster, famously distrusted the British despite being the instigator of the Revolution. The Governor occupies a position of controversy on the island, as more power rests with the Anguillian Governor than in many other territories. There have been many protests on this issue in recent years. While not a prevalent issue, independence discussions recently surfaced due to political differences between the former Chief Minister, Hon. Victor Banks, and the Governor. In 2011, there was an issue whereby the Governor refused to sign off on the Chief Minister's budget, leading to calls by some in Anguilla for a Scottish-style independence referendum. Further tension was seen in the fallout from Hurricane Irma. Successive domestic governments have experienced difficulty in engaging with the UK government, and the fact remains that effective representation is often difficult to reconcile with decisions taken by the UK at an international level affecting Anguilla. Legislation for open registers is a good example. However, despite such instances, Anguilla's Government regularly emphasises the value of the UK-Anguilla relationship. From the literature, and informal discussions with Anguillians, there appears a genuine sense of pride at Anguilla's fight to remain British (Anguilla Government 2018, 3).

Tourism is Anguilla's main economic source, yet it cannot accommodate mass tourism due to development shortcomings, such as an airport of inadequate size. It has focused on developing as a luxury tourism destination, and receives some 80,000 visitors annually. Its environment is largely protected by extensive private and indigenous ownership. In September 2017, Hurricane Irma devastated Anguilla and its people. Its tourism industry faced extreme adversity and has felt the ramifications ever since. Visitor arrivals decreased from 18,114 in January 2017 to 4,984 in January 2018, representing the lowest for January since 1993 (Anguilla Government, Statistics Department 2018).

6.2 Economy and development as a financial centre

At 2019, Anguilla's GDP per capita is $21,068 (World Bank). It is too wealthy, therefore, to receive UK aid (DfID 1.11.2018). Like many islands, Anguilla has an indirect taxation system. The IMF (2012, 13) noted that Anguilla's tax revenue was disproportionately focused on a few volatile and transitory revenue sources. Its lack of economic diversification is challenging, particularly when tourism can be unpredictable with the constant natural disaster risks. The 2017 hurricanes certainly highlighted the fragility of an economic system which relies on tourism set against this environmental backdrop. It is commonly labelled as a zero-tax jurisdiction. In 2019, Anguilla achieved a surplus of EC$25 million (*Anguillian* 22.1.2020). It collected EC$185.3 million in revenue, with 84% collected from indirect tax and 16% being non-tax revenue. Government revenue increased by EC$10.8 million from 2013 to 2014. However, as well as the generic criticisms of indirect tax systems, the IMF (2012) posited that Anguilla's system is overly complex and an accumulation of ad hoc measures. They suggested that the collection exercise for import duties was riddled with inconsistencies and approximately 40% of import duty revenue was being lost due to concessions and exemptions. Anguilla's indirect taxation model has been a notable factor in recent blacklisting efforts, such as by the Netherlands, whose criteria included whether the jurisdiction collects corporation tax (Netherlands Government 28.12.2018). Interestingly, and perhaps due to fiscal sovereignty, the recent FAC Inquiry did not once mention the fiscal circumstances of the territories.

Anguilla entered the offshore financial services market shortly after the enactment of its Companies Ordinance in 1994. At this time, Lennox-Boyd MP in the UK Parliament noted that the Government provides "considerable assistance towards developing the sector's regulatory framework and expertise".[2] Prior to the early 1990s, only international banks operated there, with Anguilla's first domestic bank opening in 1994. Since then, Anguilla's financial sector and offshore industry has grown. This market is significant relative to its size, yet small compared to Bermuda or the Cayman Islands. The IMF (2012) noted Anguilla's intention to expand its offshore service offerings as a means of economic diversification. Financial services accounted for 8.4% of GDP in 2019 (Anguilla Statistics Department 2019). Domestic banking is regulated by the Eastern Caribbean Central Bank (ECCB), and its OFC activity, including offshore banking, is regulated by the FSC. Its offerings are diverse, including IBCs, corporate and trust services, company management, captive insurance, foundations and offshore banking. In terms of the business infrastructure supporting its financial sector, there are some 40 law firms, but no major accounting firms have offices in Anguilla. The jurisdiction's financial sector comprises 2 domestic banks and 1 offshore bank. Its insurance sector has developed significantly and is among the world's largest captive insurance domiciles. As at 2020, Anguilla had 128 offshore insurance companies, 26 domestic insurance companies and 37 insurance intermediaries, along with 275 captives. There are 55 company managers and 4 trust company managers, along with 59 licensees who may provide nominee offerings. There are 3 money service businesses. There are 20 external and non-regulated service providers in Anguilla registered with the FSC. Anguilla's incorporation sector is relatively large, with over 22,000 LLCs, 40 foundations and 40 limited partnerships (OECD 2020; Anguilla FSC). As is a trend among similar islands, like Bermuda, Anguilla's FinTech offerings are increasing and, as the OECD (2020) notes the registration for Anguillian web domain addresses is projected to significantly outperform revenue than that received in respect of company registrations, fees and filings.

6.3 International concerns and implication in financial crime cases

Anguilla's financial centre has received adverse international attention. This includes being implicated in the ICIJ offshore data leaks and in various international financial

2 HC Deb (4 March 1994) Vol 238, cc25–8W, per Lennox-Boyd MP.

crime cases, or reports about its perceived lack of transparency by transparency groups. Concerns about Anguilla's financial sector and compliance with international standards have been seen at the international and supranational levels. For example, as at October 2020, Anguilla is included on the EU List of Non-Cooperative Tax Jurisdictions. It had initially avoided the list, rather being placed on the EU's greylist for ongoing review. This was partly due to the fact Anguilla was preoccupied with recovery from 2017 hurricane destruction, in common with other Overseas Territories at that time. The EU List is exceptionally narrow, although inclusion on it remains a serious problem for Anguilla and one which its financial regulatory environment needs to prioritise. Anguilla also features on the recent Dutch list of low-tax jurisdictions.

Anguilla's inclusion is partly based upon the 2nd Round review by the OECD Global Forum on Transparency and Exchange of Information for Tax Purposes in 2020, and downgrading from its earlier 2014 rating of 'partially compliant' to 'non-compliant'. The review found two significant deficiencies. These related to practical implementation of rules regarding availability of accounting records and failures by authorities to respond to requests from peers for information. They urged, however, that the latter deficiency largely related to the abrupt closure of service providers related to the Panama papers leaks and MOSSFON. In response to the Council of Europe's inclusion of Anguilla on its list, the Governor acknowledged the factors which led to it and requested the OECD's Global Forum conduct a supplementary review in order to demonstrate progress made (Governor's Office 7.10.2020).

Unlike Bermuda and TCI, Anguilla was implicated in both the Panama and Paradise papers – significantly more so in the former. Anguilla's government has in the past averred that the territory is relatively unaffected by corruption. However, evidence will now be considered which demonstrates that Anguillian offshore services, including companies and bank accounts, have been utilised for foreign misconduct or to dispose of criminal proceeds.

Drawing upon data from the Offshore Leaks, successive data breaches have presented sources of information which have been cited in policy and lawmaking. This was visible during debates about SAMLA and the Criminal Finances Act.

Anguilla was heavily implicated in the Panama papers. Consulting the ICIJ Offshore Leaks Panama papers data, the findings demonstrate that some 3,253 Anguillian-incorporated companies were named. Of these, the data shows that a significant portion of them were not active at the time of publication, leaving 1,868 active. For example, of those inactive, there were 44 dissolved companies, 13 discontinued, 1,054 that had defaulted, and 200 shelf companies. Others were in liquidation or had relocated in another jurisdictions. For active or inactive entities, other than names and registered addresses, there is no additional data provided by the ICIJ to indicate what the company's purpose was, other than the fact that it is, or was, incorporated in Anguilla.

In the subsequent case of the Paradise papers publication, Anguillian entities were mentioned sparingly. The Offshore Leaks Paradise papers database shows that only 1 Anguilla-registered company was named. While simple mention in the publication gives rise to an adverse presumption, given the negative attention attributed to countries named in the papers, data shows that the named entity's status at the time of publication was 'closed'.

The implication of Anguilla in the Panama papers is, of course, not *de minimis.* Given that there are approximately 28,000 limited companies registered in Anguilla, publication of 1,868 active entities is a significant number. What is perhaps more concerning is the purported role of MOSSFON, then the fourth-largest offshore law firm in the world. MOSSFON was essentially a wholesale provider of company incorporation. Given MOSSFON was the target of the information published by the Panama papers, and that it consequently closed due to reverberations of the leaks, its particular link to Anguilla is worth considering. There may be grounds for drawing adverse inferences with regards to MOSSFON and its use of Anguilla as a jurisdiction of choice in which to incorporate entities. This is particularly concerning in the context of serious allegations against MOSSFON for professionally facilitating criminality (US Department of Justice 4.12.2018), and given that it was reported that they had not taken steps to ascertain the ultimate identities and owners of a significant portion of its clients' companies registered in Panama and BVI, for example (*BBC* 20.6.2018). Such circumstances give increased credence to the necessity of compliance with global minimum standards on beneficial ownership registers – progress which in Anguilla has been protracted, despite their 2020 commitment to create an open register.

Given that Anguilla operates within the global offshore financial services market, it is unsurprising that it was named in the Panama papers. The evidence that Anguilla is the registered home to thousands of companies is, in and of itself, nothing revealing. However, if, as it appears, MOSSFON did not undertake DD in respect of many of its clients, it is concerning that this may have occurred with respect to those Anguilla-registered entities which it either incorporated or managed. However, this should be treated only as a rebuttable inference.

In 2009, Global Witness published a report heavily implicating Anguilla over flight capital from the Republic of Congo. Therein, Anguilla's financial services and regulators were accused of enabling Congolese officials to funnel public oil revenues through offshore entities and shell companies. It criticised Anguilla for peddling secrecy and for not publishing details of company ownership. The report claimed that the Congolese President's son, Denis Christel Sassou Nguesso, who was also head of a public sales agency for Congolese oil, paid credit card bills using offshore accounts with money relating to Congo's oil sales. It was alleged that offshore structures allowed Nguesso to spend sizeable funds from oil revenues on luxury goods, including putting shares in trust to conceal ownership and use of Anguilla incorporated entities. His reported spending, contrasted with the majority of Congo's citizens, is discussed in Sharman (2017). Global Witness concluded that the PEP provisions of the modern AML/CFT regulation are ineffectual if initial DD fails from the outset to identify that the customer is a PEP. They argued that banks should not be able to rely on intermediaries for their DD. While Global Witness takes credit for alerting the Anguillian authorities that entities in the jurisdiction appeared to be facilitating this misconduct, a year passed before the company was struck off. They criticised the regulator's protracted response and that Anguillian companies continued to provide services for Nguesso.

While there has not been any criminal proceedings emanating from the Anguillian-Nguesso connection, the allegations made by Global Witness raise questions about the extent to which Anguillian companies may have facilitated misconduct of a PEP and the extent to which its regulators may have been unaware, or wilfully blind, to this possibility. While there have been reports of members of the Nguesso family being implicated in criminality elsewhere (*France24* 25.6.2017), the extent to which Anguilla is implicated appears to be confined to Global Witness' 2009 allegations.

While this report is over a decade old, and it was 2007 when Global Witness first made contact with Anguilla's FSC about the allegations, Transparency International (2018) republished the allegations about Nguesso and Anguilla. This chapter will consider the extent to which Anguilla's response to suspect wealth has developed since the time of such allegations, thereby questioning whether the degree of reliance placed on them to indicate Anguilla's contemporary record is accurate or otherwise.

There have also been several high-profile criminal cases internationally which have implicated Anguillian entities or accounts being used to facilitate criminality in other jurisdictions, such as through money laundering. In those cases resulting in convictions, information from them can represent useful evidence. While such cases are serious, searches of publicly reported criminal cases naming Anguilla or Anguillian entities do not return many results. Moreover, many of the reported cases from jurisdictions like the UK or US go back some years, which also indicates a low level of recently reported cases. The following evidence does not suggest an endemic situation or a contemporarily representative problem. Rather, it illustrates that Anguilla's OFC has been connected to criminality elsewhere. As has been emphasised regularly in this book, this could also be said for any jurisdiction named in financial crime cases with a cross-border element.

In the English case of *R v McInerney* [2009], a private prosecution was brought against a banker who had acted for fraudulent traders operating boiler rooms. A 'boiler room' is a high-pressure selling environment whereby unduly pressurised selling techniques are used – usually by telephone – to persuade investors to engage in speculative (or even fraudulent) trading. Such practices can been deemed illegal or contrary to ethics in securities trading. In *McInerney*, the operation had defrauded some 1,700 investors of £27.5 million. McInerney was enlisted to distance the perpetrators of this fraud from its proceeds and, in doing so, opened accounts for three companies in order to receive the illicit wealth. McInerney was said to have arranged transfers to a series of worldwide offshore accounts operated by the defendants, which had been established after companies were registered in jurisdictions – including Anguilla. McInerney was imprisoned for 4.5 years. This case demonstrates the role that a financial services professional played in laundering millions with the use of offshore-registered companies and accounts, as well as implicating Anguilla as one of the relevant jurisdictions for incorporation.

Similarly, in the well-documented American case of *United States v Dreier* (2009),[3] an American lawyer convicted for operating a Ponzi scheme recovered assets under receivership included proceeds of his fraud linked to Anguilla. The report showed an account with $11.5 million therein, which were liquid remnants of the fraud. This account was maintained by a company established by Dreier and others to purchase planned residential properties in Anguilla. Anguilla was also mentioned as a destination where Dreier utilised ill-gotten gains through purchasing luxury property, as well as transferring the proceeds of his fraud into personal accounts which were purportedly used for his Anguillian properties. This reported case further demonstrates Anguilla's property market and incorporation sector being named in high-profile overseas cases.

Another example is the *Trio Capital* collapse. Anguilla was implicated in this Australian criminal case involving the collapse of the largest fraud in the history of the Australian funds management industry. One of the investment schemes proven to be a fraudulent investment vehicle was found to have extensively utilised 'tax havens' including Anguilla to perpetrate and layer the fraud (Australia Parliament 2012, 16). In the *Trio Capital* case, Palmer J, at 22, vocally criticised tax havens, stating:

> If one wants to conduct financial operations as far away as possible from the scrutiny of tax authorities, investment regulatory authorities and investors themselves . . . if one wants to conduct financial operations dishonestly or illegally – then it is to those jurisdictions that one goes.

Anguilla was also mentioned in relation to the 2010 'Flash Cash' scandal. This was a trillion-dollar US market crash which lasted just over 30 minutes, before the markets rebounded.[4] In *United States v Sarao* (2015), a UK trader pleaded guilty to wire fraud and spoofing. His actions were blamed by the US Commodity Futures Trading Commission as exacerbating the market crash. According to court documents, at the time of the crash Sarao took "significant steps to protect his assets . . . [he] established, in 2012, International Guarantee Corporation, incorporated in Anguilla" (US Department of Justice 9.11.2016). One of his wealth management assistants is seen describing the Anguillian company as having been created as part of tax planning work on Sarao's behalf.

In the American case of *United States v Currin* (2007), the defendant, a former US attorney, had established an offshore company and bank account for it in Anguilla. It was said that this was for the purpose of receiving thousands of dollars in undisclosed income. As well as tax fraud, Currin pleaded guilty to offences of money laundering and obstruction in relation to $1.45 million proceeds from a securities fraud scheme.

3 See US Government's Sentencing Memorandum, [7].

4 For background, see Supplemental Affidavit of Mr Wible, US Department of Justice Prosecutor, sworn on 18 September 2015, available at *Navinder Singh Sarao v The Government of the U.S.A.* [2016] EWHC 2737, para 7.

Anguilla was also mentioned in the case of *United States v Gordon* (2005). In this case, a former trader at the firm Merrill Lynch was sentenced for embezzling $43 million. He had told his employer he needed the $43 million to purchase insurance to cover trading losses. Instead, the funds were sent to a company he had incorporated in Anguilla.

In the case of *United States v Dandong Hongxiang Industrial Development Co. et al.* (2016), an Anguillian-registered entity was named. The company, Deep Wealth, was a front company implicated in the complaint which alleged that the defendants provided services on behalf of the Korea Kwangson Banking Corp., an organisations that was sanctioned for links to weapons development in North Korea (US Treasury Department 8.11.2009).

Many of these matters demonstrate that Anguilla's financial market has been used as a market by criminals or professional enablers to layer or conceal suspect wealth. However, given these matters span the past 15 years, they should not be taken as indicative of present circumstances but illustrative of problems which have existed in this offshore centre. Absence of controls and robust legislation means that jurisdictions which offer such sophisticated services can be, and have been, abused by criminals and professional enablers. Of course, this is not simply a matter confined to criminality within the jurisdiction, but it shows that Anguilla has been used by criminals operating in jurisdictions as far reaching as Australia or New York. While selective, they illustrate and raise an important question in the context of examining progress made in compliance with international standards. In instances where Anguilla's financial market, property sector, and professional environment have been used to facilitate overseas misconduct, has this been as a result of a lack of compliance with regulatory standards, ignorance, deliberate knowledge, or a combination?

6.4 Analysis of Anguilla's legal and regulatory response to economic crime and suspect wealth

In the context of recent high-level criticism and poor recent assessments in certain anti-economic crime areas like information exchange and practical implementation of transparency standards, as well as implication in international cases, this section analyses Anguilla's legal and regulatory anti-economic crime frameworks. In summary, the territory does show commitment and competence in some areas, while in some key areas like risk identification and legislative reform, considerable progress is needed to enhance Anguilla's international compliance and reputation. Given that international criticisms have painted a less positive view of Anguilla's framework, this analysis hopes to provide a fuller picture than the one presented thus far.

6.4.1 Anti-bribery

Anguilla has not, to date, been subject to anywhere near the level of attention or intervention as a result of corruption compared to TCI. As alluded to earlier in this book, a modern assessment of bribery necessitates an acknowledgement of corruption's many faces. There are those in some jurisdictions who have perceived rule-breaking as inherently distinct from corruption, and in others, it is seen as a necessary fact of life or a safeguarding of livelihoods. In terms of Anguilla's legislative and regulatory response to corruption, it is the least developed of the three Overseas Territories. This is not to suggest a foregone conclusion, nor is it to attempt to engage in rankings in respect of the jurisdictions. Rather, the fact that Anguilla's response to corruption is the least developed necessitates trying to better understand the causes of this.

Various anti-corruption tools have been recommended for Anguilla, including Integrity Pacts and an anti-corruption body such as a Complaints Board to oversee matters relating to conflicts of interest, corruption, misuse of office and public ethics (*Anguillian* 20.6.2014). The creation of an Anti-Corruption Commission has also been advocated by the Constitutional and Electoral Reform Commission, given that these exist in many other Caribbean jurisdictions and whose activities are visible to the wider public. Whether corruption is a problem in Anguilla, versus whether it is acknowledged as a problem, are two different things. Many in the jurisdiction, including former Caribbean Supreme Court Judge Don Mitchell QC (21.9.2017), have advocated for an increase in watchdog institutions needing to be built into a reformed constitution. Mitchell has also advocated for introducing a Code of Ethics for Persons in Public Life, which exists in other jurisdictions like TCI. UNCAC has not yet been extended to Anguilla, nor has the OECD Bribery Convention. With regards to the latter, in its 2014 follow-up report to the OECD Working Group on Bribery's Phase 3 Report and Recommendations, the UK acknowledged Anguilla to be an important target to obtain extension given its development as a sophisticated financial sector. Anguilla has achieved a ranking of 87 (100 – Good/0 – Bad) by the World Governance Indicator Control of Corruption.

There has been long-standing interest in Anguilla to establish an Integrity Commission. It was mentioned at section 79, Draft New Constitution for Anguilla in 2016, and was renewed in the 2019 Draft Constitution published by the Government of Anguilla Constitutional and Electoral Reform Committee. Mitchell observes: "The system of government that we have inherited seems almost designed to encourage us to give up our natural integrity once we achieve political power" (*Anguillian* 20.6.2014). There are functioning Integrity Commissions established in various Caribbean jurisdictions, like TCI and Trinidad and Tobago. Larger jurisdictions like Canada also have such institutions. While one has not been established in Anguilla, it will be interesting to monitor the progress made in a post-Covid-19 world with regards to constitutional reform which has long advocated for its establishment together with a register of interest to enhance accountability and oversight tools.

In 2015, the Public Accounts Committee (PAC) was established in Anguilla with a remit to prevent misappropriation and waste of public funds and to ensure transparent accounting and reporting of the government's expenditure. It has been self-styled as the surest mechanism to allow the legislature to question, scrutinise and investigate public spending. The PAC works alongside the Auditor General and is supported by the Chief Auditor. It has emphasised the need to secure buy-in to its function, particularly from the civil service, as well as changing the relationship between Ministers and Civil servants in terms of ensuring accountability. In 2011, for the first time, Anguilla published the Chief Auditor's Report on public finances, which identified serious deficiencies across all departments. While the theoretical benefits of PACs are self-evident, there are some concerning aspects such as partisan differences which can interfere with PACs operations (Woodley, Sahgal, Stapenhurst, and Pelizzo 2005, 15), as they have the capacity of being used as a tool for political targeting. In Anguilla, the Opposition Leader chairs the PAC. Proposals for an Integrity Commission as part of constitutional reform stipulate the appointment of independent Board members.

Lack of sophisticated bribery legislation can stall or lead to a collapse of corruption investigations. The then UK Attorney General Lord Goldsmith emphasised this in respect of the SFO's investigation into the al-Yamamah arms deal involving the government of Saudi Arabia and BAE Systems, which collapsed due to the inadequacy of the UK's own bribery laws (*BBC* 6.2.2010). It is concerning that Anguilla still lacks anti-corruption legislation accounting for the complexity of modern bribery. While bribery involving large multinational corporations is a focus of modern corruption laws, so too are the new offences of receiving and offering bribes as well as bribing foreign officials. For example, modern laws do not only capture bribing officials in different countries to do business therein but could include giving *prima facie* hospitality to foreign officials visiting Anguilla. Such legislation would be aimed at preventing bribery in commercial transactions – which impacts both domestic and foreign investment in Anguilla given the projected growth in its real estate and development market. Anguilla is behind its fellow Overseas Territories in demonstrating commitment to tackling corruption at home and abroad through legislative reform (Anguilla Financial Services Commission 2017).

Understanding that in close-knit communities, perceptions about corruption may be different to those which exist in larger, developed jurisdictions is an important point when assessing a country's bribery regime. Anguilla does have certain laws, such as the House of Assembly (Powers and Privileges) Act 2000 which deals with acceptance of bribes by members in relation to Assembly functions. Anyone convicted is liable to a fine of $38,400 and/or imprisonment of 3 years under section 12, House of Assembly (Powers and Privileges) Act 2000. However, nothing on its statute books is as all-encompassing as the UK's Bribery Act, or Bermuda's and TCI's legislation for that matter. Mitchell (2016a) has observed:

> In the U.K., parliamentarians have gone to jail for fiddling their expenses, and, in the U.S., congressmen have been indicted for accepting bribes . . . you will search [Anguilla] largely in vain for any punishment meted out to a politician known to have left office hugely enriched.

He has further advocated for the establishment of an Interests or Integrity Commissioner to provide checks and balances. Similar institutions have been established in other Overseas Territories and are appearing to be taken seriously in the jurisdictions by stakeholders. For example, one of the hallmarks of TCI's Integrity Commission is that since its establishment, there have not been any instances of disclosure breaches.

When reputational attacks are prevalent towards offshore jurisdictions like Anguilla, bringing its legislation up to date is important not only for its viability but also for attracting legitimate custom. If Anguilla relies on old bribery laws, then it will be guided by old case law precedents in contrast to those emanating from decisions in the higher UK courts. Such a concern was echoed in Bermuda when reforming its Bribery Act. This problem will only increase with time, and Anguilla could be seen as a jurisdiction failing to toughen up on bribery.

Further, when important legislation is lacking, the awareness-raising function and necessary trainings which ordinarily accompany its adoption are not undertaken. As such, it provides context as to how international suspect wealth might be transited into Anguilla's financial centre. While Anguilla has not experienced globally publicised corruption scandals, the lessons from TCI over a short 30-year period are valuable, particularly insofar as strengthening institutions. In Anguilla, if a construction planning decision comes before the Planning authority, and they conclude that the plans are unsuitable on environmental bases, then the Executive Council hears the appeal of this decision. The Executive Council is the cabinet of primarily elected politicians. The 1986 and 2008–9 Commissions of Inquiry in TCI demonstrate how easy it was for international developers to befriend elected politicians. If Anguilla remains behind in incorporating modern bribery law, creating and strengthening watchdog institutions and oversight initiatives, then the system invariably remains susceptible to abuse. It will therefore be of critical importance to address this when considering wider risks in the ongoing National AML/CFT Risk Assessment.

6.4.2 Anti–money laundering and counter-terrorism financing, including FATF compliance and national risk assessments

In November 2015, CFATF concluded that Anguilla had made "significant progress" in addressing the deficiencies it had identified during the 2010 MER. As such, it agreed that Anguilla should exit the follow-up process. Anguilla is not on the FATF List of AML Deficient Countries. While this sets a positive tone of Anguilla's approach to AML/CFT and implementation of international standards, it is necessary to discuss the position around 2010 in more depth. With regards to the FATF Recommendations, Anguilla was assessed as Compliant in 11, Largely Compliant in 17, Partially Compliant in 19 and Non-Compliant in 2 (CFATF 2010, 184). Many factors underlying the assessment were the inability to measure effectiveness, for example the lack of money laundering prosecutions, confiscations or seizures at the time, or that legislation and regulation had only been recently enacted.

At the time of writing, the most recent assessment of Anguilla is the 8th Follow-Up Report (2015). CFATF concluded that Anguilla had addressed deficiencies in its adherence to Core and Key Recommendations to a level at least 'Largely Compliant', with 3 achieving a substantial level of compliance. Specifically, these are Recommendations 5, 13, SRIV, 23 and 26 which were rated Partially or Non-Compliant in the 2010 MER. In terms of effectiveness since then, the report noted that Anguilla had several money laundering investigations, prosecutions and convictions (CFATF 2015, 6). Between 2011 and 2015, there were 35 money laundering prosecutions resulting in 5 convictions. On asset recovery, some EC$1 million in property was restrained, and some EC$326,000 was frozen. Confiscation, seizure and forfeiture have been less prominent, with only EC$5,022 seized and EC$4,461 forfeited in 2014, and nothing in the other years.

Anguilla's legislative response to money laundering has been strengthened since creating the POCA in 2009, later enhanced in 2013 when a consolidation exercise took place with the Financial Services (Amendment) Act 2013 and the Proceeds of Crime (Amendment) Act 2013. The report referenced that Anguilla has focused on enacting, amending and implementing key legislation. Examples relate to amendments to its AML/CFT Code 2009 and its Non-Profit Organisations Code, and to establishing the AML/CFT Legal Services Unit with Anguilla's FSC to engage in implementing a regulatory framework for non-profit organisations and DNFBPs.

As well as POCA, AML is controlled via regulations such as the AML/CFT Regulations and the AML/CFT Financing Code applying AML controls to non-profit organisations and, importantly, CSPs under Schedule 2, AML/CFT Regulations. Anguilla's POCA is modern and in line with POCA frameworks in jurisdictions like the UK. Anguilla also has confiscation provisions in its drug trafficking legislation,[5] yet from data available it is unclear whether these have been used in the Act's history. More recently, FATF was unable to measure effectiveness of legislative implementation due to the recent enactment of relevant statutes. Of course, the same could have been said of the UK Bribery Act, which took several years to see the first corporate conviction under section 7 in the case of Sweett Group plc.

In 2020, Anguilla was due to undergo FATF's 4th Round MER. This timetable changed due to the global Covid-19 health pandemic and disruption to on-site reviews. The next on-site review period in Anguilla is scheduled for 2022, whereby alongside technical compliance, Anguilla's effectiveness in implementing standards will be examined. As has been the case in other jurisdictions, and in furtherance of attaining the risk-based approach which underpins compliance with FATF standards, Anguilla announced that it would undertake a preparatory money laundering and terrorism financing NRA. As already mentioned, these are designed to identify risks across public and private sectors through multistakeholder engagements, consultations and advocacy – such as awareness-raising for DNFBPs. Anguilla successfully passed through the 3rd Round process in

5 Section 4, Drug Trafficking Offences Act (Designated Countries and Territories) Regulations 2004.

November 2015, and the NRA ought to enable an enhanced approach to identifying and mitigating against risks and complying with recommendations in previous reviews. The NRA will enable Anguilla to identify money laundering and terrorism financing risks and how to strengthen institutions which are integral for Anguilla's long-term progress and development.

The NRA was announced in February 2017, some months before the hurricane devastation. Its progress was severely hindered by the hurricanes and, since, with the Covid-19 pandemic. Provided it is not sidelined completely, the NRA ought to give Anguilla the opportunity to set the tone for positive engagement in the 4th Round assessment with risk areas identified and stakeholders, including DNFBPs, actively participating. However, given the impact on its tourism industry wrought by the 2017 hurricanes and 2020 Covid-19 restrictions, it is perhaps not unreasonable to project that rebuilding efforts will be prioritised. This also relates to one of the inevitable consequences caused by Covid-19, namely a loss of momentum on key areas of economic crime and financial regulation compliance. Given Anguilla's financial centre has been implicated as facilitating crimes including money laundering, such as through purchasing luxury property, the role of the FSC in engaging with the real estate sector will be critical. Like TCI, whose NRA identified similar risk areas, Anguilla's luxury property market presents ongoing money laundering risks. In circumstances which hinder the NRA's progress, it is difficult to assess the extent to which certain services in Anguilla are acknowledged as high risk in this regard. As at April 2020, Anguilla's NRA was underway in preparation for the 4th Round MER.

The string of successful reviews and upwardly mobile engagement with CFATF processes demonstrates willingness to engage in the global rules–based system. While FATF is the unchallenged standard-setter, it has been argued that FATF standards are incompatible with each other. For example, Recommendation 10 deals with due diligence for financial institutions, and there have been many CFATF seminars focusing on best practices that have advised licenced company managers that they should follow those due diligence requirements imposed on banks. As Mitchell (2016b) observed, under section 19 Companies Management Act, company managers cannot receive client funds or hold them on trust in the same way that financial intermediators do, such as banks. Given company managers don't engage in financial transactions, this is one example where advice on guidance may be misapplied.

Other AML assessments include the 2016 US Department of State's International Narcotics Strategy Report. It concluded that Anguilla was a "monitored jurisdiction", and cited money laundering vulnerability compounded by factors like the use of bearer shares and the ability to register companies online, as being risk areas. Drawing upon the accepted risks that IBCs can facilitate money laundering, the report notes that IBCs can hold accounts in Anguilla, despite not having required physical presence there, nor being permitted to transact business in the jurisdiction. As such, it suggests that there is a possibility for concealing the true nature of business undertakings in Anguilla (Know Your Country, Anguilla 2017, 5–7).

On the point of bearer shares, which are widely accepted to facilitate economic crime, Anguilla recently enacted legislation to prohibit the issuance of bearer shares under its International Business Companies (Amendment) Act 2018. This legislation repeals the Custody of Bearer Shares Regulations and outright prohibits issuing bearer shares from 30 September 2018, and that those issued and outstanding are to be converted to registered shares before 31 January 2019.

In terms of its regulated environment, at successive Financial Service Industry days, the FSC's regulatory efforts have been noted and praised by various stakeholders. CFATF's 8th Follow-Up indicated that the FSC's activity was responsible for bringing Anguilla up to compliance with many Key Recommendations – such as Recommendation 23 relating to DNFBPs – to a Largely Compliant rating (CFATF 2015, 3–4). Other examples include the establishment of the AML/CFT Legal Services Unit within the FSC tasked with implementing a DNFBPs regulatory regime. Its training programmes were also cited when considering the extent to which Anguilla had adopted the recommendations of CFATFs MER.

Anguilla's FSC was created via the Financial Services Commission Act 2003. As a statutory body, its role is to enable Anguilla to meet international financial regulation standards. Its wide statutory remit, outlined at section 3, includes enforcing regulatory codes, considering licence applications, supervising AML/CFT compliance of licensees and externally regulated service providers. It also takes action against those carrying on without licences and supervises the administration of the Registry Acts by the Commercial Registrar. Crucially, it monitors the effectiveness of the AML/CFT regime and advises the Governor accordingly.

As part of its broader education function, the FSC conducts trainings to educate company managers about their responsibilities under the AML/CFT Code and Regulations.[6] Between 2015 and 2017, the FSC conducted offsite reviews and published an extensive first report of its enforcement action. Publication carries a deterrent function and raises public awareness about enforcement. The purpose was to assess levels of compliance with Customer Due Diligence provisions of the AML/CFT legislation by licensees carrying on company management business. It reviewed 51 licensees and imposed administrative penalties against 13 that did not comply with the legislative obligations. Examples of misconduct included failing to conduct a customer risk assessment for 1 company, including to identify the principals as PEPs, contrary to s10(4) AML/CFT Regulations and ss10–11 AML/CFT Code; failing to apply customer due diligence measures including not obtaining official identification documents, contrary to s10 AML/CFT Regulations and ss10, 13, 14, 16, 17 AML/CFT Code; and not keeping records nor making them available on a timely basis when lawfully requested, contrary to s17 AML/CFT Regulations. While some fines were small – in one instance EC$100 for failing to conduct ongoing monitoring and to update the expired identification documentation for one principal of a customer – the total penalties were EC$178,750. Given the report omits specific information about

6 See: AML/CFT Code, R.R.A. P89–5; and AML/CFT Regulations, R.R.A. P98–1.

the entities, it is not clear whether the fines served any deterrent or punitive functions for the entities concerned, or others. Absent information about their financial circumstances, it is not possible to judge the effectiveness of the penalties. However, given some enforcement actions were completed, and that the process itself was deemed a first of its kind in Anguilla, it demonstrates proactivity by the regulator and utilisation of the offsite review process advocated by the modern AML framework.

6.4.3 Company law, beneficial ownership, transparency and tax information exchange

Given that reports have implicated Anguillian companies as being used to commit or facilitate crime overseas and that Anguillian property has been implicated as a means of disposing or concealing of criminal proceeds, it is necessary to consider the position with regards to company beneficial ownership information.

Anguilla's framework to deal with beneficial ownership information is the least developed of the three jurisdictions in terms of keeping information centrally and making it accessible to foreign governments. While its companies regime has undergone modernisation in recent times, it does not presently have a functioning central register of beneficial ownership information. Anguilla's framework on this traditionally centred on a summons procedure. If the Registrar had reason to enquire as to the ownership or control of an Anguillian-registered company, a summons could be obtained. As such, beneficial ownership was exclusively a matter for the Commercial Registrar per section 2, Companies Registry Act. In October 2020, Governor Foy, in response to the EU's inclusion of Anguilla on its blacklist following the OECD's downgrading of Anguilla to 'non-compliant', averred that Anguilla's online central commercial registry form would come online in 2021 (Governor's Office, Anguilla 7.10.2020). He stated that this would allow information to be shared on a timely basis in response to legitimate requests. While it is interesting to contrast Anguilla's progress on beneficial ownership information with other territories, like Bermuda who have collected and exchanged such information for years, it is equally interesting to compare progress with the US, which only in 2021 have approved legislation to create their central register.

In terms of its domestic companies legislation, Anguilla requires all companies to keep essential records (154[1][d] Companies Act), including keeping a register of shareholders and directors. The Companies Act requires the names of directors (legal or natural persons) to be provided to the Commercial Registrar upon incorporation, as per section 7(1)(g) of the Act. The Registry maintains the register, which includes IBCs, LLCs and foundations. While the Registry exists to also market the effectiveness of incorporation via the new online function, it makes clear that Anguillian authorities will cooperate fully with competent foreign enforcement agencies.

Anguilla has shown proactivity as regards committing to international changes on beneficial ownership and moving away from the increasingly outdated method of placing it exclusively in the hands of companies. In 2014, Anguilla's Government launched a public consultation on beneficial ownership transparency and increasing trust in Anguillian business. In furtherance of Anguilla's 2013 commitment to fully implementing FATF standards on this, the consultation was to assess the public's and other stakeholders' views on whether the register should be central or open. In the context of the EU's 4th AML Directive, and even FATF Recommendation 24, this type of exercise aligns with internationally advocated standards of that time. In 2016, the UK and Anguilla signed an Exchange of Notes Agreement enhancing mutual cooperation on beneficial ownership information sharing. The commitments undertaken in this agreement on Anguilla's side include *inter alia* updating legislation as well as establishing a central register or similarly effective system for holding such information. Under the agreement, UK-competent authorities are afforded the ability to request information and will have it within 24 hours or, in urgent cases, 1 hour.

Anguilla is one of the Overseas Territories which has made commitments to create a public register under the provisions of SAMLA. This commitment, made along with other territories in July 2020, demonstrates proactivity on the part of Anguilla in strengthening its regulated environment. As is evidenced by the Panama papers, company incorporation is an important component of Anguilla's financial industry.

Anguilla's companies regime is seeing ongoing reform, with a single piece of legislation projected to come into passage designed to consolidate other instruments and under which companies will be incorporated. The Anguilla Business Companies Act seeks to establish increased obligations regarding maintenance of corporate ownership data as well as accounting records.

Anguilla also has various MLATs in place with foreign jurisdictions, including the US. This secures bilateral cooperation in evidence gathering and information sharing in matters of crime and tax. In the most recent CFATF assessment, Anguilla reported that it had received 3 MLA requests in 2015 under the Criminal Justice (International Cooperation) (Anguilla) Act, and 2 under the MLA (USA) Act 2000. It reported sending 1 MLA request under the latter Act.

In terms of its compliance industry, while this industry is relatively small, Anguilla has engaged in various seminars and workshops relating to compliance and tax transparency for financial service organisations (*Anguillian* 15.4.2019; 20.2.2017). In 2016, Anguilla established a Compliance Association incorporated under its Companies Act, to promote the industry and engage in awareness-raising.

On tax information exchange, prior to the automatic exchange regime and adoption of obligations under the CRS, Anguilla had entered into 17 TIEAs. These included jurisdictions such as the UK, Netherlands and Canada. Since upgrading to automatic exchange, as at 2020 Anguilla has activated bilateral exchange relationships for CRS information with 56 countries (OECD 2020). Despite this demonstrating progress on Anguilla's part in engaging with international standards on information exchange on tax matters, this has to be taken against the backdrop of the OECD's 2020 downgrading of Anguilla to 'non-compliant'. The OECD's Key Recommendations highlighted poor availability of key accounting information for exchange purposes and criticised the timeliness of exchange. It also averred that no effective monitoring took place as to the practical application of recently enacted laws allowing information exchange.

6.4.4 Economic substance

In response, the EU's Code of Conduct Group on Business Taxation, Anguilla has established economic substance requirements through various amendments to its domestic laws, including the Companies Act, IBC Act, LLC Act, and the Limited Partnership Act (Formation Legislation). The regime in Anguilla came into force in early 2019 and applies to all companies and limited partnerships engaged in relevant activities. Relevant activity is defined under the Companies (Amendment) Act 2019 as banking, insurance, fund management, financing and leasing, distribution and service centre, shipping, intellectual property business, headquarters and holiday companies. There is also an annual reporting requirement to confirm engagement in relevant activities and to determine compliance with the substance requirements, per section 205C. The requirements include having an adequate number of qualified employees, operating expenditures and physical assets in Anguilla. The business must also engage in core income-generating activities in Anguilla, as well as its "mind and management" for the entity taking place in the territory (Anguilla Government 2019, 3).

Given that Anguilla had been placed on the EU greylist, the fact that it has enacted economic substance legislation recently demonstrates proactivity in adhering to international standards, including those under the BEPS regime, to subvert the form-over-substance problems which offshore jurisdictions have enabled. It demonstrates an acknowledgment of this problem, but also the need for Anguilla to adopt measures which enable it to secure its position in the international community. These reforms ensure that entities registered and tax resident in Anguilla will have adequate substance in the jurisdiction. Financial penalties exist under the amendments for non-compliance, or breaches of the reporting requirements.

6.4.5 Remaining legal considerations and constitutional reform

While Anguilla still lacks certain important and progressive legislation in the context of tackling the impact of domestic and international financial crime, there does appear to be an infrastructure in place to achieve relevant legislative apparatus and progressive reform, particularly in the area of anti-bribery. Supporting this is recent legislation abolishing bearer shares, establishing economic substance legislation, and the commitment to implementing a public register of beneficial ownership in line with UK legislation.

Anguilla is home to the Regional Law Revision Centre established in 2007, which services revision of laws in Anguilla, Montserrat, TCI and BVI, chaired by the Attorney General. The Centre has a wider training and education role in the region. Wider examples of recent legislative developments in Anguilla include the Justice Protection Act 2016 that introduced witness protection particularly for vulnerable persons, or the Criminal Justice Reform Bill 2018 that decriminalises possession of small quantities of cannabis for recreational use. Under the Anguilla Police (Amendment) Act 2016, procedural advancements include the ability to take non-intimate samples from suspects, and the introduction of the Legal Professions Act 2016 statutorily regulates the legal profession for the first time.

While some of the above legislative reforms fall outside the parameters of this work, it adds some context to relevant legislative commitments made, such as the Tax Exchange (International Cooperation) Act 2016. However, Anguilla's criminal and civil laws are still undergoing and are in further need of reform. This is important in the area of anti-corruption, strengthening transparency and AML controls, because of the cases and reports indicating that Anguillian entities have been implicated in and/or have facilitated misconduct overseas. In terms of implication in the Panama papers and consequent OECD downgrading, reform of companies laws will be needed to accommodate a surrounding infrastructure to support transition from a newly functioning central register, to operating an open register. For example, absent independent verification of information, the public register may not serve the purpose it envisions.

As a development strategy, Anguilla has also been targeting foreign investment into the jurisdiction through the Anguilla Residency by Investment (ARBI) scheme. This allows investors to bypass typical residency requirements via real estate investment of at least $750,000 or through investment into Anguilla's Capital Development Fund of at least $150,000 (Anguilla Government 23.8.2018). This will doubtless have significant economic benefit for Anguilla, although the Government has acknowledged the need to conduct significant DD on prospective investors. Given the benefits and apparent ease, investors' motivations could be tainted and therefore development of Anguilla's oversight bodies is imperative to protect this system from being abused for money laundering or evading tax.

6.5 Development concerns

Anguilla's achievements, but also challenges, in implementing and complying with international standards need to be taken against an important context of significant development-related concerns. As an aim of this work is to afford better understanding of these under-researched jurisdictions, these need to be addressed. Many issues, like capacity, affect most small island nations, and in the case of those which have less sophisticated financial sectors, attracting workers might be difficult. For example, establishing a compliance framework and recruiting people when the industry is not as visible in Anguilla presents challenges. Anguilla's development and reputation as a luxury tourist destination does not reconcile with some of its development concerns. However, combined with relatively high GDP, low crime rates, and 'tax haven' reputation, the spotlight on Anguilla's development concerns is unsurprisingly dim and often overlooked by the international community.

In recent years, Anguilla has been preoccupied with various development challenges. A powerful example demonstrating this is the account of Anguilla's then Attorney General, John McKendrick QC, who in the aftermath of the 2017 hurricanes recalled spending 3 months living in temporary accommodation without mains power or running water (Inner Temple 2018–19). Given the substantial portfolio of the Attorney General as the territory's principal lawyer (who in Anguilla's case also serves as DPP), this account demonstrates the ravages which have been wrought on Anguilla through hurricane devastation. The UK government's announcement of the public register clause in SAMLA some 7 months after the hurricanes hit was questionable.

The ECCB has regulatory function for domestic banking in Anguilla. In 2013, the island was in severe financial trouble as its two indigenous banks were placed under the control of the ECCB. Article 5(b), Eastern Caribbean Central Bank Agreement Act 1983 (as amended) provides for this in circumstances where the interests of the financial institution's depositors or creditors are threatened, or if the institution is unlikely to meet its obligations, or if the financial system of the territory is in danger of disruption. The ECCB concluded that all three conditions applied to Anguilla's indigenous banks. In 2013, they were deemed insolvent and placed under receivership (Caribbean Development Bank 2016, ii). There was a sizeable shortfall at both banks and, in the event of a run, collapse would ensue. In 2015, Anguilla's Government stated:

> The current balance sheet deficiency at [both banks] is primarily due to the quantum of non-performing loans and increasing provisions being made against such loans as a result of falling property prices in Anguilla. This problem was in part contributed to by the overreliance on the valuation of the security being advanced as collateral . . . as opposed to analysing cash-flow and the ability of the applicant to repay the loans.
>
> (*Anguillian* 9.11.2015)

In 2016, the Bank Resolution Obligations Act was passed to protect depositors' savings. It was, however, met with controversy with the Opposition Leader criticising the outcome of "the forfeiture of bank employees' pensions and the consequent default of those employees' property loans, and the institutional theft of offshore depositors' money" (*Anguillian* 8.5.2017).

Another development concern is Anguilla's dependency on neighbouring islands. It has no deep ports for large cruise liners and its airport is incapable of hosting larger international air traffic. It relies heavily on Saint Martin (French) and Sint Maarten (Dutch). As such, its direct borders are effectively with France and the Netherlands, who provide essential services including fuel, international access, excursion tourism, basic medical procedures, mail services and imports. Given this relationship of reliance, it is interesting to note the Netherland's inclusion of Anguilla on its list of low-tax jurisdictions.

Healthcare is another development issue and medical services depend upon collaboration with neighbours. Compared to other permanently populated territories, Anguilla is said to have one of the least developed public medical facilities under a British flag (Anguilla Government London Office 2017). As well as some of the more obvious implications, if Anguilla is to diversify its financial services industry, which necessitates foreign recruitment and making it easier to obtain work permits, then progress may be hindered by its healthcare infrastructure, which translates to standard of living.

Anguilla also relies on wells and rainwater harvesting as well as desalination fuel from its neighbours to make water drinkable (Pan American Health Organisation 2012, 3). According to the WHO and UNICEF (2017), while 98% of Anguilla's population in 2015 had basic access to water, it has been dependent upon bottled water and rationing at times of drought. Two-thirds of Anguilla is below sea level and the territory lies in a tropical cyclone path which can cause devastating effects (Anguilla Government 2013).

Overreliance on tourism and lack of economic diversification means that in cases of natural disaster, Anguilla's tourism season can be effectively written off. This is a problem shared by many of the Overseas Territories. This represents a serious issue which increasingly acts to incentivise diversification for Anguilla's sustainable development – at the least, diversifying its business offerings and financial services further. In a statement at Anguilla's Financial Service Industry Day 2016, then Governor Christina Scott observed that Anguilla's sustainability should not continue to depend on tourism.

6.6 Conclusion

Anguilla has been implicated in several high-profile instances of international economic crime in terms of its financial centre facilitating international criminality, or the transiting and disposal of suspect wealth in the case examples mentioned. Global Witness' investigations demonstrate the severity of allegations against Anguillian companies. While implication in the Panama papers does not necessarily show wrongdoing, it does demonstrate that a law firm proven to have facilitated international criminality utilised Anguilla as a jurisdiction of choice for incorporation or corporate services. This proved problematic for Anguilla in the fallout of MOSSFON's sudden closure with regards to obtaining and providing beneficial ownership information.

While Anguilla's response to economic crime and suspect wealth remains under-developed, Anguilla has shown willingness and commitment in several key areas, to which credit must be given. These include legislative reforms prohibiting the issuance of bearer shares, enacting economic substance laws and wider company law reforms including reporting obligations, committing to greater information exchange and establishing in 2021 a functioning central register of beneficial ownership. Open register commitments further this spirit of cooperation. These demonstrate action in trying to prevent suspect wealth entering the jurisdiction and otherwise facilitate financial crime elsewhere. Moreover, aspects of Anguilla's AML/CFT framework have been reviewed in a positive manner since the first MER.

The deficiencies in Anguilla's response to suspect wealth, however, remain a concern, particularly in the areas of broader legal and constitutional reform. The latter is imperative with regards to the development and strengthening of key institutions tasked with the delivery of these initiatives, trainings, oversight and monitoring, as well as enforcement, cooperation and the administration of justice. An example where its laws are lacking relates to bribery and corresponding institutions charged with raising standards and integrity to support a tightened understanding of bribery in the modern world.

Anguilla's commitments to operating an open register by 2023 are positive and will build upon those amendments made to its legislation relating to reporting obligations. It is positive insofar as it adheres to UK and EU standards. However, with protracted movement with developing a functioning central register, combined with the challenges even the UK has faced with its public register and lack of independent verification to date, it is unclear the extent to which this commitment will translate to meaningful improvements in the regime at this stage. This may give rise to a conclusion that such standards are not viable at present. Further, despite recently enacted legislation, there is limited data on its effectiveness. Absent a completed NRA and the consequences of a delayed 4th Round MER, the question as to whether these measures will garner positive reviews as to effectiveness is yet to be determined. It is important that Anguilla engages in preparations for the 4th Round review by completing a comprehensive NRA to identify risks. If Anguilla wishes to diversify its financial sector, then institutional and legislative reform in basic areas relating to standards, oversight and checks and balances is needed. Anguilla's compliance record needs to be taken against development challenges it has faced. With this is mind, the progress it has made is positive and demonstrates a willingness to advance its cooperation with the international community. However, commitments alone are not enough, and without meaningful institutional development, many of these commitments risk being undermined – which may translate to greater risks of abuse. In advance of the 4th Round MER, this is particularly important in the case of identifying risk in other sectors.

References

Anguilla Government (2013) 'Comprehensive Disaster Management Policy'. Available: https://www.preventionweb.net/files/74856_anguillanationalcdmpolicy.pdf

Anguilla Financial Services Commission (2017) 'Offsite Reviews 2015–2017', Report. Available: https://www.fsc.org.ai/documents/Publications/EnforcementAction/Offsite%20Reviews%202015%20-%202017.pdf

Anguilla Government (2018) 'Anguilla & Brexit: The Solution'. Available: https://westindiacommittee.org/wp-content/uploads/2018/03/Anguilla-and-Brexit-The-Solution.pdf

Anguilla Government (2019) 'Information Summary on Amendments to Incorporation Legislation to Introduce (EU) Economic Substance Requirements for Entities Conducting Relevant Activities'. Available: https://anguillafinance.ai/wp-content/uploads/2019/01/Introduction-of-Economic-Substance-Requirements-Dec-2018-final.pdf

Anguilla Government. London Office (2017) 'Anguilla and Brexit: Britain's Forgotten EU Border'. Available: http://www.westindiacommittee.org/wp-content/uploads/2017/06/The-White-Paper-on-Anguilla-and-Brexit.pdf

Anguilla Government. Residency by Investment, Information Session, 23.8.2018. Available: http://www.gov.ai/documents/finance/Anguilla%20Residency%20by%20Investment%20(ARBI)%20Presentation-%20General%20Public.pdf

Anguilla Government. Statistics Department, National Accounts 2019. Available: http://statistics.gov.ai/StatisticsDept/NationalAccountsStatistics2_2

Anguilla Government. Statistics Department, Tourism Statistics Summary, Jan-2018. Available: http://statistics.gov.ai/StatisticsDept/Tourism2_4_5

Anguillian (20.6.2014) 'Don Mitchell Advises Ronald Webster on Independence for Anguilla'. Available: https://theanguillian.com/2014/06/don-mitchell-advises-ronald-webster-on-independence-for-anguilla/

Anguillian (9.11.2015) 'Government Publishes Key Findings on NBA & CCB'. Available: https://theanguillian.com/2015/11/government-publishes-key-findings-on-nba-ccb/

Anguillian (20.2.2017) 'UWI Open Campus Anguilla Presents Workshop on Compliance Management'. Available: https://theanguillian.com/2017/02/uwi-open-campus-anguilla-presents-workshop-on-compliance-management/

Anguillian (8.5.2017) 'Message to the People of Anguilla from Pam Webster – Opposition Leader'. Available: https://theanguillian.com/2017/05/message-to-the-people-of-anguilla-from-pam-webster-elected-member-district-one-and-leader-of-the-opposition/

Anguillian (15.4.2019) 'UWI Open Campus Anguilla Launches Second Compliance Workshop – Compliance and Tax Transparency Standards for Financial Services Organisations'. Available: https://theanguillian.com/2019/04/uwi-open-campus-anguilla-launches-second-compliance-workshop-on-compliance-and-tax-transparency-standards-for-financial-services-organisations/

Anguillian (22.1.2020) 'Government Achieves Record Recurrent Surplus in 2019'. Available: https://theanguillian.com/2020/01/government-of-anguilla-achieves-record-recurrent-surplus-in-2019/

Australia Parliament, Joint Committee on Corporations and Financial Services (2012) 'Inquiry into the Collapse of Trio Capital'. Available: https://www.aph.gov.au/~/media/wopapub/senate/committee/corporations_ctte/completed_inquiries/2010_13/trio/report/report_pdf.ashx

BBC Radio 4 (6.2.2010) 'Lord Goldsmith: UK Bribery Laws are Outdated'. Available: http://news.bbc.co.uk/today/hi/today/newsid_8501000/8501758.stm

BBC (20.6.2018) 'Panama Papers: Mossack Fonseca was Unable to Identify Company Owners'. Available: www.bbc.co.uk/news/world-latin-america-44553932

Caribbean Development Bank (2016) 'Loan & Project Summary: Anguilla Bank Resolution – Bridge Bank Capitalisation Loan'. Available: https://www.caribank.org/publications-and-resources/resource-library/board-papers/loans-grants-and-project-summaries/anguilla-bank-resolution-bridge-bank-capitalisation-loan

CFATF (2010) '3rd Round MER'. Available: https://www.cfatf-gafic.org/index.php/documents/mutual-evaluation-reports/anguilla-1/2-anguilla-3rd-round-mer

CFATF (2015) '8th Follow-Up Report'. Available: https://www.cfatf-gafic.org/documents/cfatf-follow-up-reports/anguilla/6264-anguilla-8th-follow-up-report-1/file

Constitutional and Electoral Reform Committee, Draft Constitution for Anguilla (2019). Available: http://www.gov.ai/documents/anguilla_constitutional_electoral_reform.pdf

DfID (1.11.2018) 'UK Secures Change to International Aid Rules: Restrictions to Britain's Aid Support to Countries Affected by Crises and Natural Disasters that Severely Impact their Economy are Lifted', Press Release.

Don Mitchell QC, Presentation at the 'Time Kendall Public Lecture', Antigua and Barbuda Bar Association, 21.9.2017. Available: https://donmitchellcbeqc.blogspot.com/search/label/Time%20Kendall

ECCB (2018) 'Anguilla GDP (Annual) 2016'. Available: https://www.eccb-centralbank.org/statistics/dashboard-datas/

France24 (25.6.2017) 'Congo President's Daughter Charged with Corruption in France'. Available: www.france24.com/en/20170625-congo-presidents-daughter-charged-with-corruption-france

Global Witness (2009) 'Undue Diligence: How Banks do Business with Corrupt Regimes'. Available: https://www.globalwitness.org/en/campaigns/corruption-and-money-laundering/banks/undue-diligence/

Governor's Office, Anguilla, Statement, 7.10.2020. Available: https://www.facebook.com/goanguilla/posts/1569403686575565

ICIJ Offshore Leaks database, Paradise Papers; and Panama Papers. Available: https://offshoreleaks.icij.org/

IMF (2012) 'United Kingdom-Anguilla British Overseas Territory: Staff Report for the 2011 Article IV Consultation'. Available: https://www.imf.org/en/Publications/CR/Issues/2016/12/31/United-Kingdom-Anguilla-British-Overseas-Territory-Staff-Report-for-the-2011-Article-IV-25659

Know Your Country Report, Anguilla (2017). Available: https://www.knowyourcountry.com/anguillaaq

McKendrick, J. 'A Tropical Attorney General', *Inner Temple Year Book 2018–2019*, [134–135].

Mitchell, D. (2016a) 'What are the Most Important Issues for Constitutional Reform Today? In *The Anguillian* (12.12.2016).

Mitchell, D. (2016b) 'Financial Regulatory Issues', Paper presented at OECS Bar Association's Annual Law Fair and Conference, 16 September 2016, St Lucia.

Netherlands Government (28.12.2018) 'Netherlands Publishes Own List of Low-Tax Jurisdictions in Fight Against Tax Avoidance', Press Release.

OECD (2020) 'Automatic Exchange Portal'. Available: https://www.oecd.org/tax/automatic-exchange/

OECD. 'Automatic Exchange Portal, Activated Exchange Relations – CRS Information', August 2020. Available: https://www.oecd.org/tax/automatic-exchange/

OECD (2020) 'Global Forum on Transparency and Exchange of Information for Tax Purposes: Anguilla 2020, 2nd Round'. Available: https://read.oecd-ilibrary.org/taxation/global-forum-on-transparency-and-exchange-of-information-for-tax-purposes-anguilla-2020-second-round_ac228609-en#page1

Pan American Health Organisation (2012) 'Health in the Americas – Ed: Country Volume, Anguilla'. Available: https://www.paho.org/salud-en-las-americas-2017/

Petty, C. L., and Hodge, N. (1987) *Anguilla's Battle for Freedom 1967*, Anguilla: Petnat Publishing Co.

Sharman, J. C. (2017) *Despots Guide to Wealth Management*, New York: Cornell University Press.

Transparency International (2018) 'The Cost of Secrecy'. Available: https://www.transparency.org.uk/publications/cost-of-secrecy

US Department of Justice (9.11.2016) 'Futures Trader Pleads Guilty to Illegally Manipulating the Futures Market in Connection with 2010 "Flash Crash"', Press Release.

US Department of Justice (4.12.2018) 'Four Defendants Charged in Panama Papers Investigations for their Roles in Panamanian-based Global Law Firm's Decades-long Scheme to Defraud the United States', Press Release.
US Department of the Treasury (8.11.2009) 'Treasury Designates Financial Institution Tied to North Korea's WMD Proliferation', Press Release.
World Health Organisation/United Nations International Children's Emergency Fund (2017) Progress on Drinking Water, Sanitation and Hygiene: 2017 Update and SDG Baseline, Available: https://data.unicef.org/topic/water-and-sanitation/drinking-water/ (accessed 14.6.2018).
Woodley, B., Sahgal, V., Stapenhurst, F., and Pelizzo, R. (2005) 'Scrutinizing Public Expenditures: Assessing the Performance of Public Accounts Committees', World Bank Policy Research Working Paper 3613.

7 Privacy and increasing transparency

What does it mean for the future of offshore financial centres?

7.1 Introduction

There has been significant tightening of international financial regulation in recent years as well as criminal laws targeting bribery and money laundering, civil laws targeting unexplained wealth, and company laws requiring economic substance. This has culminated in an ever-developing international anti–economic crime framework. As the countless examples referred to so far which pertain to facilitative misconduct in offshore centres show, there is an increasing emphasis on the purported utility of transparency as a solution to disrupt economic crime. As far as the Overseas Territories are concerned, this has manifested through the enactment of public beneficial ownership register legislation, where fundamental legal questions arise regarding the role of privacy and confidentiality. This chapter explores this important issue and considers whether, in the present landscape, fundamental legal safeguards are gradually diminishing in favour of increased transparency, and what this could mean for offshore centres.

7.2 The right to privacy

It is first necessary to consider privacy as a broad right. It is enshrined in numerous sources of domestic and international law (ECHR, Universal Declaration on Human Rights, UK Human Rights Act 1998 and US Privacy Act 1974). Since World War II, privacy has been argued to have become an internationally accepted human right (Diggelmann and Clais 2014, 441). There are many theoretical explanations of it. Emerson (1970, 549) conjects that privacy is based on individualism and withdrawing from the collective in certain circumstances – in other words, a manifestation of individual sovereignty. Privacy protects the individual from community encroachment, whether from another person, group or state. The Universal Declaration's formulation links privacy to honour, self-respect and reputation. The value of privacy is central to realising personal dignity (Klitou 2014, 18). Privacy comprises the right to private and family life, respect for communities, correspondence, protection against unreasonable seizures and searches, and protection against attack to honour and reputation. It has been labelled a cluster of derivative rights (Thomson 1975, 307) or a curious kind of right (Marmor 2015, 3). Without privacy, people may be less likely to express individuality or form close, intimate or familial relationships (Taylor 2002, 82). Holtzman (2006, 53) suggests privacy is an enabling right which sets the foundation for other basic entitlements.

Privacy has been deemed to provide the means for greater liberty. In his essay *On Liberty*, Mill (1859/2008, 6) emphasised that "[the] struggle between Liberty and Authority is the most conspicuous feature in the portions of history with which we are earliest familiar, particularly in that of Greece, Rome and England". Liberty is closely related to privacy, and authority to security. It is the necessity of security which renders privacy a qualified, rather than absolute, right. Security in this context appears in the form of transparency as being a means for limiting privacy. Aristotle's early thinking on this posited that there is an important, discernible distinction between public and private life. In modern times, this can be applied in the context of the state's authority. In his work on the "harm principle", Mill (1859, 8) stresses that "the sole end for which mankind are warranted, individually or collectively, in interfering with the liberty of action of any of their number, is self-protection".

Another utilitarian thinker, Bentham (1789) formulated that the law can invade privacy but it must be justified on the grounds of necessary utility. In our context of finance or corporate affairs, necessary utility might be a law designed to prevent money laundering or reasonable searches in criminal investigations. It might extend to, or justify, use of transparency via public registers of beneficial ownership based on the widely accepted harm caused by money laundering through anonymous shell companies. Our conceptualisations of privacy and its different elements, and idea about the justification of the law, have changed vastly over the last century. With advanced technology increasing security threats, this is perhaps even more pertinent today. Law's intervention has had to constantly adapt to changing circumstances. A good example is technological advancement and its impact on surveillance.

Considering privacy in terms of intervention involves a delicate balancing exercise. This is prevalent in case law, with a good example being the English case of *Mosley v News Group Newspapers (No.3)* [2008], which found that a media organisation, in disclosing clandestine footage of the then President of the Federation Internationale de l'Automobile engaging in sadomasochist activities in a private residence, had invaded privacy. The Court held there was no public interest or other justification for the recording, disclosure and publication. Another example is the case of *Silken v Beaverbrook Newspapers Ltd* [1985], where Lord Diplock, at 745, emphasised that freedom of speech, like other freedoms under the law, must be balanced against other fundamental freedoms. In the case of *United States v Jones* (2012), a drug trafficker's convictions were quashed because law enforcement monitored his vehicle for 28 days via GPS, which was held to have violated his constitutional right to privacy. Warren and Brandeis (1890, 193) observe "that the individual shall have full protection in person and in property is a principle as old as the common law". Privacy has been argued to have become an internationally accepted human right following World War II (Diggelmann and Clais 2014, 441). While the balance is inevitable in the context of qualified rights, some scholars have argued that rights like freedom of expression should not be viewed as more important than privacy (Moore 1998). Posner (1978) has advocated that while conceding the necessity of a balancing act and that the state's interest might sometimes exceed that of the individual, the presumption ought to be on individual freedom. This ties in with other thinkers, such as Rousseau (1762), who observed that the government's interference in individual rights ought to be necessarily minimal for society's well-being.

Given the common law's eternal youth, there is sometimes the need for the recognition of new rights or the ability to adapt to society's needs. A contemporary example demonstrating this is recent legislation in many jurisdictions recognising same-sex marriage, while it remains criminalised in many other countries.

While technological advancement has been argued to pose the greatest threat to privacy (Maple 2017), it might be the case that there is growing acceptance by individuals to dispense of privacy in favour of convenience that technology provides. There have been interesting studies about the varying degrees of value placed by individuals and businesses on privacy (Acquisti, John, and Loewenstein 2013). Some have argued that privacy is an expression of triviality (Negley 1966, 321) or individualistic ideology (Sevignani 2016, 191) which lends itself to the notion of convenience created by technology. While Sevignani falls short of attacking individualism, he priorities the role of social circumstances (giving the example of social media services regularly changing privacy policies). He suggests that an alternative response to the struggle against surveillance is needed, rather than default insistence placed upon the notional value of privacy.

7.3 Confidentiality

While there is no internationally accepted right to financial privacy *per se*, financial information and confidentiality in private matters are well understood to have significant legal protection. This sits within the general right to privacy and in the context of confidentiality duties which can arise under contract, professional activity including legal privilege, and common law fiduciary duties. It would be misconceived to think confidentiality in financial affairs is confined to business adventure. Rather, it is a central component of criminal enforcement and financial regulation, for example the 'tipping off' provisions in money laundering legislation, the confidentiality which applies to the filing and processing of SARs, or the non-disclosure obligations placed on Integrity Commissions or FIUs.

Confidentiality is a material component to the provision of certain offshore services. This has evolved into what Antoine (2014) describes as the offshore confidentiality norm. Then there is bank secrecy, which can materialise through legislation and culture which prohibit banking information disclosure. However, there are significant nuances within these strands of privacy formulations. Privacy in financial affairs has been a hallmark of financial asylum, whereby wealthy and targeted individuals domiciled in unstable or oppressive societies seek to hide their wealth in alternative, safer investment environments.

Confidentiality is vigorously protected by law. Common examples include non-disclosure, confidentiality agreements, or contractual terms within contracts. Through this, the law serves a deterrent function to prevent breaches and disclosure of confidential information. These are often boilerplate provisions in commercial contracts with obvious rationales, such as protecting trade secrets, intellectual property, or price-sensitive information. The main bases upon which insider dealing laws were created in the 1980s in the UK were to preserve the financial market's level playing field and prevent insiders making private gain by abusing information unauthorised for public disclosure (Rider and Ashe 1993).

Typically, the role of confidentiality in financial affairs acts to safeguard information which facilitates commerce, competitiveness, expansion or privacy. For example, premature publicity of merger negotiations or particulars of a deal might devalue share prices, harm investors and destabilise the market. Protecting commercial secrets from competitors has long been recognised in case law (*Securities and Exchange Commissioners of the U.S.A. v Guaranty Trusts Ltd* [1985] [Bahamas]). However, confidentiality agreements are not direct remedies *per se*, as their deterrent function cannot guarantee the information remains confidential and an award of damages may not provide adequate restitution.

7.4 Legal privilege

Another important strand of privacy and confidentiality, which is important in the context of professional facilitators like lawyers, is the doctrine of legal privilege. This protects the confidentiality of communications between lawyer and client under strict rules for the purpose of legal advice. Typically, only the client can waive this privilege, as only they should be able to authorise who possesses information relating to their affairs.

The implication from the Panama and Paradise papers was that law firms were knowingly or otherwise facilitating wrongdoing. There is a legitimate line of inquiry which these data breaches opened, notwithstanding the questionable bases upon which the information came to be disseminated. That is, the extent to which lawyers might hide behind legal privilege to facilitate clients' wrongdoing – whether through advice or services they provide. Similar to the way individuals can hide behind the veil of limited liability, the concept of privilege only waivable by the client represents the problem at the heart of the offshore leaks.

As emphasised already, regulating the professions is a necessary component of the global AML risk-based approach. However, there have been challenges to these attempts in certain jurisdictions, whereby lawyers have considered that increased obligations upon professionals potentially subverts legal privilege and fundamental rights. In the Jamaican case of *Jamaica Bar Association v The Attorney General Law Council* [2017], the local Bar objected to new AML requirements under its POCA legislation which, they argued, were unconstitutional and contrary to ss13(3)(a), (j) and 16 Jamaica's Charter of Fundamental Rights and Freedoms, including subjecting law firms to searches and seizures. They argued that the right to legal representation and the implied right to confidentiality thereof would be undermined. Alongside the doctrine of privilege is the extent to which lawyers are aware of, and adhere to, their rights and obligations to clients while being alive to the risk of inveiglement or manipulation from clients with nefarious intent. Particularly for those lawyers who handle client money, it is critical that the professions are aware of their due diligence obligations.

7.5 Confidentiality norm in offshore financial centres – and the limits of confidentiality

There are legitimate reasons why one might seek confidentiality and privacy in this context. This is a central element of the criticism of offshore financial centres, however it is an important aspect to acknowledge. In the context of offshore centres, privacy as part of the broader provision of offshore services has equated to profitable business and financial independence. Given that its provision has become the linchpin in many islands' development strategies, it is unsurprising that confidentiality has been so vigorously guarded, particularly if it manifests as permissible under law, both in their jurisdiction and in others. Of course, reforming onshore tax loopholes is a much-used retort to the criticism of offshore models. While simplistic, it is not without merit, and the question arises about the extent to which jurisdictions that rely upon financial services and confidentiality ought to be the moral arbiters of the laws in other countries. Scholars have argued that the whole structure of offshore finance is designed to be confidential. Antoine (2014, 38) avers that "the notion of a fiduciary relationship must be even stronger within offshore financial circles where legitimate clients invest on the understanding of priority given to confidentiality". As such, it is important to understand why there is a legitimate expectation of privacy in financial and business matters, why it is valued in the offshore context and whether it remains justified.

Confidentiality has been seen in many civilised societies to be more than a legal requirement. Countries which place great value on individual liberties have tended to place greater emphasis on confidentiality, rather than something simply confined to professional relationships. An example is Switzerland which, as well as respecting confidentiality through the Swiss Civil Code, has traditionally placed significant importance on the values of personal liberty and independence. While far less prevalent today, a rigorous campaign to largely eradicate bank secrecy in Switzerland through a referendum in 1984 was significantly defeated with 73% voting against it (Aubert 1984, 273), implying the value of privacy held by the Swiss at that time.

Privacy as a desirable feature of financial affairs must be distinguished from its abuses. It is clear that any attempt to undermine confidentiality should have law enforcement as its objective, particularly in fighting crime. Through exchange mechanisms implemented in offshore jurisdictions to provide information to onshore ones, additional to the well-established MLA doctrine, it is clear that there is an acceptance that in certain cases privacy rights can be curtailed in the case of suspected wrongdoing or investigation efforts. It is, however, the criticism of countries' unwillingness to go further in light of adverse revelations which calls into question whether striving to safeguard confidentiality more generally is acceptable or not in this context.

It is worth examining the confidentiality norm in offshore financial centres. Trusts are a good example, whereby courts in various offshore jurisdictions have emphasised confidentiality's importance. In the Bermudian case of *Guardian Ltd v Bermuda Trust Co* [2009], the court considered the issue of disclosure of a trust's identity and beneficiaries with regards to the implementation of a trust deed clause excluding spouses. It also concerned publishing a Chambers ruling (i.e. in 'closed' court), as there was a public interest in publishing the judgment, but only if it did not reveal confidential information. Prioritising non-disclosure, the court considered Bermuda's status as an offshore jurisdiction and the development of its law of trusts. Kawaley J, at 25, stated:

> Having regard to Bermuda's status as an offshore trust domicile, this Court is bound not just to be sympathetic to the privacy needs of those who establish trusts here, but also to the need to promote the development of Bermuda's trust law.

Other examples of courts finding in favour of confidentiality include the Cayman Islands case of *Re H* [1996], whereby a US subpoena requiring disclosure of information about assets of a Cayman trust as evidence in foreign proceedings was irreconcilable with the confidentiality obligations thereunder, per Smellie J at 4–25. Likewise, in the Belize case of *Securities and Exchange Commission v Banner Fund International* [1996], confidentiality obligations relating to trusts in Belize law were interpreted strictly in response to a request by US enforcement bodies. When considering legal safeguards, in the Jersey case of *Macdoel Investments Ltd v Federal Republic of Brazil* [2007], the court paid particular attention to the fact that Jersey had developed as a major financial centre. A similar view was taken in the context of a confidential banking relationship by the Bahamas Supreme Court in the case of *Pindling v Douglas* [1994], where Strachan J, at 250, emphasised the statutory nature of banking confidentiality, and with this the necessary public importance of preserving confidentiality considering the Bahamas as an important financial centre with public confidence therein needing to be safeguarded.

For jurisdictions which have developed significant offshore business markets over time, including those Overseas Territories this book focuses on, it is an inescapable fact that confidentiality has attracted clients, thereby carrying a more practical policy justification and perhaps an unsurprising stance taken by decisions in offshore courts over the past decades. Antoine (2014) makes the comparison that there are many types of onshore laws designed to stimulate economic growth, such as laws on compulsory arbitration or relating to non-unionism in labour law. There are also considerable laws and policies in onshore jurisdictions which provide fiscal incentives for businesses to locate rurally to stimulate growth in such areas. These commonly include reduced or deferred business rates and tax incentives. One only has to consider the swathe of fiscal incentives announced during the Covid-19 pandemic. There is an imperative link between law and economic development which is important in examining the justifications of a particular legal provision. The territories' financial centres were not set up for nefarious purposes, and confidentiality in financial matters was created due to the realisation in larger countries that providing such services promoted sound commercial relations (Antoine 2014). Therefore, when revised standards aim to restrict confidentiality for the purpose of fighting crime (based on the presupposition that such features of an offshore centre can facilitate crime), it could be viewed as misguided to revert to a narrow conclusion that the common law should no longer afford individuals the protections of privacy.

It is unsurprising that recent offshore leaks have been celebrated for their probative value. However, there must remain a clear line between that which is in the public interest (e.g. exposing a conflict of interest of an elected official) and disclosing information which is simply interesting. While exposing criminality featured prominently in the aims of the publications, so too did the sensationalism of wealthy athletes or actors being found to have engaged in tax avoidance – a legally permissible, if controversial, activity. As Campbell LJ, at 84, stated in the English case of *R v Inhabitants of the County of Bedfordshire* [1855]:

> "Interested" here does not mean that which is interesting from gratifying curiosity or a love of information or amusement, but that in which a class of the community have a pecuniary interest, by which their rights or liberties are affected.

This principle was also espoused by Griffiths LJ, at 553, in the case of *Lion Laboratories Ltd v Evans* [1985], who reinforced the necessity of distinguishing that which is in the public interest and that which is interesting to know. This principle demonstrates that public interest should not be taken broadly. An example was the implication of the then UK Prime Minister David Cameron, who was exposed in the Panama papers as having benefited from his father's offshore investments. The fact he paid UK income tax on the proceeds was far less interesting than the implication he had investments offshore for those with other agendas.

Set against the increasing backdrop of negative reputational harm caused by the offshore data breaches, many offshore jurisdictions are eager to obviate the adverse connotations in such publications. As was recently seen in Malta with Standard & Poor's assessment of heightened reputational and operational risks in the banking sector (*Malta Today* 2.8.2018), financial de-risking presents significant challenges to both institutions and markets. Legitimate investors and institutions can be put off conducting business in jurisdictions which have been negatively reviewed – whether in terms of money laundering allegations against domestic institutions, or if controls are lacking more broadly.

It has been argued that there is a significant policy imperative of maintaining the offshore confidentiality norm in financial matters, which looks to be at risk with the passage of legislation compelling greater transparency. Antoine (2014, 44) suggests: "Just as onshore states have the right to protect their economic interests by attacking offshore law and policy, all things being equal, offshore states have a similar right to safeguard their economic and political interests by upholding them". This is important in the context of offshore jurisdictions, which rely on services and the ability to offer a respect for confidentiality, notwithstanding any disclosure mechanisms already in place. As well as economic considerations, there is also a constitutional basis for offshore jurisdictions striving to maintain confidentiality. In the case of the territories, this pertains to their devolved systems of governance on matters such as economic policy, tax legislation, financial market regulation and company law. While the UK government considered the growing perception of opaqueness and the risk this presents to national security enough to warrant intervention, if company law has been devolved in good faith by the UK Parliament in legislatively recognising the territories' individual constitutions, then any attempt to appropriate autonomy in such matters gives rise to constitutional tension.

With all this said, many aspects of confidentiality in financial matters are equally protected onshore as offshore. This undermines certain criticisms which portray offshore centres as being more associated with confidentiality. The public beneficial ownership register is a good example, whereby jurisdictions worldwide are still not reconciled on the extent to which they regulate such information and whether it should be provided to domestic authorities, foreign investigators or civil society. Even for those who have opted for public transparency, there is then the issue as to whether it is freely accessible or in exchange for payment. The UK has led in this regard with its free, publicly accessible register. It is one of the only major countries to have this. Hence, the argument which has until recently been prevalent in the Overseas Territories: If onshore countries do not yet change their own policy to make beneficial ownership information accessible, then why should offshore countries bow to criticism of their same model? It certainly raises questions of proportionality and legitimacy of international standards if they are not equally applied. The US, which only in 2021 approved provisions in the Corporate Transparency Act to effectively outlaw anonymous shell companies via the creation of a central (not public) register, is a good example.

An increasing level of disclosure obligations necessitates an approach by individuals mindful of their privacy to seek to rely on constitutional provisions insofar as possible. Disclosure of private financial information is legally permitted in clearly defined circumstances, as the *Tournier* principle demonstrates. While privacy and confidentiality are legally recognised by the courts to be legitimate safeguards, there is another side to this. It would be naïve to conclude that a diminishment of bank secrecy necessarily eradicates the notion of secrecy in offshore jurisdictions. Offshore services can provide various layers of protection which can be difficult or impossible to permeate. For example, one of the primary uses for offshore trusts is to protect assets whereby the trustee acts as a fiduciary in holding assets on behalf of the trust's beneficiary. Or, one could create a private bank subject to far less regulation and reporting requirements to offer additional privacy and transaction layers. Secrecy might be achieved through operation of an anonymous shell company, or a company registered in a jurisdiction which has lax beneficial ownership reporting requirements. Absent accurate information, bilateral information exchange agreements may prove unfruitful. It could also be said that layering within complex trusts or foundations, for example, inhibits transparency (Griffin 2017). Entire overhaul of a jurisdiction's beneficial ownership regime of companies may serve to disperse activity to other, less regulated vehicles.

7.6 Bank secrecy

Bank secrecy is something which is often associated with offshore financial centres and usually refers to domestic law prohibiting banks from disclosing information about their clients or accounts. It goes further than the express or implied confidentiality duty in such professional dealings. Less prevalent today, the G20 (2009, 15) claimed, "[The] era of bank secrecy is over". Subsequently, in 2013 the G8 stated, "tax authorities around the world should automatically share information to fight the scourge of tax evasion". The OECD has continued to pressure countries to enhance tax evasion controls since the 2008 financial crisis. The OECD (26.10.2011) averred that tax evasion is now accepted to be facilitated by offshore centres, and in particular, bank secrecy. As well as bank secrecy, the phrase 'secrecy jurisdiction' is often interchangeably used with reference to offshore jurisdiction. However, many offshore centres do not have bank secrecy legislation. The most renowned jurisdiction in the last century for bank secrecy was Switzerland where, prior to the Swiss Money Laundering Act 1997, secrecy laws and practices were stringent (Stressens 2000, 101). Sharman (2017, 86) suggests Switzerland was the "most secretive and secure host of illicit money", yet it also has become perhaps among the most active asset recovery practitioners in respect of looted funds.

International AML strategy has largely diminished bank secrecy, particularly with information exchange frameworks. There is also increasing compliance with FATF Recommendation 37 that countries should not refuse a MLA request on the grounds of bank secrecy. This standard exemplifies growing global intolerance to such laws. According to Nakajima (2017, 115), the increasing AML initiatives have led to financial institutions implementing measures to facilitate disclosure. However, Nakajima suggests that there is a conflict placed upon banks that have to comply with international commitments yet also owe a confidentiality duty to customers. Nakajima highlights sentiment that in previous decades, the FATF obligations on bank secrecy would have been seen as corporate social responsibility and thus perceived as voluntary. Placing institutions in a position of conflicting demands results in exposing banks to increasing legal, regulatory and reputational risks – for example, civil actions brought by clients whose confidentiality might have been breached.

Bank secrecy has, however, typically been subject to exemptions under the common law which have been upheld by various courts. For example, in the English case of *Tournier v National Provincial Bank* [1924], an implied contractual duty of confidentiality was found on the part of the bank not to disclose client information to third parties. The *Tournier* principle prevents disclosure except in select circumstances including by compulsion of law or public interest, or with the express or implied consent of the client. This principle has been applied in subsequent cases. For example, the US case of *Peterson v Idaho First National Bank* (1961) involved a bank that had disclosed to its client's employer that its client's cheques were not being fulfilled. The Idaho Supreme Court held that the bank was held liable for a breach of an implied duty of confidentiality to its client.

7.7 Transparency offshore and the 'nothing to hide' conjecture

A common argument presented by transparency campaigners and critics of offshore centres is that if you have nothing to hide, then you should have no problem having your financial business transparent for public scrutiny. This shall be referred to as the 'nothing to hide' argument. It implies that simply providing this information to the government, which can in turn provide it to any other government they have obligations to exchange it with, is inadequate. This view has been expressed by many British parliamentarians, including former International Development Secretary, Andrew Mitchell MP, who stated:

> The territories may well allow access to law and order agencies, within an hour in the case of terrorism, through closed registers, but that does not allow civil society – charities, NGOs and the media – to expose them to the sort of scrutiny that the Paradise and Panama papers did".[1]

The suggestion that individuals engaged in legitimate business should be subject to scrutiny by anyone other than the state (and only then in circumstances relating to the prevention of crime or preservation of national security) is now a firm, albeit concerning, characteristic representing the fast-moving transparency landscape. Similarly, in another recent debate on money laundering, then Economic Secretary to the Treasury and City Minister, Simon Kirby MP, said "people with nothing to hide have nothing to fear" with increased transparency requirements.[2] Likewise, Global Witness (2018) argued that there are "many secret companies registered in U.K. tax havens, many of which are not vehicles for crime or corruption and have nothing to fear from greater transparency". This overly simplistic view is ideologically flawed, as it presupposes the benefits of transparency while insisting on a disregard for well-established protections of privacy, and legitimate reasons why individuals or businesses may seek this. While it is indisputable that transparency will likely deter crime, a sensible balance needs striking. If Gordon and Morriss' (2014) formulation is to be preferred, then 'efficient enterprise'

1 HC Deb (1 May 2018) Vol 640, Col 203.
2 HC Deb (21 March 2017) Vol 623, Col 790.

theory would prioritise legitimate financial flows over a 'control first' theory aimed single-mindedly at disrupting crime. There is, of course, no easy answer. As this chapter has demonstrated, the concept of privacy remains qualified and often subject to a balancing exercise.

The 'nothing to hide' argument is more commonly seen in national security or crime prevention literature (Marsh 2003). Perhaps its most famous opponent was Benjamin Franklin (1755), who contended that "those who would give up essential liberty, to purchase a little temporary safety, deserve neither liberty nor safety". This formulation appears to find privacy and liberty sacrosanct. One prominent scholar on this issue is Solove (2013), who contends that the 'nothing to hide' argument is flawed due to the fact that protecting privacy is not necessarily fatal to preserving security. Solove's empirical work presents responses to the 'nothing to hide' argument. These include: "Do you have curtains?"; "Can I see your credit card bills?"; "I don't have anything to hide, but I don't have anything I feel like showing you either"; and "It's not about having anything to hide, it's about things not being anyone else's business" (Solove 2008, 750). Arguing that the balancing act often short-changes privacy while inflating security, Solove suggests that privacy is pluralistic and 'nothing to hide' represents a narrow conception. There are conceptual similarities here with the modern transparency campaign. When the impact of offshore privacy can include the facilitation of trafficking, corruption, terrorism financing and money laundering, it is unsurprising that transparency momentum is increasing from supranational bodies and legislatures alike.

7.8 International transparency standards: beneficial ownership registers and information exchange

This book has highlighted the standardised nature of international responses to economic crime. While FATF's AML/CFT standards are a good example of an internationally accepted approach, the one-size-fits-all element does not always work, as there are sometimes different rules being conceived and imposed by certain members of the same international group. As was clear from the chapters on the three islands, beneficial ownership information is a central component of the global AML/CFT framework. However, there has been considerable disparity in the application of standards around this. If international standards are to carry legitimacy and be viewed as viable and ultimately successful, then it is unhelpful if some members of the international community set their own standards which contrast with the broader regime. A good example was the UK compelling the Overseas Territories to implement public registers, despite FATF standards (i.e. Recommendation 24) not specifically advocating this, nor it being applied equally across large, developed jurisdictions. Another example is the recent blacklisting attempts at both EU and individual state levels. While many territories have avoided the EU's blacklist (or been successfully removed following commitments made), they have found themselves on the Dutch blacklist.

Ascertaining the ownership of companies is widely acknowledged to be an effective tool in preventing serious crime. When considering the weight of the

Panama papers and consequent influence on UK legislation, it is concerning that in June 2018, it was reported that MOSSFON (the law firm targeted in the Panama papers) could not identify the owners of up to three-quarters of companies it administered (*BBC* 20.6.2018). These findings add weight to arguments for public registers and the 'nothing to hide' conjecture. Exchanging this information between competent authorities on beneficial ownership and tax matters is fast becoming normative policy. However, there are those which think this is not enough, which has culminated in a campaign to impose more transparency. Traditionally, most companies never had to provide beneficial ownership information to government bodies, but only some information confirming and relating to the company's existence (Sharman 2016, 4). Much is the same internationally. Many jurisdictions have only recently implemented central registers of beneficial ownership information. For example, the Serbian government created legislation for a central register in June 2018, and Portugal implemented its central register in August 2017. The US with the approval of the Corporate Transparency Act has only in 2021 committed to a central register in law. As Sharman (2016, 11) discusses, even as recently as 2016 the US presented a significant problem due to it having "neither licenced CSPs nor registries of beneficial ownership information (and had opted out of the worldwide CRS on tax information exchange as well)". The UK's public register, which leads the world, has only been operational since 2016.

International standards are, however, ill-defined. This is at odds with the general standardised nature of the global AML movement. At the EU level, the 5th AML Directive adopted by the European Council rapidly updated the also recently implemented 4th AML Directive (2015/849). The latter introduced the requirement for central registers. The 5th AML Directive (2018/843) goes further by requiring beneficial ownership information to be accessible to "any member of the general public". At the country level, at 2018 only 6 G20 countries operated functioning central registers. Despite the Directive's ascent to public registers, at March 2020 only 5 EU Member States had implemented public registers. The 4th EU Directive gave members a choice between a central or public register. The 5th Directive removed this choice. There are those who have suggested irreconcilability between the trend on the one hand towards data-protection seen with the General Data Protection Regulation (GDPR), and increasing public registers on the other hand which appear to subvert confidentiality in financial matters. Noseda (2018) posits that while registers may be an effective tool, the question of privacy makes their necessity rather more questionable. While GDPR aims to give citizens control of personal data and create high-level protection across the EU (European Parliament 14.6.2016), it is clear that in other areas privacy is not considered to carry the same degree of importance. The concept of informational privacy is well-established (Westin 1970), encompassing the trend towards increased ownership emphasis, privacy and regulation of personal data. Antoine (2014) suggests there is similarity between the individual's desire to protect sensitive financial information located in a financial institution and protecting personal information located in a government or public data bank.

Transparency International (2018) conducted an international study on G20 Beneficial Ownership Principles. Its findings demonstrate that public registers are not yet a global standard and imply that it is a long way from being so. Specific findings include that Canada, US and China scored "zero points on requiring companies to collect and maintain accurate and up-to-date beneficial ownership information". The modern public register campaign relies at its core on the 'nothing to hide argument' and powerful messaging that high-tax jurisdictions have difficulty managing deficits and implementing austerity while not being helped by offshore centres. Moreover, large OECD countries are concerned about large multinationals' tax avoidance using loopholes to save billions. Public registers are not as relevant for multinationals because information as to ownership, majority shareholding and directorships are generally publicly accessible under company records. If a large multinational wants to avoid tax, this is less to do with ownership transparency and more to do with making use of legislative loopholes, which perhaps reshapes the debate toward reforming domestic tax law, something the EU is addressing with its Anti–Tax Avoidance Package. TI also found that in 9 G20 countries, including Australia, Canada and the US, financial institutions can still proceed with transactions if they cannot identify the beneficial owner. Despite greater participation in international regulation, TI found that 8 G20 countries, including Argentina, Australia, Germany and South Africa, had not conducted an AML risk assessment in the 6 years preceding the report. In stark contrast to some larger jurisdictions, previous chapters showed that Bermuda and TCI have already completed national AML/CFT risk assessments.

The UK's register, established in 2016, was designed to complement the existing public register containing some company information. It now applies to some 4.1 million UK-registered companies. Ninety-six per cent of UK companies are micro-businesses employing between zero and 9 persons (Rhodes 2017, 4). The government recently announced that the "vast majority of U.K. companies contribute positively to the U.K. economy, abide by the law and make a value contribution to society. But there are exceptions" (Department for Business, Innovation and Skills 30.6.2016). Thus, it is prioritising controls on all companies to eradicate the exceptions – something resembling a 'control first' (Gordon and Morriss 2014) regulatory philosophy. The UK's register is not presently independently verified and only annually updated when companies file confirmation statements. Under such a framework, the point of scrutiny is lost, or at least undermined if information is inaccurate or outdated. Of course, despite the emphasis on the general public's right to scrutinise, the extent to which they would wish to scrutinise or be able to understand all of the information and its implications is unclear.

In a joint assessment in 2017 by Open Ownership and Global Witness, the point is made that certain privacy safeguards exist for the UK register. These include publishing only contact addresses and only the month and year of beneficial owners' dates of birth. This argument omits reference to the fact that the majority of companies are micro-businesses, and while it is difficult to argue with certainty, it is likely that a significant portion of these relate to individuals with limited companies, whose company address may also be their home. The

UK government acknowledged that there is some information which is useful to law enforcement but would create an unacceptable risk to people in terms of identity theft and fraud should it be publicly accessible. Some may be at serious risk of harm if their association with certain companies is publicly known. Consequently, an application can be made to remove certain information. At the time of the study, there were 30 beneficial owners who had successfully applied for privacy. Wealth invariably carries the risk of being targeted, even in the most civilised societies, including by blackmail, extortion, ransom, kidnap or defamation. The protection provisions raise interesting questions of fundamental rights. The UK government has led with transparency as the default position but allows individuals to apply for privacy if there are exceptional circumstances rendering serious risks of harm to them or family. For those people, their right to privacy and confidentiality may be protected. It does not take account of individuals already on the register who later become involved in circumstances to which their public information may retrospectively put them at risk. It also risks facilitating a two-tiered system predicated on respect for needs rather than rights. There are a whole manner of reasons individuals may wish to keep information private which, for them, may be serious yet not amount to 'exceptional' to warrant its removal. The subjectivity implicit in this framework is concerning, as it acknowledges that privacy is valued only in some instances and only afforded to some individuals.

There have been instances of false representations on the register, a criminal offence under s1112 Companies Act 2006. One alleged launderer is reported to have filed his occupation as 'truffatore' and director's name as 'Il Ladro di Galline' (Italian translated as 'fraudster' and 'Chicken Thief', respectively; *Evening Standard* 17.7.2017). Enforcement action came against one individual, Kevin Brewer, for deliberately and falsely naming directors and shareholders as well-known UK politicians (Companies House 23.3.2018). He was fined £12,000 in an unprecedented prosecution for providing false information on the register. The defendant averred that he was exposing a loophole as a whistle-blower, while Companies House praised the prosecution rather than perhaps addressing the concern that this occurred on more than one occasion. Brewer's actions came to light when he contacted the politicians he had named in the hope of facilitating a discussion about the register's deficiencies (*CityAM* 5.4.2018).

While public registers are being advocated as essential components of the global fight against economic crime, the above deficiencies – particularly regarding independent verification – are concerning. In September 2020, Companies House announced a reform package to make identity verification compulsory for directors and beneficial owners, and the same for company agents – including use of digital, document and knowledge-based verification (Department for Business, Energy and Industrial Strategy 18.9.2020). If public registers are implemented around the world without accounting for the deficiencies inherent in a register which lacks these safeguards, then the silver bullet label as a tool to disrupt criminality is ambitious at best. It will also be necessary for these mechanisms to be rolled out in those offshore jurisdictions which have made high-level commitments. If it's taken the UK this long to strategically upgrade its system and seek to make the information on the register more reliable as a result, then this does not augur well for territories which, at present, are not even operating functioning central registers.

The UK government announced that the territories had until the end of 2020 (later extended to 2023) to commit to operating public registers or face having them imposed. This became law under section 51 SAMLA. This decision emanated from placing corporate transparency on the international agenda during the Lough Erne G8 Summit in 2013. Public registers are a radical move for many countries, particularly those narrower economies reliant on financial services or desirous of maintaining a confidentiality norm upon which their economies have prospered. It also disregards existing frameworks in place, which is particularly so in the case of Bermuda but also those territories like TCI which have recently remodelled their company laws to create a central register and more stringent reporting and exchange requirements. Given transparency activism in the UK and a precarious minority government at the time, it was unsurprising that this amendment was again tabled in Parliament. However, the incongruity of it was demonstrated by the lack of consultation with the territories. It was justified as an extreme circumstance, relating to foreign policy and national security, relying on money laundering concerns. In the context of the Panama and Paradise papers, however, it appears the move was motivated as much by tax avoidance as money laundering. It was arguably premature and idiosyncratic, given that the UK has still not at the time of writing addressed deficiencies in its own register.

The move created tension, as has been mentioned previously. When decision-making powers devolved to the territories are unilaterally removed, disenfranchisement and resistance is inevitable. The impact of public registers will affect each territory differently. It is conceded that once a central register system is in place, which is the case in many territories, making it public ought not to require significant resources. However, it was viewed by some of the territory leaders as a renegade in relations. It therefore represents a deeper issue, which may affect buy-in, than simply the technical practicalities of implementation. Bermuda's Premier David Burt said it showed a "wanton disregard" for Bermuda's unique constitutional position and an "egregious breach of well-established constitutional conventions". He stated, "The government rejects this regressive colonial mindset that some in London hold, that a Parliament 3,000 miles away can impose anything on Bermuda that does not fall under the areas of defence, internal security, the judiciary, and external affairs".[3] TCI's Premier Sharlene Cartwright-Robinson called it "destructive, constitutionally regressive, offensive and disappointing [and will] cause additional burden and hardship".[4] The Anguillian Opposition Leader and Chair of the PAC, Pam Webster, noted the inconsistency in approach between the territories and Crown Dependencies, as well as the disastrous impact on the financial industry and financial well-being of

3 Bermuda Government (4 May 2018), [3–4].
4 TCI Government (4 May 2018) Statement from Premier.

the territory's people (*Island Sun* 21.6.2018). Over 1,000 people protested in BVI – a country with a population of 29,000 – and its government announced an intention to legally challenge the UK Parliament's authority on constitutional grounds (*BVI Beacon* 25.5.2018). Cayman's Finance Minister criticised the UK's ignorance of Cayman's level of ongoing cooperation with over 100 tax authorities around the world, including HMRC (*Cayman Compass* 1.5.2018).

Section 51 ignored the wider implications of budget issues and financial constraints in many of the territories, for example significant recovery being underway following hurricane destruction. Prioritising a public register with all the infrastructural development required for successful implementation – including educating company officers and agents about the changes, enabling professionals to provide accurate timely advice and raising awareness – seemed mistimed when recovery efforts were so prevalently underway. As the Covid-19 pandemic has demonstrated, crises expose the fragility of legal infrastructure. This is particularly important when considering the extent to which the central register frameworks in Bermuda and TCI, for example, may arguably be already viable and adhering to international standards.

Further, the process of implementing sophisticated international standards, particularly those envisioned 'elsewhere' and often with far greater resources and technical infrastructure to assist, requires a shift in attitude. There has to be consultation periods with citizens and the public and private sectors in order to assess likely effectiveness, buy-in and constraints. Only then will there be a chance of successful implementation and compliance. These societies are not monoliths, as was evidenced by their various commitments to transparency and compliance. Their legislatures have to operate in a way tantamount to any other democratically elected government. It is incumbent on the UK, as emphasised in successive White Papers, to support this in furtherance of its responsibility to ensure the territories' good governance.

Set against this backdrop, in a seemingly unexpected U-turn, in 2020 the territories announced their agreement to work towards complying with the public register demands by 2023. Equally surprising, given SAMLA did not apply to them, the Crown Dependencies also announced pre-emptively their intention to comply and implement public registers. This brings these jurisdictions into a highly select group internationally which have made these commitments. Of course, with the necessity for the islands to rebuild their devastated economies having had to effectively write off their tourism industries during the Covid-19 pandemic, it is unclear the extent to which this will be achievable by the appointed time. This is perhaps more concerning for those jurisdictions like Anguilla, which have only recently committed to a central register, compared to Bermuda whose central framework has been established for decades. It will also be interesting to monitor the position of BVI, which operates a significant incorporations market upon which their economic sustainability relies. Despite being the last of the territories to make the commitment, and even after publicly defending their central register while other territories like Bermuda announced their intention to go public, BVI changed its position in September 2020. Their commitment is subject to caveats such as implementing them once they develop into a global standard, collaboratively exploring other models and examining the potential to limit access to some levels of data. It is interesting to contemplate this acceptance and the reasons for it, as it came during a time of a global pandemic and also at a time when the UK is leaving the EU. It may be the case that the territories considered pre-emption may serve their longer-term interests better than being compelled, particularly if delays are expected in implementation and, at least, some goodwill is forthcoming. Set against the non-optional nature of SAMLA, this at least represents a sense of positivity and demonstrates cooperative engagement. For any jurisdiction interested in enhancing its regulated environment, increasing their regulatory toolkit and perception of international cooperation is a positive move.

7.9 Remaining paradoxes

In researching offshore jurisdictions, one cannot help but find significant paradoxes in the discourse. This goes beyond legitimate criticism of facilitative misconduct, which is warranted in respect of any jurisdiction, or their financial sector, wilfully or inadvertently playing host to suspect wealth or failing to comply with reasonable standards. Rather, legitimate criticism is often undermined by fundamental mischaracterisations and misunderstandings borne from ignorance or other agendas.

The first example to note is the disproportionate focus on the Overseas Territories in the aftermath of the Panama and Paradise papers as targets for implementing public registers. Notwithstanding that SAMLA applied only to Overseas Territories and not Crown Dependencies, it is unseemly that the pressure was largely applied to the former. Bermuda's regulatory model, for example, has been traditionally viewed as more aligned with Jersey than its Caribbean counterparts like BVI. While the UK government cannot pass Orders in Council on the Crown Dependencies, the policy demonstrates inconsistency of approach when Crown Dependencies have also been targeted in the same way, for like reasons. The Panama papers motivated this policy, so it must be noted that the Isle of Man was mentioned in the Panama papers, yet Bermuda and TCI were not.

It is also contradictory that historic blacklisting efforts have come from large international organisations like the OECD, in which various remuneration structures are tax exempt in most member states. Famously, the OECD has not been in the business of blacklisting its own members such as the UK, Switzerland or Luxembourg. Rather, it has been the less powerful nations such as those this book concerns who were traditionally subject to this discriminate approach. Also, little is said of the tax failings of source jurisdictions, although it is interesting to see the shift in mindset of tax justice advocates and legislators who have recently averred that the EU's and other blacklists omit the worst offenders (European Parliament 10.12.2020). International organisations and high-tax nations have been in the business of encouraging others to raise their taxes and making it increasingly prohibitive for small, low-tax and offshore jurisdictions to operate in their traditional form. It is unclear still why such jurisdictions prioritise interference or pressure on other jurisdictions before first examining or reforming, where applicable, their own taxation systems.

The argument that public registers will prevent corruption or money laundering is too simplistic, as they may encourage a race to the bottom for illicit finance to far less regulated environments than even the least developed Overseas Territories. As Geoffrey Cox MP emphasised in Parliament: "All it will mean is that the money goes to where it is darkest",[5] and he characterised public registers as a "one hit wonder".

Finally, it is worth remarking that the ICIJ's offshore databases are effectively examples of freely accessible public registers. The most concerning paradox is the disclaimer which users have to consent to before accessing the data: "There are legitimate uses for offshore companies and trusts. We do not intend to suggest or imply that any people, companies or other entities included in the ICIJ Offshore Leaks Database have broken the law or otherwise acted improperly". The ICIJ clearly acknowledge legitimate uses of offshore and, more crucially, they do not imply criminality or wrongdoing. In other words, the publication expresses total disregard for the privacy of legitimate persons and entities whose data has been misappropriated and published. As with the principle of confidentiality, once information is published, the damage may already be done for which there is no redress. It therefore questions the legitimacy of the arguments behind operating public registers if the motivation is to scrutinise accountable persons or detect criminality.

7.10 Implications for the British Overseas Territories

As Piercy (1982) aptly observed, "There are clearly times when [one] must make a stink to survive". While the question of beneficial ownership and transparency is important, the manner in which it is manifesting necessitates consideration not only about the role of fundamental legal rights but also about future political and financial stability in the territories. As Sir Alan Duncan MP acknowledged when announcing section 51 SAMLA, "Legislating for [the territories] without their consent effectively disenfranchises their elected representatives".[6] Geoffrey Cox MP warned, in relation to Cayman yet applicable to all those territories with democratically elected legislatures, "[They] were given a constitution in which the responsibility for the governance of their financial and economic affairs was solemnly conveyed to them by this Parliament?"[7] It has deeper implications than just affecting the financial industry. Disenfranchising the territories' representatives, particularly through interference in a field important, for many of them, to their economies is perhaps misjudged. It is their autonomous systems of governance and constitutional convention, together with UK partnership, which

5 HC Deb (1 May 2018) Vol 640, Col 203.
6 HC Deb (1 May 2018) Vol 640, Col 181.
7 HC Deb (1 May 2018) Vol 640, Col 183.

distance the relationship from its former colonial past. If elected local officials are disenfranchised, then it is likely that the independence and self-determination debate will reignite in some territories – much like it did in TCI during direct rule.

Importantly, it also has the capacity to lower standards in public life and diminish progress made with regards to promoting integrity. If these achievements are sidelined, then it has the capacity to add to local disenfranchisement. While Parliament can theoretically intervene, doing so without consultation acts as a direct threat to their self-governing autonomy. Similar tensions and problems have been experienced in the devolved legislatures of Wales, Scotland and Northern Ireland.

It is also worth briefly remarking on the principle of comity. Comity is the recognition which one nation allows within its territory to the legislative, executive or judicial acts of another nation, having regard both to international duty and convenience and to the rights of its own citizens or other persons who are under the protection of its laws (*Hilton v Guyot* [1894], 163–164). Antoine (2014, 307) avers that this is an extension of the principle of territorial sovereignty, and that the underlying concept is to recognise that states have sovereign interests that need reconciling. The common issue in this context is when onshore jurisdictions call upon offshore ones to provide certain information – the provision of which risks infringing confidentiality. Antoine (2014, 26) calls this a "jurisdictional deadlock", particularly when confidentiality is the linchpin of all offshore activity and not confined to banking confidentiality. The problem is exacerbated through an increase in disclosure requirements in onshore states as well as frequent use of subpoenas – notwithstanding the presence of an increasing number of bilateral agreements such as TIEAs which ought to redress the dilemma. While the principle of comity typically rests between states, it is illustrative of the importance of reconciling competing interests between metropolitan, sovereign powers and their dependencies.

Prior to the territories making commitments to go public with their beneficial ownership registers, it might have been the case that they regarded information exchange and sharing as an acceptable abrogation of privacy rights only in circumstances clearly defined under law, and necessitated via bilateral agreements. Further erosion beyond this may have been viewed as an irreparable surrender of fundamental protections. Compared to the position in some Commonwealth Caribbean states where such information is still not adequately collated or exchanged, the position in many Overseas Territories whereby central registers and bilateral disclosure agreements existed could be viewed as modern. For critics, however, nothing short of public registers will suffice. In the end, succumbing with caveats appeared to be the least worst option.

In the 2012 White Paper, the then Commercial Secretary to the Treasury, Lord Sassoon, commented at 57:

> [The territories] have developed as important financial centres. . . . I welcome the significant progress territories have made in complying with international standards on tax transparency and dealing with the threat of terrorism financing and money laundering. HM Treasury will continue to

represent the interests of those territories which meet these standards in international fora and will strongly support their right to compete freely in international markets.

SAMLA and the surrounding policy does not account for the acknowledged successes in the territories and does not reconcile with the principle of being freely competitive in international markets. While the US is being celebrated by transparency campaigners for approving legislation for a central register which may effectively see the end of anonymous shell companies, the territories have no say on maintaining their central registers in circumstances under which they are subject to a legislative ultimatum.

7.11 Conclusion

Having acknowledged that criminality has been facilitated by offshore financial centres, and in the case of those Overseas Territories this book focuses on, the transparency debate is an important one. While conceding that privacy has its pitfalls, there are important legal bases for its justification. Whether protected under common law principles or constitutions, privacy is rightly safeguarded as a fundamental right – notwithstanding its qualified nature and the necessity to often balance it against other important rights. However, in the context of offshore financial centres, the offshore confidentiality norm is an important consideration in circumstances where international standards presuppose an increasing expectation towards openness as an exhibition of both compliance and cooperation. Anything short of this attracts reputational criticism and even legislative interference as evidenced by section 51 SAMLA. Confidentiality has been a linchpin for the islands' economic development and an increasing problem for the international community. While some of these territories are wealthy or 'middle income', the provision of financial services is an economic mainstay, without which the territories are left to rely on tourism – which, as we have seen from hurricanes and the global coronavirus pandemic, is volatile. Therefore, it should come as no surprise as to why privacy and confidentiality, rather than secrecy legislation, are so closely guarded as hallmarks of their financial sectors. This chapter has sought to distinguish privacy from its abuses and to rebut the 'nothing to hide' argument as an overly simplistic characterisation of the legitimate use of these legal safeguards which are rightly enshrined in law, rather than acting as some inherently nefarious tool.

Public registers which seek to abrogate privacy in the context of legal entities are not yet a global standard, and despite the Overseas Territories making high-level commitments in 2020 which should be viewed positively by the international community, some, like the BVI, remain quite clear that the commitments are made subject to public registers becoming a global norm (*BVI News* 6.1.2021). Conventionally, the UK would only intervene in the Overseas Territories' economic affairs on establishing exceptional reasons. While evidence of money laundering and terrorism financing engages national security concerns, this high bar arguably has not been met, particularly when territories like Bermuda could argue that their long-established central register frameworks are viable and that these key elements of their AML/CFT regime are positively rated by FATF. The move also demonstrated an ignorance that the incorporation sectors in the territories differ fundamentally.

This chapter has engaged the important issue of whether privacy and confidentiality in financial affairs appear threatened by the increasing emphasis on transparency in international economic crime standards. When countries like the US and the UK take such a different stance, and it being likely that a public register in the US will take years to materialise, it is right to question the proportionality of compelling small island territories to take the lead. Moreover, an important yet concerning reality is that influential transparency campaigners, who are impacting law and policy, predicate their work upon the inarguable fact that there are legitimate uses to offshore centres and that the data they publish to support their arguments does not imply wrongdoing or criminality. A legitimate question, therefore, is what's the purpose in breaching the rights of legitimate individuals or entities beyond an agenda to indiscriminately disrupt offshore centres? The net in this debate is cast wide. However, what is axiomatic is that public registers are not the global norm, despite commitments now made by the territories. If only a select few jurisdictions around the world implement them, then it could further the race to the bottom for suspect wealth. Moreover, unless all countries which implement them address the deficiencies identified in the UK's register early in their establishment, then it is likely that their purported utility in terms of being a reliable resource for scrutiny, due diligence and enforcement investigations will be useless at best if information is public but not verified.

References

Acquisti, A., John, L. K., and Loewenstein, G. (2013) 'What is Privacy Worth?', *Journal of Legal Studies*, 42(2): 249–274.

Antoine, R.-M. (2014) *Confidentiality in Offshore Financial Law*, Oxford: Oxford University Press.

Aubert, M. (1984) 'The Limits of Swiss Banking Secrecy under Domestic and International Law', *International Tax and Business Lawyer*, 2(2): 273–297.

BBC (20.6.2018) 'Panama Papers: Mossack Fonseca was Unable to Identify Company Owners'. Available: www.bbc.co.uk/news/world-latin-america-44553932

Bentham, J. (1789/1988) *An Introduction to the Principles of Morals and Legislation*, New York: Prometheus.

BVI Beacon (25.5.2018) '1000-plus Protest UK Public Registers Decision'. Available: www.bvibeacon.com/1000-plus-protest-uk-public-registers-decision/

BVI News (6.1.2021) 'Governor's Statement on Publicly Accessible Registers Misleading'. Available: https://bvinews.com/governors-statement-on-publicly-accessible-registers-misleading/

Cayman Compass (1.5.2018) 'Full Statement – Cayman Islands Government'. Available: www.caymancompass.com/2018/05/01/full-statement-from-cayman-islands-government/

CityAM (5.4.2018) ‘Government’s Pride over the Companies House Sage Completely Misses the Point’. Available: www.cityam.com/283377/governments-pride-over-companies-house-saga-completely

Companies House (23.3.2018) ‘UK’s “First Ever” Successful Prosecution for False Company Information’. Available: www.gov.uk/government/news/uks-first-ever-successful-prosecution-for-false-company-information#:~:text=Companies%20House%20dissolved%20the%20company,Court%20last%20Thursday%2015%20March

Department for Business, Energy and Industrial Strategy (18.9.2020) ‘Corporate Transparency and Register Reform’. Available: https://assets.publishing.service.gov.uk/government/uploads/system/uploads/attachment_data/file/925059/corporate-transparency-register-reform-government-response.pdf

Department for Business Innovation and Skills (30.6.2016) ‘People with Significant Control Companies House Register Goes Live’, Press Release.

Diggelmann, O., and Clais, M. N. (2014) ‘How the Right to Privacy Became a Human Right’, *Human Rights Law Review*, 14(3): 441–458.

Emerson, T. I. (1970) *The System of Freedom of Expression*, New York: Random House.

European Parliament (14.6.2016) ‘Data Protection Reform – Parliament Approves New Rules Fit for Digital Era’. Available: https://www.europarl.europa.eu/news/en/press-room/20160407IPR21776/data-protection-reform-parliament-approves-new-rules-fit-for-the-digital-era

European Parliament (10.12.2020) ‘EU Tax Haven Blacklist not Catching Worst Offenders’, Press Release.

Evening Standard (17.7.2017) ‘Occupation: Fraudster. Address: Street of 40 Thieves – How Italians Mocked UK Company Rules’. Available: www.standard.co.uk/business/occupation-fraudster-address-street-of-40-thieves-how-italians-mocked-uk-company-rules-a3589906.html

G8 (18.6.2013) ‘G8 Lough Erne Declaration’. Available: https://www.gov.uk/government/publications/g8-lough-erne-declaration/g8-lough-erne-declaration-html-version

G20 (2.4.2009) ‘London Summit, Leaders Statement’. Available: https://www.imf.org/external/np/sec/pr/2009/pdf/g20_040209.pdf

Global Witness (2018) ‘The Time Has Come to Address the Issue of the UK Overseas Territories’. Available: https://www.globalwitness.org/en/blog/time-has-come-address-issue-uk-overseas-territories/

Gordon, R., and Morriss, A. P. (2014) ‘Moving Money: International Financial Flows, Taxes and Money Laundering’, *Hastings International and Comparative Law Review*, 37(1): 1–123.

Griffin, J. (2017) ‘The Need for the Abolition of Secret Rusts’, *Trusts and Trustees*, 23(4): 373–382.

Holtzman, D. (2006) *Privacy Lost: How Technology is Endangering Your Privacy*, San Francisco: Jossey-Bass.

ICIJ (2016/2018) ‘Offshore Leaks Database’. Available: https://offshoreleaks.icij.org/pages/database.

Island Sun (21.6.2018) ‘Anguilla’s Opposition Leader Praises BVI’. Available: www.islandsun.com/anguillas-opposition-leader-praises-bvi/

Klitou, D. (2014) *Privacy-Invading Technologies and Privacy by Design: Safeguarding Privacy, Liberty and Security in the 21st Century*, New York: Springer.

Malta Today (2.8.2018) 'Updated: Maltese Banking Resilient and Profitable, MFSA Reacts to S&P Risk Warning'. Available: www.maltatoday.com.mt/business/business_news/88616/maltese_banking_resilient_and_profitable_mfsa_reacts_to_sp_risk_warning#.YAD_iZP7TOQ

Maple, C. (2017) 'Security and Privacy in the Internet of Things', *Journal of Cyber Policy*, 2(2): 155–184.

Marmor, A. (2015) 'What is the Right to Privacy?', *Philosophy and Public Affairs*, 43(1): 3–26.

Marsh, J. (2003) *Rights vs Public Safety after 9/11*, Lanham, MD: Rowman and Littlefield.

Mill, J. S. (1859/2008) *On Liberty*, Oxford: Oxford University Press.

Moore, A. D. (1998) 'Intangible Property: Privacy, Power, and Information Control', *American Philosophy Quarterly*, 35(4): 365–378.

Nakajima, C. (2017) 'The International Pressures on Banks to Disclose Information', in S. A. Booysen and D. Neo (eds.), *Can Banks Still Keep a Secret? Bank Secrecy in Financial Centres around the World*, Cambridge: Cambridge University Press.

Negley, G. (1966) 'Philosophical Views on the Value of Privacy', *Law and Contemporary Problems*, 31(2): 319–325.

Noseda, F. (9.6.2018) 'Public Registers in the Age of GDPR', Mischon de Reya LLP. Available: https://www.mondaq.com/uk/data-protection/711144/public-registers-in-the-age-of-gdpr

OECD (26.10.2011) 'The Era of Bank Secrecy is Over: The G20/OECD Process is Delivering Results'. Available: http://www.oecd.org/tax/exchange-of-tax-information/48996146.pdf

Open Ownership and Global Witness (2017) 'Learning the Lessons from the UK's Public Beneficial Ownership Register'. Available: https://www.globalwitness.org/en/campaigns/corruption-and-money-laundering/learning-lessons-uks-public-beneficial-ownership-register/

Piercy, M. (1982) *Circles on the Water: Selected Poems of Marge Piercy*, New York: Alfred Knopf.

Posner, R. (1978) 'The Right of Privacy', *Georgia Law Review*, 12(3): 392–422.

Rhodes, C. (28.12.2017) HC Library Briefing No.06152, 'Business Statistics'. Available: https://www.alejandrobarros.com/wp-content/uploads/2017/10/SN06152.pdf

Rider, B. A. K., and Ashe, M. (1993) *Insider Crime: The New Law*, Bristol: Jordans.

Rousseau, J. J. (1762/1998) *The Social Contract*, London: Wordsworth.

Sevignani, S. (2016) *Privacy and Capitalism in the Age of Social Media*, Abingdon: Routledge.

Sharman, J. C. (2016) 'Solving the Beneficial Ownership Conundrum: Central Registries and Licenced Intermediaries', Report for Jersey Finance.

Sharman, J. C. (2017) *Despots Guide to Wealth Management*, New York: Cornell University Press.

Solove, D. J. (2008) "I've Got Nothing to Hide" and Other Misunderstandings of Privacy', *San Diego Law Review*, 44(4): 745–772.

Solove, D. J. (2013) *Nothing to Hide: The False Tradeoff between Privacy and Security*, New Haven: Yale University Press.

Stressens, G. (2000) *Money Laundering*, Cambridge: Cambridge University Press.

Taylor, N. (2002) 'State Surveillance and the Right to Privacy', *Surveillance Society*, 1(1): 66–85.

Thomson, J. J. (1975) 'The Right to Privacy', *Philosophy and Public Affairs*, 4(4): 295–314.

Transparency International (2018) 'G20 Leaders or Laggards? Reviewing G20 Promises on Ending Anonymous Companies'. Available: https://www.transparency.org/en/publications/g20-leaders-or-laggards

US House of Representatives (1756) 'Votes and Proceedings in the House of Representatives, 1755–1756, Remarks of Benjamin Franklin, 11.11.1755, para 6'. Available: https://founders.archives.gov/documents/Franklin/01-06-02-0107

Warren, S. D., and Brandeis, L. D. (1890) 'The Right to Privacy', *Harvard Law Review*, 4(5): 193–220.

Westin, A. F. (1970) 'Privacy and Freedom', *Washington and Lee Law Review*, 25(1): 166–170.

8 Conclusion

A pertinent issue across the fields of law, international relations and development is whether it is reasonable to expect small states to be able to shoulder the same kinds of responsibilities as larger, better-resourced jurisdictions. In this context, this book has examined the ability and willingness of the three selected jurisdictions with regards to the various standards that have been set internationally as to the handling of suspect wealth, economic crime and financial regulation. This section reflects on the key arguments and points raised in this book which, it is hoped, shall be of use to legislators, policymakers, practitioners and researchers alike. It is envisioned that these will be of utility not only to those with specific interest in the British Overseas Territories, but also those from other offshore jurisdictions which face challenges similar to those identified in this book. For those at the table in larger jurisdictions, or supranational organisations, and influential campaigners, it is further hoped that the findings of this book add deeper context to the compliance and cooperation records of these jurisdictions, which are often outrightly maligned.

The analysis proceeded on the basis that suspect wealth, and the various predicate and facilitative activities which create or sustain it, has an inimical impact on the legal and institutional development of jurisdictions. A problem not confined to poorer jurisdictions alone, it harms stability and sustainability more generally. The profound concerns manifesting at international and supranational levels, particularly from inter-governmental organisations insofar as recognising the risks that suspect wealth and economic crime pose will likely intensify. The impetus of protecting countries against handling suspect wealth has been proclaimed through many international conventions and legal instruments such as UNCAC, the OECD Bribery Convention and in the UN's Sustainable Goal 16. Within these concerns, the criticism of offshore financial centres as conduits of crime have become industrial. This book did not set out to discuss the morality of tax havens, given so many arguments against them are rooted in the concept of unfairness – which many legal scholars may agree is an emotive and unsound basis for invoking criminal law. The importance of fundamental legal safeguards in an international rules-based system in which transparency is in a state of freefall, was emphasised. The book's aim was to critically assess the legal and regulatory structures in place in three jurisdictions which, individually and collectively as Overseas Territories and offshore centres, have been criticised for being harmful actors in the international financial system. In doing so, evidence was considered which provides context as to their business models, domestic legal frameworks and levels of international engagement.

Of course, insofar as international standards are generally regarded as a form of soft international law, it would be shocking to conclude that there was a reluctance, let alone antipathy, to their implementation in any jurisdiction wishing to secure its place in the international community. In the context of the territories examined in this book, their willingness to accept and adhere to these standards varies. Before conclusions are derived, this is not a simple case of offshore centres having different degrees of political will, as is often described in the discourse. The research has not encountered any serious argument or evidence that these jurisdictions are unwilling to meet international expectations. The analysis demonstrates the ability across the territories to shoulder burdens which are, at times, perhaps disproportionate. The research found that their abilities in this regard also vary. The work identified important underlying development considerations which ought to be accounted for when considering commitments, technical compliance and effectiveness of standards within the jurisdictions. In the coming section, the main findings will be summarised, however at this juncture one axiomatic conclusion is that while safety in numbers has empowered these small jurisdictions and their voice on the international stage, externally viewing them as a collective is problematic in legal and social science discourse, despite their commonalities. Criticisms manifest and consequently solutions materialise for them as a group, rather than fundamentally different jurisdictions. A key example flagged in the research was the passage of the public register provisions of SAMLA – indiscriminately applied to all relevant territories while ignoring differences in their financial service offerings with greater or lesser emphasis on corporate services and incorporations. While international best practices presuppose a degree of standardisation, treating the territories in a one-size-fits-all manner when it comes to law and policymaking in this context is flawed. With this said, some of the criticisms seen at the international level are not without merit. The research found that these jurisdictions have, to differing degrees, been implicated in international economic crime cases, various data breaches such as the Panama and Paradise papers, controversies surrounding aggressive tax avoidance and domestic instances of corruption or related misconduct.

8.1 Bermuda

Bermuda has established a sophisticated business environment over time which has translated into a capacity to comply with international standards to tackle suspect wealth. It has developed a robust regulatory framework in support of its key international markets like reinsurance. Its institutions are highly developed and there is a significant body of professionals regulating its business environment, evidenced by substantial increase in its compliance sector in recent years. Its statutory bodies visibly engage with relevant stakeholders indicating a multi-party approach to strengthening risk awareness and response. International standards are not only visible but prevalent in the jurisdiction. The research found that Bermuda has proactively modernised key legislation, such as bribery laws, to a level which exceeds the scope of internationally advocated legislation. This indicates will and ability in adopting standards to a high level. The fact that Bermuda has had a central register of beneficial ownership, reviewed positively by FATF, for decades – while other major jurisdictions like the US have only recently legislated to establish one – speaks to this level of commitment to securing its place in the global community. This is further supported by recent commitment to make this register public by 2023. This brings Bermuda into a highly select group of countries which have committed to going public and further associates Bermuda with the principles set out in the 5th EU AML Directive on beneficial ownership registers. Its record on compliance with AML/CFT measures is evidenced by positive ratings from organisations like CFATF. This has been helped internally by several national money laundering and terrorism financing risk assessments, a number greater than many fellow Overseas Territories and larger, better-resourced jurisdictions. On cooperation, Bermuda engages in various internationally accepted exchange mechanisms on beneficial ownership, tax and investigations including under MLATs, TIEAs, and the CRS. It has also enacted economic substance legislation to enhance substance over form.

Finally, Bermuda has benefited from various multi-stakeholder initiatives designed to promote the compliance industry, prepare for AML/CFT implementation reviews, identify risk and raise awareness of the risk-based approach to suspect wealth. It was also notable that Bermuda has a specific task force within its police service focused on economic and organised crime. Bermuda was significantly mentioned in the Paradise papers, and its financial market has been implicated in criminal and civil cases internationally. Further, there have been considerable reports of multinationals appearing to use Bermuda for aggressive tax avoidance. These factors have led to blacklisting and greylisting. Notwithstanding consequent removals in some cases such as the EU's list, this can cause reputational damage to the jurisdiction which is more difficult to assess. For these reasons, as well as the more general criticisms against offshore centres, it is likely that pressure on Bermuda will continue.

In terms of considering how Bermuda may better protect itself from suspect wealth entering its financial centre, maintaining the level of engagement with AML/CFT monitoring bodies is necessary in order to ensure that ever-developing risks are controlled. Further, it will be necessary to monitor effectiveness of recently enacted legislation and to ensure that stakeholders across sectors understand their obligations in the course of business, but also the underlying awareness-raising functions as to why compliance benefits the jurisdiction. For economic substance, it will be critical to balance the need to attract and maintain business while ensuring such are in full compliance with legal obligations. Otherwise, the whole point of substance over form will be a futile endeavour. Further, while it is clear that high-level commitments on public registers will enable Bermuda to strengthen its regulated environment for legal entities, it will only be effective if Bermuda goes further than simply making things public, and ensures that the register contains adequate protection provisions and accurate information through independent verification, and achieves buy-in from stakeholders including corporate service providers and businesses themselves. Bermuda's national campaigns surrounding AML reviews indicate that on beneficial ownership, the same level of work in awareness-raising, training and infrastructure will be deployed. This is perhaps underscored by the fact that Bermuda does not have a significant incorporation sector relative to other territories, like BVI, which indicates that implementation may well be more straightforward.

8.2 Turks and Caicos Islands

TCI's ability and willingness to comply with international standards can be most accurately characterised as progressive in the past decade. The analysis of its legal and regulatory frameworks was set against a unique history of both development-hindering events, and losses of sovereignty through public sector corruption allegations, the disposal of which TCI is still dealing with. TCI's recent history involves two periods of direct rule. This history, being different to that of Bermuda's, called for a nuanced approached when considering its compliance records with international standards on economic crime and suspect wealth. While this history is contextually important, TCI should not be judged on outdated instances of misconduct precipitating on its shores. Rather, the research found that international standards are, to quite a significant degree, visible and prevalent in the jurisdiction.

TCI demonstrates willingness and ability to comply with sophisticated standards, and has engaged in the past decade in legal reform in some key areas including anti-bribery legislation. Reforms to its company laws include implementing a central register of beneficial ownership and more stringent reporting requirements placed on companies and CSPs. Importantly, TCI has also made recent high-level commitments to make this register public, in line with UK demands. During and before the FAC Inquiry, many territories like Bermuda and BVI exhibited resounding opposition to this move, while evidence from TCI to the Committee suggested that it was more open to the idea of going public if that was the direction in which the river was moving. What is perhaps more challenging is TCI's technical ability to go public so shortly after establishing a central register. Unlike Bermuda's, which has been established for decades, TCI will have gone from a relatively young central register regime to complete transparency in a matter of a few years. However, TCI's willingness to adopt a risk-based approach to AML/CFT has been positively reviewed by CFATF – with it being ranked largely compliant with Core and Key Recommendations. It successfully completed an NRA in preparation for the 2020 CFATF report, which helped raise awareness and identify money laundering and terrorism financing risks to its market. Willingness was further evidenced by TCI establishing an Integrity Commission, placing a higher emphasis at island level on higher standards in public life. Of particular note, TCI has incorporated this into its educational curriculum to teach youth about integrity and its nuances. In terms of visibility of international standards, simply enacting legislation is not enough, as TCI's history demonstrates an imperative for addressing cultural and social change. Certain areas whereby standards have been implemented require further attention, such as the level of SARs and requirement for greater risk aversity in the real estate and construction sectors. These points are concerning on the basis that these industries have been at the core of findings of unaccountability in the Auld Report.

As an offshore centre, criticisms of TCI have been fervent and will likely continue, despite high-level commitments and implementation of international standards. However, TCI did not feature in the Panama papers and only sparingly in the Paradise papers, although there have been instances whereby TCI entities, and by extension its offshore sector, have been implicated in foreign economic crime cases. Despite a stable legal environment, the research found some concerning aspects of TCI's administration of justice with reference to the ongoing trial of former Ministers. While demonstrating proactivity in holding defendants to account, the excessively long case is now in its fifth year, which raises important constitutional questions.

In order for TCI to better protect itself against suspect wealth, it appears that continued regional engagement with FATF is necessary, but in particular raising compliance in certain areas such as real estate and DNFBPs – which represent a key growth area for the islands. For TCI's longer-term development, it will also be necessary to maintain momentum in community and multi-stakeholder initiatives to raise awareness of integrity and compliance and strengthen educational focus on standards and accountability.

8.3 Anguilla

The research into Anguilla found the jurisdiction to be the least developed in its legal and regulatory approach to economic crime and suspect wealth. Anguilla was heavily mentioned in the Panama papers, and was implicated in foreign economic crime cases and allegations by NGOs of misconduct. An example was the allegations surrounding the transiting of Congolese oil revenues into Anguillian-registered entities controlled by the Congo's ruling family.

However, Anguilla has demonstrated some will to implement international standards and has made several high-level commitments to this effect, such as signing an Exchange of Notes agreement with the UK and entering into a relatively high number of TIEAs. Recently, it committed to implementing a central register of beneficial ownership of companies, and shortly thereafter made commitments to work towards making this a publicly accessible register in line with UK demands and moving international standards. In terms of the risk-based approach, Anguilla has embarked upon a money laundering and terrorism financing NRA in preparation for the next round evaluation by FATF. While commitments have been made, processes like NRAs require significant effort and resources.

Anguilla's preoccupation with various development-hindering circumstances, such as post-hurricane recovery, has affected progress. The NRA was announced shortly before the hurricanes. Other development factors include the recent collapse of its banking sector, narrow reliance on financial services and tourism, healthcare deficiencies and connectivity and dependence on neighbours like Saint Martin. These are important factors to understand when considering progress and ascertaining the jurisdiction's ability and willingness to comply with international standards. In terms of implementation of AML/CFT standards to date, Anguilla has received some positive reviews across various measures. From a conclusion in 2010 that it was in the preliminary stages of implementing a risk-based approach, to significant progress being concluded in 2015, Anguilla has demonstrated action in a positive direction. However, challenges exist which make Anguilla's overall framework susceptible to risk, given its underdevelopment. A good example is that modern bribery legislation is still lacking, and its constitution is in need of reform. There have been other challenges for the jurisdiction in terms of strengthening governance and issues with the effectiveness of its PAC. A broader, comprehensive framework is needed for Anguilla to better protect itself against suspect wealth. Given that Anguilla is home to a regional law revision centre, reforming its anti-corruption legislation and empowering oversight institutions to strengthen standards in public life and its regulated sector ought to be a priority. *Prima facie* it could be argued that Anguilla's compliance with certain standards to date, such as beneficial ownership, appears to be no more than window dressing. It is unclear how a jurisdiction so young in establishing a functioning central register in line with international standards can be expected to ascend to the same degree of compliance with beneficial ownership as, say, Bermuda will when the time comes to implement a robust, publicly accessible register.

When taken with the point that Anguilla's developmental concerns are among the more pressing of all Overseas Territories which operate sophisticated financial centres, the conclusion might equally be drawn that compliance with international standards has not been correctly prioritised. Therefore, issues relating to resources and capacity need to be borne in mind. While recently enacting or amending legislation is positive, institutional strengthening as part of constitutional reform will enable the territory to achieve more effective implementation of standards and better protect its offshore market from the threats of suspect wealth.

8.4 Implications for the future of these jurisdictions

The modern international regime which this book has focused on, particularly relating to risk-based AML/CFT compliance, is characterised by standardisation. The influence of soft law has been shown in this work to be a significant underpinning of countries' anti–economic crime regimes, driving domestic legislation, regulatory initiatives and international cooperation. The amalgamation of various sources of law, rules and best practices strives to achieve harmonisation. However, the point has been made that many standards remain ill-defined, susceptible to frequent change or amendment, or left deliberately vague to allow for interpretation. For example, while small island offshore centres make high-level commitments to implement public registers of beneficial ownership to avoid being placed on the blacklists of larger jurisdictions, many larger jurisdictions do not yet comply with minimum requirements such as a central register. Despite momentum towards complete openness as the price of security, it is unclear whether the international standard on corporate transparency is best characterised as a register which is a central, public or pay to view. For many jurisdictions, even a central register remains non-existent. It will be interesting to note the effects this is likely to have on small island nations that disproportionately rely on incorporation and related services, while many of their independent neighbours exist beyond the legislative compulsion of large, metropolitan governments. Only 6 G20 countries have central registers, while adoption at EU level remains protracted.

Blacklisting and greylisting is likely to continue and intensify. Public registers will not, in and of themselves, cure the ills of economic crimes like corruption, money laundering and tax evasion. They risk encouraging the race to the bottom and stand to be useless if they are poorly implemented without independent verification as to the validity and accuracy of data, coupled with enforceability of sanctions for non-compliance. Acceptance of UK demands will invariably strengthen the relationship each territory has with the UK, which is perhaps more critical than ever with Brexit. However, as the problems of international financial crime continue, it is unlikely that attention will simply divert from offshore centres just because they have implemented certain standards. We have seen the inconsistency in approach with blacklisting. The EU's blacklist originally omitted jurisdictions like Bermuda, TCI and Anguilla – the latter two on the basis of hurricane recovery efforts shifting immediate compliance priorities. Within a year, the Netherlands blacklisted them. Bermuda was later added to the EU list on the basis of a technical breach but then removed again. The EU has not traditionally been in the business of blacklisting any of its own members. Despite blacklisting others, the Netherlands has been implicated in large-scale tax avoidance by multinationals using the 'sandwich' structure to shift profits to jurisdictions for fiscal efficiency. While such structures are being eradicated, it is worth observing that the Dutch have significant interests in the Caribbean including their own territories like Aruba and Sint Maarten – the latter upon which Anguilla's development heavily relies.

Blacklisting is not simply sensational but constitutes a sanction capable of damaging the reputation of jurisdictions which heavily rely on financial services. Even during Covid-19, calls to limit financial assistance to companies that were registered in jurisdictions on the narrow EU list highlighted the adverse perceptions such countries have and the adverse effects of being included on such lists can have. At times of crisis, the perceivably harmful role of offshore is exacerbated.

In the face of such growing criticism, which is unlikely to cease, the question arises as to how these jurisdictions can better protect their financial centres from accepting suspect wealth and thereby continue to engage in the necessary process of compliance with international standards. As the earlier chapters of this book showed, this is imperative not only for their effects on others but on their own stability, reputation and sustainability. Strengthening oversight in certain sectors (particularly real estate, construction and other DNFBPs), as well as enhancing core values through multi-stakeholder initiatives, are useful strategies which have been tested through processes such as NRAs. However, the research demonstrated that some of the territories may, actually, not need to make any radical changes to protect themselves in the context of certain elements of their regime. For example, Bermuda and TCI demonstrate an up-to-date approach with regards to bribery legislation and strengthening of integrity-related institutions in support of technical compliance and awareness-raising. Specific betterment of this seems to be inapplicable at this stage, but such may be required once a passage of time enables accurate measuring of effectiveness – something the FATF follow-up process will achieve. Of course, Anguilla needs to address this as a matter of urgency along with constitutional reform. Given the international concerns about economic crime, it remains the case that making commitments to implement internationally advocated standards enables these small jurisdictions to enhance their positions in the international community.

However, jurisdictions with economies which rely on financial services may risk too much in meeting standards which may jeopardize their business, particularly during the economically challenging times in which we presently live. This is exacerbated when such standards are not yet equally applied by all, particularly some larger economies with whom they may compete and have no influence over. Island jurisdictions have to make political decisions in the allocation of resources, which may be difficult to justify internationally.

Finally, a word on the relationship between the UK and its Overseas Territories. There is a *prima facie* case that the UK intervening in the company laws of all territories disregards the fact that problems may be more pertinent in some territories than others. This leads to a conclusion that the UK government needs to further its understanding of the challenges each individual territory faces and reconcile this with specific partnership action, rather than generalised policies which indiscriminately and insensitively apply to all irrespective of the important differences in their financial sectors and contrasting stages of development. Ironically, the FAC Inquiry sought to improve understanding of the territories, yet viewing them as a collective in terms of financial services undermines this. Care should be given in requiring, by law, small jurisdictions to comply to the same or higher degree as larger countries, for reasons including capacity, resources and, importantly, their individually differing records of compliance with international standards. Despite the territories making high-level commitments on public registers, one concern remains unresolved. This book highlights the constitutional difficulty in interfering in matters of, arguably, devolved legislative function. Some leaders thought that this set a dangerous precedent for future restrictions on their ability to operate their business sectors. With the territories being afforded an inalienable right to determine their futures, it will be interesting to monitor the position to 2023 where public registers will go live.

This book has shown that international criminality has found safe haven in some Overseas Territories. That said, some have also shown significant ability and willingness to comply with internationally advocated standards, reform legislation and engage proactively with AML initiatives. While many aspects are positive, there are still those lacking and requiring significant attention, particularly in Anguilla's case. Protecting themselves from risks emanating from suspect wealth abroad is paramount, as well as robustly acknowledging domestic risks and enhancing controls within the jurisdiction – particularly in terms of those charged with upholding the highest of standards and guarding the rule of law. In circumstances of compliance achievements, it is only correct that the territories are supported in international fora and their right to compete freely is supported. In order for each territory to better protect themselves from the risk of suspect wealth, it is right that local initiatives surrounding risk analysis, awareness-raising of compliance and engagement with international monitoring and reviews continues and increases. Not only does this demonstrate a clear message of adherence to the global risk-based approach, but it can strengthen institutions and, in turn, the countries' legal and regulatory response. Of course, this does not translate to blindly adopting standards whose likely effectiveness remains unclear. However, jurisdictions which have long been perceived adversely will continuously need to innovate their regimes to demonstrate international cooperation and compliance, as is evidenced by considerable legislative reforms across the territories to take account of the modern scope of economic crime.

Through this discussion, it is hoped that greater understanding of these important jurisdictions is contributed. Externally dictated controls are not always consistent with development priorities or even viable in terms of implementation. As such, a holistic view of their frameworks and responses to suspect wealth, including those standards they have successfully implemented, as well as those which are yet to be, is needed. It is hoped that a more meaningful discussion to these important issues is facilitated by this book.

Index

For Product Safety Concerns and Information please contact our EU
representative GPSR@taylorandfrancis.com
Taylor & Francis Verlag GmbH, Kaufingerstraße 24, 80331 München, Germany

www.ingramcontent.com/pod-product-compliance
Ingram Content Group UK Ltd.
Pitfield, Milton Keynes, MK11 3LW, UK
UKHW021720240926
475702UK00029BA/1712
* 9 7 8 0 3 6 7 6 5 1 1 0 7 *